A REAL LIFE STORY
RUI MARQUES
TRIUMPH
TRAGEDY
PECOENSE STORY
THE GAFFER TAPES PRESENTS
THE A-Z OF FANTASY FOOTBALL
A HILARIOUS GUIDE FILLED WITH ANECDOTES AND EXPERT ADVICE
TOM HOLMES, CRAIG HAZELL AND ASH KERNSWORTH
THE THIN WHITE LINE
The Inside Story of Cricket's Greatest Scandal
Taking it to EXCESS
Footballers ALCOHOL ADDICTION
BENJAMIN ROBERTS
Sport
THE HOLLOW CROWN
ENGLAND CRICKET CAPTAINS
FROM 1945 TO THE PRESENT
BARBED WIRE
AND CUCUMBER SANDWICHES
The Controversial South Africa Tour of 1970
COLIN SHINDLER
FOREWORD BY SIR MICHAEL PARKINSON CBE
FILIPE D'AVILLEZ
One Thousand Miles to JAMOR
A JOURNEY INTO PORTUGUESE FOOTBALL
GRANDAD WHAT WAS FOOTBALL LIKE IN THE 1970s?
RICHARD CROOKS
EVEN HESKEY SCORED
EMILE HESKEY
MY STORY
WITH DEAN ELDREDGE
SECOND YELLOW
THE FURTHER ADVENTURES OF OUR FOOTBALL HEROES
JOHN SMITH AND DAN TRELFER
LUKE FLETCHER
Tales fro
the Front Lin
'Relevant, pithy and amusing... a terrific piece of work'
Daily Telegraph
GROVEL!
The story and legacy of the summer of 1976
England v West Indies
David Tossell
Foreword by Tony Greig
The Telegraph SPORTS BOOK AWARDS 2020
SHORTLISTED
MY SONG SHALL BE CRICKET
FRANKLYN STEPHENSON
With Dave Bracegirdle. Foreword by Sir Garfield Sobers.
THE PRIDE OF THE LIONESSES
The Changing Face of Women's Football in England
Carrie Dunn
FOREWORD BY RACHEL BROWN-FINNIS
BRIAN HORTO
A Life in Football
FOOTBALL'S
WHY ARE WE ALWAYS ON LAST?
STEVEN SCRAGG

'Every now and again a book crops up that can only be described as extraordinary, and *Too Black to Wear Whites* most certainly falls into that category... what is remarkable is the man that authors Parry and Winch have chosen to write about, and the lengths that they have had to go to reconstruct his life.'

Martin Chandler, *CricketWeb.net*

‘Every now and again a book crops up that can only be described as extraordinary, and *Too Black to Wear Whites* most certainly falls into that category ... what is remarkable is the man that authors Parry and Winch have chosen to write about, and the lengths that they have had to go to reconstruct his life.’

Martin Chandler, *Cricket Web. Net*

‘An immensely valuable piece of revisionist sporting history from a country still striving to make sense of the past.’

Paul Edwards, *The Cricketer*

‘Winch and Parry have done the game a great service by delving deeply into their subject to knot the loose ends of Hendricks’ previously barely-told story, and in the process weave a vibrant vision of the South Africa of the time.’

Telford Vice, *CricBuzz*

‘The authors have done South African, and world cricket, a huge service in articulating a non-White sporting heritage fraught with adversity, sacrifice, courage and humanity.’

Mushtak Parker, *New African*

‘In recording the true history of South African cricket, Parry and Winch are driven by a commitment to correct an injustice against a player such as Hendricks, who has been airbrushed out of history.’

Ryland Fisher, *Weekend Argus*

‘From a few footnotes a few years ago, we now have a rounded picture of an early South African bowling star and the almost unbelievable dramas that surrounded his life and career.’

André Odendaal, *Cricket World*

‘The central aim of the project, to recover the career of a player whom the authorities would rather have ignored, is resoundingly successful.’

Geoff Levett, *Sport in History*

‘This comprehensive piece of sporting history is a triumph of commitment.’

Nancy Richards, *South African Country Life*

‘Winch and Parry paint a picture of a vibrant and engaged cricket community, of which Hendricks was a part ... So much for the later narrative that people of colour are not interested in cricket.’

Firdose Moonda, *Cricinfo*

‘Had it not been for the forensic feat of Jonty Winch and Richard Parry, the compelling story of Hendricks and the nefarious shenanigans of Rhodes would not have been unearthed in their fascinating book *Too Black to Wear Whites*.’

Mushtak Parker, *Cape Times*

JONTY WINCH | RICHARD PARRY

TOO BLACK
TO WEAR WHITES

KROM HENDRICKS

The Remarkable Story of a Cricket Hero Rejected by the Empire

pitch

This edition published by Pitch Publishing, 2021
First published by Penguin Books, SA, 2020

Pitch Publishing
A2 Yeoman Gate
Yeoman Way
Worthing
Sussex
BN13 3QZ
www.pitchpublishing.co.uk
info@pitchpublishing.co.uk

A CIP catalogue record is available for this book
from the British Library.

ISBN 978 1 78531 825 2

Typesetting and origination by Pitch Publishing

Printed and bound in India by Replika Press Pvt. Ltd.

Contents

For Norma, Matthew and Jamie

– Jonty

For Helen and Carolyn

– Richard

Dr Jonty Winch studied at the University of Rhodesia; De Montfort University, Leicester, and the University of Stellenbosch. He has been involved in photography, journalism and education, and has written six books on sporting history in southern Africa. He also co-authored *Cricket & Conquest: The History of South African Cricket Retold 1795–1914* (2016); co-edited *Cricket & Society in South Africa 1910–1971: From Union to Isolation* (2018), and has written articles for accredited international academic publications.

Dr Richard Parry studied African history and politics at the University of Natal, Durban, and his post-graduate work at Queen's University, Canada focused on Cecil Rhodes and resistance to colonialism. After a career in international taxation, he now divides his time between advising African countries on implementing effective tax systems and uncovering the hidden histories of black cricketers in South Africa. He was a contributor to *Empire and Cricket: The South African Experience 1884–1914* (2009) and co-editor of *Cricket & Society in South Africa 1910–1971: From Union to Isolation* (2018).

Foreword

THIS IS A book that desperately needed to be written, and that I, as a historian of South African sport, have been awaiting for a long time. It is about a fast bowler of exceptional ability who played cricket in Cape Town in his prime in the 1890s. His name was William Henry 'Krom' Hendricks and he was someone who came to life on the cricket field. His hostile and skilful bowling was a thrilling sight. He delivered high-speed yorkers which burst through defences and electrified the big crowds who queued to see their hero bowl. Week after week he turned in exceptional performances. He was in constant demand and played for more than a dozen teams in his long career. English professional cricketers who saw him play compared him to the first great Australian fast bowler, Frederick 'The Demon' Spofforth, and rated him one of the best in the world.

But, until comparatively recently, you had to look hard to find the name of Krom Hendricks in the official records of South African cricket. In the massive 848-page history of South African cricket written by Maurice Luckin in 1915, he appears as 'the Cape coloured boy, Hendriks [*sic*]' whose selection for the 1894 tour would have been 'impolitic' and is listed in a single scorecard hidden away on pages 517 and 518. He was one of 18 cricketers who serendipitously got a chance to play in an unusual match, described in Chapter 1 of this book, against the 1891/92 English tourists.

Those 18 cricketers were unusual because they were described as 'non-Europeans' and later 'non-whites' under the terminology of the time. And they were the only players so described who made it into the 'official' record of South African cricket for the 85 years from the beginnings of competitive cricket in this country in the mid-1870s to 1960. Not one other person not classified white was included in the four dense volumes written by Luckin, Louis Duffus and Brian Bassano covering that period.

The clear implication arising from Luckin's and other histories like his was that cricket was a 'white man's game', and that the natives never played it or showed an interest. The exclusions and silences in the history books mirrored the horrible real-life discrimination that people suffered under the violent and exclusionary systems of colonialism and apartheid. The ruling classes assumed for generations that others who did not look like them were somehow less human and did not have the same capabilities or deserve the same opportunities.

However, in the past few decades a determined group of historians has been hard at work rewriting the story of South African cricket to disprove these supremacist notions. As they proceeded with their searches, amazing stories started to unfold – in terms of both Krom Hendricks and the broader South African cricket canvas, revealing an infinitely richer story than that which has been known.[1] The researchers, with Jonty Winch and Richard Parry prominent, first found a newspaper report about the 1891/92 match and then the comments by the English professionals regarding Hendricks. They went on a systematic search of the newspapers of the time and the name Hendricks kept jumping out at them. Three books and a doctoral dissertation emerged from these searches, but still Winch and Parry persisted until finally this lovingly crafted, intimate biography emerged.

A truth stranger than fiction has come to the fore. It turned out that William Henry Hendricks suffered cruelly for his temerity in being both black and better than the empire at its own game, and that no less a person than the prime minister of the Cape Colony decided that his face did not fit with their notion of cricket as an essentially British pastime. Therefore, though good enough, it was decided that under no circumstances should he be selected to play cricket for South Africa.

Arch-imperialist Cecil John Rhodes and his right-hand man William Milton, a former England rugby full-back and South African cricket captain, were at the heart of the plot. Working together with their acolytes in the Western Province Cricket Club – which styled itself as the MCC of the Cape Colony – and the Western Province Cricket Union, these diehard, high-society British racists set out to systematically hound Hendricks out of the game. A panoply of exclusion followed as grand empire intersected with virulent social racism.

Although Hendricks was selected for the squad for the first tour to England in 1894, the Cape cabal ensured he was banned from playing for South Africa, Western Province and the 'Colonial-born' team in what was then the annual cricket showpiece versus the British 'Home-born' XI. Then he was prohibited from plying his trade as a professional playing in the Cape Town club 'Championship' and the second-tier 'Peninsula League', and forced into the subservient status of 'net bowler' for whites. For more than a decade, the bigoted and incompetent club and union officials obfuscated and held the line about Hendricks's status despite being forced to consider his eligibility on several occasions in the period between 1894 and 1905. On every occasion they failed to revisit let alone change their original decision, frustrating Hendricks's career step by mean step until he was past his prime and irrevocably denied the opportunities he so deserved. This was cruel, systematic discrimination carried out over a long time by poker-faced bigots parading as society's leaders upholding 'civilisation' and standards.

When journalist and founding secretary of the South African Cricket Association Harry Cadwallader championed Hendricks's inclusion in the team for England, Milton unceremoniously dumped him as manager for the tour. Having been virtually assured of the position because he had been the tour's main organiser, Cadwallader was held responsible for the 'Hendricks affair' and subsequently relieved of several influential positions in national rugby and cricket affairs. Pushed out by the system, he relocated to the Transvaal where he died in 1897 in 'such grievous need' that a public fund was set up to assist his wife and children.

As a bowler, Krom Hendricks's pace and aggression viscerally challenged white batsmen and the social order they inhabited. The better he was, the more threatening he became. He regularly demolished senior clubs when he had the opportunity to play against them, making a point of dismissing those who had been selected for the provincial or Test teams. Whether or not leading Cape batsmen were frightened of his pace, they were certainly unhappy at being shown up by a coloured player. White supremacy required white control. A humiliation on the pitch was intolerable. And Hendricks was not alone, but the first in a catalogue of hundreds of black cricketers, up to Basil D'Oliveira and beyond, who despite their talent were denied the opportunity to represent their country.

His contemporaries Ebrahim Ariefdien, Robert Grendon, Armien Hendricks and Lamarah Samsodien would all have been certainties for representative honours in a fair, non-racial system. Hendricks was the key to a non-racial sporting door. That was the real threat to the colonialists.

The Hendricks affair showed that cricket in South Africa, and globally, was not simply a game – it was a vehicle for culture, ideology and politics. South Africa's 300-year experience of colonialism and empire encompassed slavery, forced labour, segregation and apartheid. But oppression could not crush the human spirit, and the colonised never stopped challenging the colonial narrative, until eventually their vision of an inclusive game prevailed with the arrival of cricket unity and democracy a century later in the 1990s.

William Henry 'Krom' Hendricks's struggle against the forces of imperialism and colonialism has now finally been told. We owe our colleagues Jonty Winch and Richard Parry a huge debt of gratitude for their ground-breaking research and imaginative reading of the sources. They have given Hendricks back his humanity. Depicted as less than a man, the 'boy' and unseen statistic in the colonial record has become a rounded personality. In a multi-faceted analysis of the evolution of early South African segregation, they describe Hendricks's struggle to retain his integrity and dignity despite his vindictive treatment by the Cape cricket establishment.

In the process, the authors have recreated the world in which Hendricks lived as a young man, a father and a grandfather; someone who refused to go quietly, who played on into his mid-sixties and who, above all, loved the game.

Hendricks's background was complex and obscure, but his Malay connections sealed his fate within Cape Town's cricketing and social underclasses. In examining his life, the authors also shine fresh light on the ambiguity and contradictory nature of identity and racism in South Africa, touching on themes of intersectionality, which have become popular in recent youth protests and debates in the country. In a twist to the tale, this work suggests that in addition to the deliberate suppression of the Hendricks saga by the cricket establishment, contemporary chroniclers and subsequent South African historians, Krom Hendricks the cricketer possibly had his own reasons for disappearing. His life story illustrates how the genesis of segregation lay in a tangled web of ideas and political imperatives, including British imperialist ideology formed in the crucible of the public schools in the late nineteenth century; a local colonial struggle over economic opportunities and the nature of the social order; an alliance between Rhodes and J.H. Hofmeyr in the interests of the mining industry and incipient white South African nationalism; and the violence of the struggle for mineral resources culminating in the Anglo-Boer War.

South Africa was not a united country until 1910, but not everyone thought racism trumped cricket talent. The Transvaal enforced draconian provisions against African labour on the mines, but was less bothered by challenges from the coloured population. Barberton Halliwell, South African captain in 1896, tried to select Hendricks for the Johannesburg Test against Lord Hawke's tourists only to be thwarted by Milton. Nor was the 'coloured issue' a problem for Natal, obsessed with driving their Zulu population into the colonial workforce. Charles 'Buck' Llewellyn, whose origins were apparently similar to those of Hendricks, grew up in Natal and played for South Africa.

The vast majority of cricket followers at the Cape supported Hendricks, that most exciting and charismatic of players. Besides

Cadwallader, his case was pressed by the influential Frank Robb, who had close connections with Hendricks throughout his life and employed him as a cricket professional for the Woodstock and Metropolitan clubs. Robb had been educated at the multiracial Zonnebloem College in contrast to the Western Province cricket establishment, which learnt its imperialism at Bishops and SACS or the English public schools. For Robb, the Western Province Cricket Union was there to encourage cricket and not judge a man's social position. This story of struggle and ambiguity was not just about race, but class as well.

Hendricks himself was undeterred. He played on in the coloured community he called his own until well into his sixties. His reputation and personal integrity shone as brightly as ever, his enthusiasm and passion for the game undiminished.

As for Rhodes and his cricket cabal, their decisions formalised segregation and apartheid as official policy and took South African cricket on a 100-year journey into a dead-end street. Wasted opportunity and the deliberate suppression of human potential were the biggest outcomes of their folly. That meme was to become the destructive legacy of the tragedy that was apartheid. It is a great historical irony that 120 years after Hendricks was unfairly barred from representing his country, students at the University of Cape Town should deface Rhodes's statue and cause it to be removed from its plinth overlooking the suburbs because it symbolised dishonour.

ANDRÉ ODENDAAL
NEWLANDS
NOVEMBER 2019

Acknowledgements

THIS BOOK HAS its origins in the research on Hendricks that we began independently during the 1990s – Richard in London and Jonty in Johannesburg. Inspired by Hendricks's courage, boldness, talent and sheer magnetism, we published pieces on him and early South African cricket, some in Richard Hill's *Cricket Lore*, which provided fertile soil for cricket writing too specialised, too detailed, too obscure or too opinionated to be welcomed elsewhere.

Thanks to Bernard Tancred Hall, in the early 2000s we assembled a London-based steering committee – which also included Dale Slater, Geoff Levett and Keith Booth – to develop a project on rewriting South Africa's early cricket history, in line with a growing historiographical tradition based on the 'transformation' initiative, which for two decades has recreated colonial history as the key to a liberated society. Historians including André Odendaal, Krish Reddy, Christopher Merrett, Bruce Murray, Ashwin Desai, Goolam Vahed and Vishnu Padayachee have interrogated the past not as a neutral space, but as an expression of the experience of the colonised, recording the impact of segregation and white supremacy. These new authoritative narratives have emphasised the relationship between cricket and politics, and are beginning to fill the gaps in the histories and experience of black South African sportsmen and women and those who formed resilient communities in the face of oppression.

The London group developed strong links with Bruce Murray, Goolam Vahed and Heinrich Schulze in South Africa, and as a result published *Empire and Cricket: The South African Experience, 1884–1914*, a series of essays examining the central themes of race and politics in early South African cricket. A subsequent volume, *Cricket and Society in South Africa, 1910–1971: From Union to Isolation*, expanded the pool of writers to include Rafaelle Nicholson, Albert Grundlingh, Patrick Ferriday and Jon Gemmell. We owe a debt of gratitude to all these scholars who shared their knowledge and most importantly their enthusiasm as we worked collectively to shine light on the role of sport in the growth and development of South Africa.

No references to the 1890s are complete without mention of Krom Hendricks, although few historians provide detail beyond the disputes over his selection for South Africa and his efforts to play as a professional in Cape Town in the mid-1890s. The most significant piece has been Drew Forrest's chapter on the fast bowler in his book *The Pacemen: 100 Years of South African Fast Bowlers*, but a biography of the player has remained a lacuna in South African sports history.

Establishing his life and achievements and grounding them in the Cape context necessitated wide reading of primary sources and secondary literature, while detailed references to his cricket achievements were gleaned from the South African and overseas press. Collectively, the Cape newspapers – particularly the *Cape Argus*, *Cape Times*, *South African Review*, *South African News* and *The Owl* – created an invaluable record by providing contrasting views on Hendricks. Other centres – notably Johannesburg's *Standard and Diggers News* – made important contributions, as did English newspapers during South Africa's 1894 tour.

The primary records for this period are almost non-existent. Minutes of meetings and other records of the various clubs are limited. Finding Hendricks has been even more challenging. But detailed digging, some detective work and help from others inspired by our quest have provided enough clues to establish the reality of the man himself. Genealogical research has also proved key.

Hendricks 'disappeared' partly because the archival materials relating to his employment on the Cape Railways and the Table Bay Railways and Harbour Board are incomplete, as are those relating to schools. In addition, the turbulent history of the Cape, including the waves of forced removals, meant that little has survived relating to coloured sports clubs or institutions that existed more than a century ago. Historians never have the last word and we anticipate that more on this fascinating story, perhaps buried away in a long-forgotten hatbox in an attic somewhere, will eventually come to light.

Some of the mysterious aspects of Hendricks's life may not simply have been a matter of the destructive nature of the passage of time or human collusion. It was partly down to Hendricks himself. He spent his life treading a racial tightrope and had plenty of reason to obscure the already incomplete and ambiguous historical record.

Our research has allowed us to enjoy the privilege of working in impressive libraries, archives and museums. A special debt of gratitude is extended to the staff of these institutes. The bulk of the research was undertaken in the National Library of South Africa (Cape Town); the British Library (at Colindale and, latterly, St Pancras); the MCC Library at Lord's; the Archives of the Western Cape; Johannesburg Public Library; the William Cullen Library at the University of the Witwatersrand; the Archives of the Western Province Cricket Club; and the Bo-Kaap and District Six Museums. David Studham, librarian at the Melbourne Cricket Club, kindly provided further assistance.

As part of the ongoing research into providing alternative narratives of South Africa's cricket history, it is particularly appropriate that André Odendaal should have kindly written the foreword to this publication. We would like to extend our deep gratitude for his support over this complex and difficult project. His impact on the growing historiography of South African cricket through his chairmanship of the Transformation Monitoring Committee and his lead role in the four-volume *History of South African Cricket Retold* and other projects have been fundamental to the ability of South Africans to understand their history and themselves.

The key element of the Hendricks puzzle came down to identifying Krom Hendricks, the man. Heather MacAlister, one of South Africa's leading genealogists, is an enthusiastic and knowledgeable expert who provided invaluable information, moral support and red wine. She played a key role in helping locate Hendricks's descendants and built on the earlier work of Ivy Trott, a meticulous genealogist who was also an author and journalist with the *Cape Times*. Ivy's research has been of considerable importance in detailing Hendricks's life.

We are extremely grateful to Ivy's daughters, Josie and Lesley Trott, and to Vicki Priday for sharing their family reminiscences. Josie was very enthusiastic about the project, hospitable and most helpful. She provided details of her own sporting family and assisted us in locating important information and photographs. Vicki told us of Hendricks's grandson who had played football for Liverpool and who, like his grandfather, never lost his own commitment to the coloured community in the Cape.

We were also fortunate in being able to make use of the records of FamilySearch through which we were able to confirm numerous details from the spelling of Vollie van der Byl to the first names of the Samsodiens.

A central theme of this book is the subjective and ephemeral nature of racial categorisation, based primarily on culture and economic position. But the Hendricks story is about racism and we have used contemporary expressions – 'coloured' and 'Malay' – though we understand such terms are inevitably value-laden and ideological. On occasion we have quoted from sources where racist, offensive and demeaning expressions are used and with which we are uncomfortable. We have retained these in the interests of historical accuracy and to reflect the reality of the linguistic violence of the past.

In addition, while we use the term 'Test' for all matches played between a representative South African XI and an English touring side from 1889 onwards, such matches were only retrospectively designated as Tests in 1907.

A long list of people played an important role in the project, sharing information and filling gaps. We are once again indebted to Robin Isherwood, whose work on South African cricket records and biographies has been of great importance to the *South African Cricket Annual* and numerous cricket publications. He kindly read through the manuscript and gave us the benefit of his expertise. We also greatly value Dale Slater's input. His insights into South African cricket history and its place in the overall political economy have helped us to shape and situate the Hendricks story. Both Robin and Dale have been supportive throughout this process of remapping the evolution of a very particular society.

We have received generous assistance from Terry Wallace, president of the Cape Town Cricket Club, and Phil Hartmann, the club's historian and co-author of *Playing the Game: The Story of the Cape Town Cricket Club*. We would like to thank Sigi Howes of the Education Museum for her most important insights into aspects of early Cape Town history, while Dr Francois Cleophas from Stellenbosch University and John Young, an independent historian, were both helpful in developing our views on different periods of Hendricks's cricket career. Sincere thanks are also due to Merle Martin of the impressive South African St Helenian Heritage Association for background on the history of Islanders in South Africa. When visiting Bo-Kaap we spent a memorable afternoon with Shafiek Allie who lives opposite Basil D'Oliveira's former home and who, as a small boy, watched legendary players practise on a concrete slab alongside Upper Bloem Street.

We are grateful to the Port Elizabeth artist Bella Forsyth, who worked from small and fading images of Hendricks to produce an impression that has been used in various reviews and to assist subsequent illustrations.

We greatly appreciate the patient and professional cooperation we received from our South African publisher, Penguin Random House. The managing editor, Robert Plummer, guided us through the various stages of production while the senior editor, Bronwen

Maynier, undertook the demanding task of copy-editing the manuscript. We thank them both and everyone else involved in the production and promotion of the first edition of this book.

We were very fortunate that the leading independent sports publisher in the United Kingdom should agree to produce the second edition of the book. We would like to thank the Pitch Publishing design and production team (Paul and Jane Camillin, Duncan Olner and Graham Hales) for their expertise and unwavering support. They were able to link with Natasha Muluswela who created the most effective drawing which highlights the cover.

Introduction

'The story of "Krom" Hendricks has assumed romantic and mythical proportions over the past few decades, both for those trying to gloss over past inequalities – "things weren't always that bad in the past, there was this player, that match etc" – and those deeply angry about white domination and its impact.'[1]

– Professor André Odendaal

'KROM' HENDRICKS WAS an exceptional cricketer in extraordinary circumstances. He was caught in a political machine that dehumanised him, denying his talent, his identity and his pride as a South African. His deselection for the cricket tour of England in 1894 by Cecil John Rhodes, the arch-imperialist bestriding southern African politics and finance, fixed the colour bar in cricket. Rhodes acted within a broader political alliance with J.H. ('Onze Jan') Hofmeyr, the leader of the newly formed Afrikaner Bond. Driven by labour demands and a class-based belief in social segregation, the Cape formalised racial exclusiveness into a concrete system of segregation that 50 years later would be ideologically encapsulated in apartheid. This book is not only about how Hendricks became the central figure in the genesis of sports segregation in southern Africa; it also rescues this most elusive of cricketers from historical anonymity.

It tells the true story of William Henry Hendricks, his cricket talent and his bravery over several decades as he fought the oppressive forces ranged against him. It provides insight into how he built the best life he could for his family in a time of frenetic and bewildering change, and above all as a cricketer whose love for the game shone through everything he did despite the efforts of the authorities. Hendricks's struggle exemplified the efforts of the coloured community in Cape Town to fashion its own destiny under the framework of colonial power.

The significance of the Hendricks affair in 1894 is well known to cricket historians, but there is little analysis of the political and institutional context within which this injustice was perpetrated, and nothing at all about Hendricks's personal history and the long struggle he waged against the cricket authorities.

Hendricks has been a footnote for 100 years as historians have sought to tell the story of South African cricket. Despite much interest, it is remarkable how few significant efforts have been made to establish who he really was, or even to confirm his name. At the Cape, Hendricks is a common name with spelling variants, notably 'Hendrickse', which was used in his own family. He signed himself 'H. Hendricks' in a letter to the *Cape Times* in 1894, but many contemporary sources simply referred to him as 'Hendricks', his fame perhaps sufficient for no other name to be needed.

After a generation of being ignored by cricket writers, Hendricks was discussed by Wally Hammond in 1949. Hammond described how it was 'typical of South Africa's perverse fortune that a faster bowler than Kotze or Ochse, a man who seems to have combined Larwood's accuracy with what was possibly the fastest trajectory ever seen on any cricket field – never came to England at all ... The bowler in question was a negro called Hendricks, a black Hercules about six foot four inches tall, with extremely long arms who was employed in some capacity by a Pretoria cricket club and displayed as a local wonder who could bowl down anyone's wicket, no matter how good the batsman, within half-a-dozen balls, because of his ferocious pace'.[2]

Hammond may have been hazy on the details ('Negro' and 'Pretoria' were a garbling of the truth) but Hendricks's significance was clear. Nonetheless few showed any interest in following it up. Twenty years later, he was referred to as 'T. Hendricks' in 1970 by Rowland Bowen in *Cricket: A History of Its Growth and Development Throughout the World*.[3] Other historians confused him with A. or Armien Hendricks, another talented bowler from the late nineteenth century. In 1977, South African cricket historian Syd Reddy was the first to mention his nickname 'Krom', and this is the name by which he is now most widely known.[4] It is testament to how little is known about Hendricks that the origins of this nickname have never been discovered. Establishing the player's identity and his full name, William Henry Hendricks, has been a complex task.

The failure by previous historians to rescue the real Hendricks from the haystack of history is indicative of the failure of South African cricket writing prior to transformation to undertake detailed research into black and coloured cricket. It is a product of apartheid thinking that covered up the pain and inhumanity inflicted by the system and did not see such cricket as demanding of attention and analysis. This book, building on the recent insights of historian André Odendaal and others, plays a role in setting the record straight. It is the story of an unfulfilled cricket career but a fulfilled life, and Hendricks's indefatigable courage as both a cricketer and a man.

The historical record, however, is as elusive as the man. Contemporary documents have been culled from the archives of the cricket establishment by those who do not understand the importance of history or by those who understand its power as a witness to truth only too well. Any 'Hendricks' archival materials held by the Western Province Cricket Union were destroyed to cover up apartheid-era embarrassments or sweep out the dust of the historical record. And family and community memories 120 years later are often no more than a glimmer of light from a distant era, a star in a far-off galaxy.

But the reports in the press written contemporaneously on cricket, politics and Hendricks provide an entry point, even if the content needs careful interrogation. They provide a patchwork of his cricketing achievements, an indicative rather than comprehensive view of his career for 'Malay' teams, as a professional for 'white' clubs and his final long cricket swansong when he played again for a 'coloured' team in the community in which he felt most at home. Mostly, though, they document his ongoing struggle to comprehend and oppose the forces of the imperial and colonial establishment that stood against him; they describe the monstrous injustices that Cape politicians and cricket administrators systematically visited on him over two decades; they reflect the voices of the many people who recognised his ability and talent; and, on occasion, they demonstrate the sympathy of those who resented the segregation that deprived this great fast bowler of the chance to reach his potential and spectators to witness him in action on a wider stage. Hendricks and his struggle were part of the warp and woof of a society busy drawing its red lines.

By the latter part of the nineteenth century, the British Empire was a complex matrix of economic, military and ideological ties aimed at building a greater Britain, with the British establishment the spider at the centre of the web. Colonial outposts, initially established as refreshment stations for accessing the riches of the East, soon developed physical presences – convict settlements and trading posts – and their own independent interests. This inevitably encompassed a dual identity: the colonial settlements were part of the wider imperial family, but also became increasingly fractious separate entities, with their own economic and political imperatives competing against one another and the metropole. This created a clear tension between the English establishment and the colonial middle classes who saw their interests as being above those of the empire itself.

The British civil servants who administered the colonies were largely drawn from public schools, the source of the widely held theory that there was a strong link between the qualities that public schoolboys derived through games-playing and those they would need to administer the empire. The year that Hendricks was born in Bo-Kaap – 1857 – saw the publication of *Tom Brown's Schooldays*, a novel that emphasised the doctrine of athleticism and helped inspire the belief in public schools that team games were a key instrument in building character, manliness and an understanding of fair play. The most prominent late nineteenth-century figure in developing the imperial games in South Africa was William Henry Milton, who had played cricket for Marlborough College against Rugby at Lord's and rugby for England against Scotland and Ireland. Milton's sense of 'fair play', or lack of it, was shaped by prevailing assumptions of the moral and physical superiority of the white English race. At Marlborough, he came under Dean Farrar, whose work, *Aptitudes of Races*, gave clear expression to Semitic and Aryan superiority over the Mongoloid and, lower still, the Negroid. Milton's subsequent actions exposed the obvious hypocrisy of the self-serving creed that products of public schools were able to exercise authority over other races in a reasonable and selfless manner.[5]

That Milton was keen to transplant what was happening at 'Home' appealed to the influential editor of the *Cape Times*, Frederick York St Leger, who, like Milton, saw the significance of the colony as an imperial project. St Leger sought to impose English values and hegemony, and recognised the advantages attached to promoting 'Englishness' through imperial games. Milton would assist St Leger in helping southern Africa take its place in the cultural exchange that was being fostered within the empire and, in doing so, would become Hendricks's leading adversary.

The tendency towards increasing colonial independence was one reason for England's propensity to promote cricket. Entrepreneurs took their cricket shows on the road to North America, Australia and (for the first time in 1888/89) South Africa. These were financial gambles, but they provided significant rewards for participants who represented the British establishment, whether 'professionals', amateurs or 'shamateurs' (paid amateurs). From the perspective of the periphery, these tours promoted empire and were an opportunity to showcase the colonial environment to increase immigration and investment in a crowded field. They hoped the southern African colonies could demonstrate ability on the cricket field, as well as economic opportunities off it; in particular, they publicised the extent to which the periphery was a repository of British values. It was this that lay at the heart of the Hendricks saga.

Milton, who headed the Western Province Cricket Union and organised the first English cricket tours, not only became the dominant personality in the South African game, but also headed Cecil Rhodes's Prime Minister's Department. He carried with him the baggage of empire with its focus on a hierarchy of races, arriving in a profoundly stratified society where social and economic segregation took place along class lines where the establishment was white. To his separatist thinking was added a direct political imperative. His rise in the political world coincided with the changing nature of Cape politics as Rhodes and Hofmeyr set out to replace mid-nineteenth-century Cape liberal notions of individual opportunity and advancement with a policy of segregation. Milton became Rhodes's subordinate in all matters, and his sometime spokesman. In turn, the Western Province Cricket Union slavishly followed its political masters, quickly ensuring that the process of segregation became an overriding philosophy of the game under its jurisdiction. It might have hoped the arrangement would fall into place seamlessly and unnoticed, reflecting as it did the organising principles of the establishment as well as the new political dynamic. That this did not happen can be largely attributed to Hendricks's personal qualities and successes, and the attention that was consequently focused on him as a household name created unprecedented controversy.

When the time came to select a South African touring team to England in 1894, there was almost universal support on cricketing grounds for Hendricks's inclusion. Those who opposed him constituted a small group of individuals who were influential in higher levels of politics and cricket administration in the Western Province, and who were not prepared to countenance a coloured player representing South Africa. A South African–born cricketer, agreed to be the best fast bowler in the country by a considerable distance, was thus omitted, while visiting English professionals were included in the tour party, along with an Irishman who had been in South Africa for four months. It was clear that Hendricks's selection was not approved for political reasons. Had this not happened, the South African cricket landscape may have turned out differently.

This was just the start of the Hendricks saga. The Transvaal Cricket Union continued to press for the strongest South African XI and began a process through which it hoped to select Hendricks for the South African team against Lord Hawke's tourists in Johannesburg in 1896. But Milton once again intervened, and Hendricks was prohibited from travelling to Johannesburg. In the same year, the Western Province Cricket Union passed its infamous 'Hendricks resolution' (known as Bye-law 10), which refused to allow coloureds to play 'championship' cricket in the Western Province. This was challenged by Woodstock in 1897, but the governing body proved its intransigence and, despite Hendricks's personal qualities and demeanour, would not consider a special exemption for him.

Hendricks was the first cricketer to be banned from playing the game at a senior level at the Cape and in South Africa as a whole, and probably the first in the world to be formally excluded from playing because of his colour. He would be followed by thousands of coloured and black players. They suffered huge injustices, being denied access to opportunities, adequate facilities and the right to play representatively. In this setting, Hendricks's history is one among many – the fate of most South Africans who, over hundreds of years, were faced with the tragedies of conquest, slavery, segregation and apartheid. But Hendricks's story is also peculiar to the Cape in the 1890s: it involved a dividing line being drawn between white and coloured. It was a matter of complexion, but perhaps more fundamentally a matter of economics, culture and community.

The Cape community at that time was an amalgam of dozens of different identities and hundreds of histories. It included remnants of indigenous hunter-gatherers (San and Khoi peoples), white settlers, Xhosa immigrants from the expanding eastern frontier, and freed slaves from Batavia and Madagascar. Many of the latter were Muslims and became identified as Malays at the Cape, their non-colonial culture and traditions defining the whole blended community in the mind of the colonial establishment. But what of those who were part of the Christian community who happened to live in predominantly Malay or mixed-race areas, such as Bo-Kaap, and who played cricket for local community teams? They were generally perceived as part of the greater coloured identity, occupationally often interconnected with the white working classes. When it suited the establishment, an individual could be treated as racially inferior, denied opportunity, relocated or exploited. Such was the fate of Hendricks and, some 70 years later, that of Basil D'Oliveira.

This racial exclusivity was as painful to individuals and families as any of the other community-slicing devices used by the white establishment to maintain their social, economic and political control. In fact, by sundering one from another on the flimsiest of excuses, according to a set of undeveloped values and prejudices, it was arguably the worst kind of discrimination – arbitrary in form, substance and impact.

William Henry Hendricks was brought up by his mother who was from St Helena (which meant that she would be considered coloured in the Cape's complex informal racial tapestry), and it is possible that he did not know his father. His marriage in 1880 would subsequently produce 11 children over more than 20 years. He would also delight in his more than 40 grandchildren, one of whom would go on to play football for Liverpool. They were a happy, close-knit family who regarded themselves as European.

In the aftermath of the vicious Anglo-Boer War of 1899 to 1902, little changed for Hendricks, at least on the cricket field. There were crucial developments taking place in South Africa: when the exhausted troops finally laid down their arms and (much later) the concentration camp survivors returned to their burnt-out farms, the war had claimed more than 100,000 victims in and out of uniform and the empire had won political control over the goldmines. The long-suffering black and coloured populations, who had fought on the side of the British, gained nothing from the peace and were to lose even more in the reconstruction of the country in the interests of the mining industry.

In 1904, at the age of 47, in the year in which he was promoted to foreman in the Salt River railway works and his eldest daughter married an English soldier, Hendricks again applied for the right to play senior cricket, previously denied under Bye-law 10 of the Western Province Cricket Union rules. He argued that his parents were European and that in any event there were coloured cricketers playing at senior level without challenge. The union, composed of the same establishment figures as in the 1890s, simply ignored his claim to have European status and, without discussion, refused to accept his application.

In the end, the question of race was a subjective rather than an objective classification. Whether or not Hendricks was of European stock was irrelevant; he was not treated as such by the Cape cricket establishment. They did not care whether he was coloured or not, or even how this was to be defined. The committee said it could not make any exceptions, while praising Hendricks personally in its infuriating and hypocritical manner. They had no idea how to answer the question that the one delegate who supported Hendricks asked: 'Where is the line of colour to be drawn?' The committee had already decided he was coloured. There was no suggestion that they should be looking to achieve some measure of belated justice or right a long-standing wrong.

One might wonder as to the intransigent racism of the Western Province Cricket Union. The common view was that current players serving as delegates, such as Murray Bisset (erstwhile captain of South Africa), were scared of facing Hendricks's express pace bowling – he regularly demolished senior clubs when he had the opportunity, invariably making a point of dismissing those who had been selected for the provincial or Test teams. There was no delivery more dangerous for an incoming batsman than a yorker from Hendricks. A remarkable feature of his bowling figures was the number of times he hit the stumps, while some of his feats would not be matched in South Africa for many years. Whether or not leading Cape batsmen were frightened of his pace, they were certainly unhappy at being shown up by a coloured player.

And it was not just Hendricks. There were plenty of other good coloured cricketers around: the Malay side that won the Glover

Cup in 1891/92 could all have challenged for a place in the team of the Western Province Cricket Union, and several – Krom Hendricks, Ebrahim Ariefdien, Edward Adams and Lamarah Samsodien – would have been certainties in a fair, non-racial system. Cricket as the elite symbol of white social status, or 'snobbery' as the locals called it, could not risk anything other than racial segregation. Rhodes, with Milton as his right-hand man and the Western Province Cricket Union as his loyal servant, moved the Cape rapidly to a segregated society where race became congruent with class in a political economy based on cheap black labour and endless efforts to co-opt the white working class into the establishment.

This process occupied the next decades of Hendricks's life. He continued to play cricket into his sixties, and while his performances as a grandfather may have been less eye-catching than in his glory days, his reputation as the 'great and mighty' Hendricks shone as brightly as ever. He was not a man driven by fame or glory, but by personal integrity. The representative honours that he deserved were denied him in the cruellest way imaginable, but he played on, his enthusiasm and passion for the game undiminished.

1

Origins of a legend

> 'The very ablest bowler he had ever met he believed to be, not Spofforth, but a South African black, [Krom] Hendricks.'[1]
>
> – William Chatterton (Derbyshire and England)

ON THE EVENING of 3 January 1892, more than 3,000 jubilant cricket fans streamed towards Cape Town station. Elated Malay supporters came from Bo-Kaap, District Six and Woodstock to celebrate the triumphant return of their Union Cricket Club (CC) from Kimberley. Cricket was a ritual as well as a recreation and provided the social glue that bound together the community. Male choir clubs and bands in elaborate costumes led processions down the narrow avenues. The station was alive with song and music, interrupted by the wild cheering that greeted the arrival of the Kimberley train. Fans crammed the station platform, jostling for position to welcome back their cricket heroes, who shook off the dust and soot of the long journey and tumbled into the throng of well-wishers.

The tidal wave of humanity swept towards the Parade where a chorus of demands to display the newly acquired silverware punctuated the warm summer air. Abdol Burns, the half-Scottish half-Malay president of Union CC, delightedly held aloft the gleaming Glover Cup to riotous cheers and applause. The underdogs from Cape Town had dramatically defeated the might of Kimberley in its own backyard. For Burns, the victory was a combination of talent, team spirit and the passionate support received from those gathered on the Parade. But it was also a triumph for unity beyond religion. Cricket was a means of breaking down barriers and strengthening the coloured community, both Muslim and Christian.

Burns hailed the turnaround in fortunes since the first Glover Cup contest, played at the Diamond Fields (as the region around Kimberley was known) some nine months earlier. In that inaugural inter-town competition, Robert Grendon – a Christian of Irish-African parentage – had scored a brilliant 111 out of a total of 191 to lead Kimberley to a convincing victory. This time, Burns had decided to fight fire with fire and called upon Krom Hendricks to strengthen his Union club against Kimberley's best players, mainly drawn from the Red Crescents. Hendricks, a Christian from Bo-Kaap's Star of South Africa CC, formed an unstoppable strike force with the impressive Ebrahim Ariefdien. They destroyed the strong Kimberley batting line-up, steamrolling them for 41, Ariefdien claiming 6-13 and Hendricks 4-24. Cape Town replied with 106 (Ariefdien 26), which provided a commanding if not unassailable 65-run lead. It gave Hendricks the chance to become a new star in the cricket firmament. His intimidating deliveries flew from a length off the matting laid on rolled red earth, forcing his opponents on to the back foot and opening their defences to a venomous yorker. In an innings analysis of 6-39, all six of his dismissals were clean bowled, including the classy Grendon who top-scored with only 24 in Kimberley's 91. Cape Town were left to knock off 27 runs to secure victory and won with nine wickets in hand.

The bare details of the game do not describe its intensity or its drama and excitement. Rivalry on and off the pitch between Cape Town and Kimberley was exacerbated by incidents in a game that was played at fever pitch. The umpires (the Powell brothers), who were pillars of the white Kimberley cricket establishment, stoked the strength of feeling among the Cape Town travelling support. They had apparently planned to neuter the visiting side by no-balling both of their match-winning fast bowlers, Hendricks in the first innings and Ariefdien in the second, for throwing. This tactic failed to win the game in the end, but it clearly upset Ariefdien, who bowled just five overs in the second innings without taking a wicket.

'Feeling ran very high,' said the *Cape Times*.[2] Such outrageous partisanship demonstrated the lengths that Kimberley – or, more accurately, the tournament sponsors – were prepared to go to keep the trophy on the Diamond Fields. The Glover family, who ran a sports and entertainment business based around the Pirates ground, was only too keen to expand its market and encourage cricketers of whatever race or religion to spend their money at the club. The Glover Cup, which the Glovers valued at 50 guineas, was intended to attract lucrative cricket business to Pirates. They had no desire to see their investment head south in the hands of their bitter rivals and to lose control over the Glover Cup competition and the lucrative inter-town coloured cricket market.

Under Abdol Burns's effervescent leadership, the coloured cricket community in Cape Town was a force to be reckoned with in a sport that the colonial establishment held in almost sacred regard. Malays had always been subject to social and economic segregation, which separated them from the middle classes. As descendants of freed slaves, they had few economic resources to challenge the colonists, and theological differences meant they were permanently at odds. Nonetheless, Burns sought to simultaneously support the Malay community and build a broader coloured base. He was the community spokesman and fought the city council for decades to retain a cemetery on Signal Hill near enough to District Six and Bo-Kaap to allow bodies to be carried on foot by mourners, as required by Cape Muslim tradition. He encouraged regular cultural performances based on Turkish Muslim traditions, including music and Khalifa. He also worked to strengthen the wider community of Christians and Muslims who lived, worked and played together in Bo-Kaap, District Six, Woodstock and across the Cape peninsula. He strove for community acceptance, combining active engagement in the political process

– supporting liberals such as Saul Solomon – with a focus on celebrating empire as good imperial citizens.

The casual, deeply entrenched racism of the ruling-class establishment meant that whites generally paid little attention to either Muslim or coloured culture. They made no effort to consider who was of 'Malay' descent, who was Muslim and who was Christian. Members of the coloured community were heterogeneous by racial background, culture and class grouping. They were categorised less by what they were than by what they were not – that is, middle-class Anglo-Saxon immigrants or their descendants. Coloureds populated Cape Town's lower social classes, but some, through religion and skin colour, assimilated into the skilled or unskilled European working classes.

Cricket was one means through which coloureds might have sought the economic advantages that followed entry into the white working class. When the first Malay inter-town cricket tournament was organised by Burns in January 1890, it prompted an editorial from the *Cape Times*. The newspaper commented on 'olive-complexioned cricketers' whose younger generation had taken enthusiastically to the game in recent years and would be observed with interest. The 'Malay people', said the writer, were 'capable of a higher degree of civilisation than the simpler African races, of that there can be no doubt'. He admitted:

> However we may have lamented the spread of the Asiatic influence in Cape Town, we have always had a saving cause for the Malays. They have not come here to try their own fortunes against the Europeans; but their fathers were brought here against their will as slaves for the convenience and comfort of our predecessors, and they have the same right to regard this country as their home.[3]

This leader article, probably written by the editor, Frederick St Leger, was characteristically condescending in tone and its racist rhetoric followed the prevailing model of higher and lower standards of civilisation. Where the coloured community stood was the essence of the Cape Town social battleground. For the 'liberal' St Leger, the Malays had become 'an integral part of the population of Cape Town ... they have proved themselves most worthy'. But being an integral part did not mean unqualified acceptance. The arrangement through which Malays played at Newlands was contentious. The *Cape Times* reported that 'several people occupying some standing in Cape society have indicated their disgust and others their surprise at the action of the Western Province CC in allowing the Malay cricketers the use of Newlands'. Some were 'perfectly scandalised at the idea that so large a number of respectable persons actually found their way to matches and so gave countenance to the action of the Western Province CC'. There were other comments in the columns:

> 'What next?' exclaimed an indignant dame. 'Where will respectable people be able to go? I expect the Malays will go and call on the Governor next'. A shrill voice was heard in the carriage-park: 'Oh I say, it is a decided shame to allow the Malays to play on the beautiful ground at Newlands. Let them go to the Flats that's their proper place.'[4]

William Milton's spokesman on cricket matters, Thomas Lynedoch Graham, answered the complaints in a letter to the newspaper. A decade later, Graham would become the colonial secretary responsible for overseeing the removal of hundreds of mixed-race residents from District Six, an action repeated several times until its ultimate demolition. But, as secretary of the Western Province CC, he could not afford to ignore the bottom line. After all, Newlands had been purchased a mere five years before and financing was proving to be difficult. He noted that an estimated 5,000 spectators attended the tournament, adding that their conduct 'has been admirable ... an entire absence of rowdiness, not a single policeman employed on the ground ... In no case was the rules of cricket infringed or the decision of the umpires criticised.' He defended his club against the criticism it had received in the press, openly stating that they needed to pay for the ground. He did not ...

> …in any way regret their action in lending the Malays the use of their ground, whereas the share of the gate money has been a welcome and needed assistance to the funds of the club. As to the cricket itself, the comparatively high standard of excellence attained is a matter of surprise, considering that it is only within the past few years that cricket has been played by the Malays as a body…I may add that the get up of the players, barring an odd pair or two of braces was flawless.[5]

Times would change, but in the early 1890s there was no reason for Krom Hendricks to believe that he was jeopardising his future in the game by playing with Malay cricketers. He had grown up in Bo-Kaap with the players and was part of the community. Abdol Burns had offered him the opportunity not only to play representative cricket to a high standard, but also to impress at Newlands. Hendricks's ability as a fast bowler was attracting attention and he was playing matches before large crowds. Further opportunities were to come his way.

Walter William Read's English team toured South Africa in 1891/92, an arrangement that had been agreed to at the eleventh hour. Milton exercised rigid control over the whole project as president of the Western Province Cricket Union, as chief clerk and accountant of the Cape Civil Service, as Rhodes's private secretary, and last but not least, on the pitch as captain of the South African team in the Cape Town Test match. Nineteenth-century cricket tours were entrepreneurial exercises and teams required a delicate balance between being strong enough to provide a drawcard for spectators, but not too strong that they simply annihilated the opposition. Given the role that gambling played in the success of the enterprises, the popularity of the cricket depended on a contest with an uncertain result. After significant interest in Cape Town where the venture began with two draws, the tour proved a failure at the turnstiles. Read's negative tactics and the restrictions on batsmen facing 18 or 22 men in the field were important factors in the tour's lack of popularity. Invariably, shot-making was nullified against odds and batsmen reduced to ineffective plodders. On this tour, the only batsman to enhance his reputation was the patient and phlegmatic professional William 'Bill' Chatterton. The bowling was spearheaded by J.J. Ferris, a left-arm swing bowler who had represented Australia with distinction and scythed through an almost endless procession of ill-equipped batsmen in various southern African teams.

Milton was assisted in the organisation of the tour by Frank Hearne, the Western Province CC professional who had been part of Major Warton's 1888/89 tour and had settled in Cape Town. Hearne was considered by the Cape Town establishment as part of the working-class aristocracy, rising in due course to lower-middle-class status through his ownership of a sporting-goods shop. He was a friendly man as well as one of the best cricketers in the country. Within a month of his arrival in Cape Town, he had already developed a strong rapport with the coloured cricket community.

The final match of Read's tour, in March 1892, was the only game played on even terms against a representative South African team. Given Read's plain sailing so far, few were anticipating a strong showing by the locals. The English team came into the game unbeaten and determined to preserve their record. Ferris, as he had throughout the tour, again proved too good for South African batsmen, most of whom were not from Cape Town and were less familiar with the Newlands matting-on-grass surface than the visitors, who had already played several games on it. Ferris exploited his knowledge of the local conditions taking 6-54 out of South Africa's first innings of 97.

The crowd sat back expectantly awaiting an English run-fest, but the intensity of the response took them by surprise. Dante Parkin and English professional Charles Mills dismantled their top order, which had three wickets down for less than 40. They received excellent support from the fielders, particularly the athletic Charlie Fichardt at cover point. Then Harry Wood, in a classic cricket reversal, came in at 144 for six and hit South Africa out of the game. His 134 not out was scored out of his side's commanding 369. South Africa, clearly shell-shocked, replied with 83 – Frank Hearne top-scoring with 23 – and were defeated by an innings and 189 runs.

Ferris was again dominant with figures of 7-37 in 25 overs. He lifted his final tour tally to an outstanding 234 wickets.

This heavy defeat has been presented as evidence of the weakness of South African cricket and the Marylebone Cricket Club's (MCC) mistake in belatedly awarding the match Test status.[6] This may be true, but it is interesting that Lord Sheffield's English team, with W.G. Grace, began a Test against the Australians less than 48 hours later and won by an even greater margin – an innings and 230 runs. Johnny Briggs, who had humiliated South Africa at Newlands in 1888/89, once again created havoc, this time claiming 12-136 on a rain-affected wicket. Remarkably, the Australians, with C.B. Turner prominent, still won the series by two games to one.

The Cape Town Test may have concluded the official programme, but it was not the end of the tour, because a team described as the 'South African Malay XVIII' took on Read's 11 professionals. The game started about an hour after South Africa's final wicket fell and was played on the same matting. Later efforts to denigrate the significance of the fixture described it as an 'unplanned arrangement' to entertain the paying public when it became clear that the Test was going to end early. It was in fact the culmination of much organisation – it would be a benefit match for the English professionals. They would play against the Malay team that had won the Glover Cup, the *Cape Times* adding, 'Doubtless the Mohammedan community will turn out in great force in addition to the Europeans who will get to see the conclusion of the present match.'[7]

Frank Hearne had hatched the plan for the benefit match with Abdol Burns and the Malay team. There was a clear class basis to this. During the 1888/89 tour, the professionals had sat with the Malay community in the ground, and Hearne and his colleagues had apparently developed a friendly relationship with Cape Town's coloured players, who performed much the same working-class tasks – groundsmen, caretakers and particularly net bowlers – as the professionals did in England. The closeness of the relationship was illustrated a few days after Read's team arrived at the Cape in

December 1891. The professionals in the tour party were invited to a Malay wedding feast at Hearne's behest. Not surprisingly, no amateurs attended.

The day after the wedding, the English cricketers headed for Newlands. The professionals observed the trial match for the Glover Cup team at Cape Town CC's ground, which was shared with the Western Province Rugby Football Union, while the amateurs headed across the railway line to watch a match at the elite Western Province CC. One of the professionals noted in *The Sportsman* that the Malays 'seem to have a fair amount of knowledge of the game, the bowling and fielding reminded one of the style of the Parsees'. He added: 'The bowlers go in for pace, disregarding their fielders entirely, and just pelting as hard as possible at the wickets.'[8]

The coloured cricketers staged another 'trial' fixture on 14 March with the intention of extending their Glover Cup squad to 18 players. The Union CC, captained by Ariefdien, played against the Star of South Africa led by Hendricks at the Cape Town CC ground while the white Western Province XV simultaneously challenged the English on the Western Province CC ground.

Armien Hendricks from Kimberley was selected as captain of the Malay side to play the English a week later. The side would have been further strengthened if it had included Robert Grendon, who smashed 187 out of 260 for the 'Malays' against the 'Europeans' in Kimberley at the New Year, but he was not available.

Excitement among the coloured community was intense in the period leading up to the fixture. At last they would have a chance to test their skills against an international team. Thousands of excited supporters poured into the mountain-framed amphitheatre, filling the ground with colour in contrast to the more sober dress of the white spectators. All 11 professionals in the touring side played. Frank's brother George Hearne stepped in as captain and lost the toss to Armien Hendricks, who decided to bat.

'Naturally the crack professional bowlers were not put on first,' said the *Cape Times* of the Malay innings. Bill Chatterton and Victor Barton opened the bowling, and Lamarah Samsodien made solid progress. The Hearne brothers (Frank's brothers George and

Alec, both making their debut for England) soon joined the attack. Meanwhile, Samsodien was getting his runs 'in fine fashion cracking the bowlers for threes and fours to the great glee of the majority of the spectators'. Jack Hearne (a cousin of the Hearne brothers), who had taken 162 wickets on the tour at an average of less than 7 runs, was spanked for 10 in a five-ball over. Eventually, Samsodien was induced into spooning a catch to Edwin Leaney behind the wicket off Alec Hearne's bowling, having contributed an invaluable 55 in a total of 113. Remarkably, this was the highest individual score against the visitors in all 21 tour games.

In reply that evening, the English found the going more difficult than anticipated. The large coloured crowd delighted in seeing the professionals struggle to cope with the extreme pace of Krom Hendricks and the nagging accuracy of Armien Hendricks and Ebrahim Ariefdien. They bowled five consecutive maidens before a run was scored. When Chatterton hit out in frustration, he lifted a ball from Ariefdien towards square leg. It 'was being cheered for a "sixer"', reported the *Cape Times*, 'but [Krom] Hendricks finely caught the ball close on the boundary'.[9]

Krom Hendricks bowled even faster the next morning, with speed and power generated effortlessly off a relatively short run. Press reports described him as 'loose-limbed' and 'a regular "demon" with his very swift deliveries'. The batsmen attacked the bowling in fear or desperation, and several shots fell just out of reach of the fielders. Unfortunately, the fielding of the Malays did not match their bowling – Barton was missed three times and too many runs were given away. The most memorable moment, however, was the dismissal of Jack Hearne for a brave 67. The *Cape Times* recalled the crowd 'gasping in astonishment when J.T. Hearne, who had been very venturesome, had his off-stump shot some yards out of the ground in trying to drive a fast ball from [Krom] Hendricks'.[10]

It was more than ironic that the South African team had failed in the Test primarily because of the lack of a penetrative fast bowler who could put pressure on the English batsmen. With ball in hand, Hendricks would make this point many times over the next decade. The English captain, George Hearne, described him as 'the fastest bowler in South Africa'. He spoke about the match in an interview in *The Cricket Field*:

> A Malay named Hendricks was very fast indeed. In our last match against the Malays, the wicket was very bad and we didn't like facing the man at all. I was captain during the match and everybody began to ask me to let somebody else go in his place. [Harry] Wood, for instance, [the century maker the previous day], was rapped on the glove and said I ought to think of the danger to his fingers but I told him to get double figures and then he might get out which he did very promptly [retired hurt]. [William] Brockwell, however, managed to slip off. He said that he absolutely must go into Cape Town – on business which would brook no delay – and he went, coming back just after the game was over, cheerily waving his handkerchief. I was in a long time with Jack Hearne but it wasn't pleasant. The balls flew over our heads in all directions and we exasperated [Krom] Hendricks by telling him that we had been told that he was quite a fast bowler and were surprised to find that he was only medium. Of course, he bowled faster than ever then but couldn't get them straight which was what we wanted.[11]

Over the two days, the Malays had performed well in comparison to the other opponents faced by Read's team, scoring 113 and 70 in reply to the tourists' 176 and 8 for no wickets.

After the match, George Hearne recalled being surrounded by the Malay team. 'One of them begged for a piece of my necktie which has in it the team's colours. I cut off a piece and pinned it to his coat and he said afterwards that it would be buried with him.'[12] The match was a huge boost as coloured cricket came under the spotlight and the community, aware of the historic nature of the occasion, rendered enthusiastic support. The thoughtful Bill Chatterton also provided a positive view of coloured cricket: 'The Malays ought to have a future ... they are exceedingly earnest in their desire to play the game properly, and the bowlers try to make better use of the ball. The worst of it is that the colonists will not play against them and so they do not get opportunities of measuring themselves against others.'[13]

William Milton, whose South African team had been annihilated earlier, was almost certainly closeted in the pavilion with members of the South African Cricket Association. The governing body of cricket, including Transvaal and Orange Free State delegates for the first time, was due to meet in the course of the day. Milton presided over the meeting and may also have watched the Malay match with some ambivalence. He must have wondered what might have been when he saw the torrid time that the English professionals were being given by the Malay pace bowlers. He should have been aware that Krom Hendricks – and others – would be an asset to the South African team. But, despite the added attraction of a large crowd witnessing aggressive cricket from a local side, he was reluctant to see his side infiltrated by the lower orders.

The game involving the Malays made sure that paying punters could not reasonably demand their money back for the last day of the Test. In fact, it was considerably more competitive and entertaining than the official match had been. It also enabled the professionals to squeeze a last few shillings out of the tour. And it was a handy means of diverting attention away from the compelling drama that surrounded the arrest of the English captain, Read, and the tour manager, Edwin Ash. On the day they were due to return home, they were served with a sheriff's order refusing to allow them to leave without a legal promise to repay a £1,000 loan from James Logan. After being forced to kick their heels for several hours, a local businessman, Jack Richards, finally did the necessary and Read and Ash arrived humiliatingly by rowing boat to climb the ladder up the ship's side and find Milton with their farewell party in full swing. They would all be meeting in the High Court in the following year.

The administration of cricket in the Western Cape had been criticised rightly and regularly over the years. The main complaint invariably concerned the unilateral manner through which Milton and the Western Province CC – the 'MCC of the Cape' – controlled the game. The latest gripe involved the clubs objecting to their not being given a voice in the costs of hosting Read's team. They declined any responsibility for expenses incurred, notably 'a large amount for rent of the ground charged by the Western Province CC'. The *Cape Times* vented its spleen on being unable to gain entry to the meeting and decided to investigate the way cricket was being administered. It referred to 'some little friction in the Western Province Cricket Union arising again out of some disagreement with the Western Province CC who possess a distinct preponderance of voting power on the Union which is therefore a union in name only'. There were further complaints that all Western Province Cricket Union meetings were held in camera and that there needed to be a fairer distribution of club representation. The report concluded: 'The Province club will take a step forward if it works in the same direction instead of attempting to wreck what may be made a very useful organisation.'[14]

The following day, 'Longstop' submitted a damning indictment of Western Province CC's strategy to the *Cape Times*. He provided an accurate assessment of the administration of the game as it stood in 1892:

> Everything considered there can be no question that the Union is, as a union, a complete fiasco. It is really the old thing over again for the Western Province CC cannot be outvoted. Worked on equitable representation from all clubs wishing to join as at Kimberley and elsewhere – the Union – which it would be then – must succeed; but at present it appears to be the strengthening power of our strongest club. That club has never shown a desire to be the nursing club it should, and in the Cape under notice we have it further exemplified that it has no intention of becoming so.[15]

Beyond the ivory tower of the Western Province CC, coloured cricketers were desperate for the facilities to improve their game. Abdol Burns wrote to the *Cape Times* on behalf of 'the Mahommedan community' to thank the English players and to congratulate their own players for 'the fair stand they made against the professionals, considering the drawbacks they have as regards practice grounds, etc.' Although they were grateful that they were able to play at Newlands, they hoped that 'local cricket teams will, in future, show us a similar kindness in allowing us a better field to practise on'.[16] It was a reasonable request; the facilities for coloured cricket were limited and nets and practice grounds non-existent.

It encouraged a less than positive response. 'Straight Tip' condemned the Malay 'impudence' and regretted the indecent encouragement they received to take part in matches with senior players: 'they will ask for the Cathedral next for their singing clubs to practise'.[17] 'Son of Japhet' skewered the correspondent by suggesting that if 'my little brother Straight Tip' should become a Muslim then he might have a chance of making the highest single score against the tourists, 'which is the sore point when you knock all the padding out of it'.[18]

The bittersweet nature of this game gave way to the tragedy of South African cricket history. Straight Tip was eager to condemn the coloured population to an ignored and oppressive isolation. Tragically his was to be the way of the future, produced by empire and directed by Rhodes. The result was the indescribable loss suffered by the many thousands of black cricketers who lost their birthright – the chance to be citizens of, and to represent, their own country. It was a huge loss to South African cricket as well. South Africa's Test team had struggled for pace and paid the price at Newlands. The same day, on the same surface, the two Hendricks had proved there were fast bowlers ready to lead the South African attack.

The most striking feature of the match – the lightning pace of Krom Hendricks – would become the major focus of debate in South African cricket for more than a decade. Albert Knight, an England player and author of *The Complete Cricketer*, recorded a conversation he had with the touring team's opening batsman, Bill Chatterton. The latter mentioned that he had 'played at home against Richardson, Lockwood and Mold, and against the greatest of Australian genius, Spofforth and Turner'. According to Knight's impressions, Chatterton 'shook his head as the great name of Spofforth passed his lips and agreed that much might be urged on his behalf in a claim as the world's greatest bowler ... Yet the very ablest bowler he had ever met he believed to be, not Spofforth, but a South African black, Hendricks. The memory of this man's pace from the pitch, his quick swing away, alternating with a fine break back, stirred a cold and critical nature to enthusiasm.'[19]

2

'A place not inhabited by white men'

> 'Cricketers who for years have knocked about the Parade stones and spoored holes in the Green Point sand, rather than give up their favourite sport, have surely earned the consideration of the Cape Town public.'
>
> – *Cape Argus* (6 March 1873)

WILLIAM HENRY HENDRICKS was born on 15 October 1857 in the area known as Bo-Kaap ('Upper Cape'), a five-minute walk from the Cape Town city centre. Once popularly referred to as the Malay Quarter, it is regarded as the traditional home of a population that emerged through the influx of thousands of labourers, slaves and political exiles, transported in chains by Dutch settlers from the colonies that formed the East Indies. Today, Bo-Kaap is a popular tourist destination, with picturesque terraced houses on steep, cobbled lanes.

They present a charming mixture of Cape Dutch and Cape Georgian architectural styles, with the oldest house in the area on 71 Wale Street now serving as the Bo-Kaap Museum. It was built by Jan de Waal, sexton of Groote Kerk, on land he bought between 1763 and 1768. He began building small *huurhuisjes* – rental houses – which he subsequently leased to his slaves. The boundaries of his holdings were roughly formed by Rose, Chiappini, Shortmarket and

Wale streets, with the area stretching in ragged formation up the side of Signal Hill.

After the emancipation of the slaves, most of whom were Muslim, in 1834, property developers built further dwellings in terraces as Jan de Waal had done more than half a century earlier. These flat-roofed houses were structured in rows with narrow frontages but considerable depth to accommodate the large families of the time. The mainly Muslim community that occupied the new parts of Bo-Kaap comprised fishermen, tailors, shoemakers, bricklayers, carpenters and silversmiths. They built up their small businesses alongside the successful merchants, with many of the families who now inhabit Bo-Kaap having lived there for generations. Houses that were painted white while on lease have since presented brightly coloured facades, which some say were an expression of freedom by the new homeowners. Others attribute the development to the Eid al-Fitr celebration at the end of Ramadan, a time to dress up in bright costumes and repaint homes in distinctive colours. A modern street might feature lime green, turquoise, canary yellow, sky blue, pastel purple and even bubblegum pink facades.

In his early years, Hendricks resided on Chiappini Street, which runs through the heart of Bo-Kaap. His mother, Anne, brought him up, but there is no record of his father on their death certificates. Many years later, in 1894, during the debate over his potential selection for South Africa, Hendricks wrote to the *Cape Times* to state that his father was born of Dutch parents in Cape Town and that his mother hailed from St Helena. Immigrants from the island had been imported as indentured labour in the second half of the nineteenth century, and as descendants of English soldiers and local slaves, were generally considered to be 'coloured' by Europeans. Family legend, however, perhaps with a twist in the telling, suggests that 'Anne came from Holland as a young, pregnant girl in search of her lover who had preceded her to the Cape, and whom she did not find'.[1]

The extent to which Hendricks was 'objectively' coloured or European was of no significance to his early life in Bo-Kaap, an area which the Reverend Thomas Fothergill Lightfoot said consisted of 'many nations'. It was a melting pot in a port city, reflecting a diverse population of seafarers, settlers, freed slaves and adventurers from around the world, along with indigenous African peoples. This was the world of the old 'liberal' Cape where racial identity mattered little in the town, but much more in the socially and racially exclusive white suburbs.

The part of Cape Town in which Hendricks grew up was under the watchful eye of the remarkable Thomas Lightfoot, who had moved there in 1858 at the high point of Cape liberalism under Sir George Grey. On arrival, he had marvelled at 'the flat summit of Table Mountain and the peaks of the two hills on either side, which like arms, seem to hold the town beneath in a gigantic embrace', and he described the scene which met him at the jetty 'as extraordinary: Kaffirs, Hottentots, Malays – all mixed up together'. He commented on the flat-topped, whitewashed houses of the city and, just as numerous, the old Dutch mansions with their stoeps projecting into unpaved streets, and how, 'when the wind blows, especially the dreaded "south-easter", the clouds of red, gritty dust are overwhelming'.

Lightfoot's life work was 'to be a mission amongst the coloured people of Cape Town – I am afraid a rather discouraging field of labour, but I must try to do my duty and leave the rest to God'. Lightfoot served the community until his death in 1904, a period of nearly 50 years. He became 'a household word in Cape Town, as well as the length and breadth of the vast Diocese of South Africa', and his memory, according to his contemporaneous biographers, was 'so cherished and revered by all, whatever their colour or creed ... particularly the grief-stricken, the afflicted and poor ...'[2]

Almost as soon as he arrived at the Cape, Lightfoot was confronted by the 1858 smallpox epidemic that claimed up to 2,000 lives out of the city's population of 24,000. His fearless support for those afflicted made a lasting impression, particularly among the 5,000-strong Malay community. St Paul's Mission was established in 1859 to cater for the emancipated slaves and their descendants, and efforts were soon under way to raise funds to build a church. A day school catered for 300 children, a few hundred metres from Hendricks's home. There was also a night school running three times a week, which would attract '50 to 70 men, 40 to 50 women'.

Lightfoot took lessons in Dutch and became sufficiently fluent to conduct church services in the language. By the early 1860s, he and Dean Henry Douglas were providing ten different services on Sundays in St George's Cathedral and its dependent chapels. This resulted in them attracting people from all levels of society. Lightfoot had 'so much to be thankful for in that I have been permitted to see such fruit from my labours', but lamented that 'owing to the impoverished condition of the Colony, it seems just now impossible to raise the necessary funds for the support of others'.[3]

There are no details on the life of the young Hendricks, but when he was seven years old he would have witnessed one of the greatest catastrophes since the settlement was formed. On Tuesday, 16 May 1865, 28 ships were anchored in Table Bay, unprepared for a great north-westerly gale that struck with shattering force and caused untold destruction and misery. Contemporary accounts graphically described the drama and the anxiety, frustration and disbelief of those who gathered on the central jetty to watch the unfolding disaster. They looked on helplessly as vessels were driven ashore and crews and passengers drowned in the surf. Table Bay boatmen had long been recognised for their courage and skill in coping with the greatest dangers in the most violent gales, but this was exceptional. Several boats were employed to convey anchors to ships that had dragged or lost their own. The *Stag* was engaged on such an 'errand of mercy to the imperilled and distressed' when it capsized. The *Prince* made directly for her and saved two; 'the remainder were already lifeless, although they retained with a death grasp their hold on the mast and rigging'.[4] The *City of Peterborough* struck upon the reef off Papendorp (the village that became Woodstock) and within half an hour went to pieces; the *Athens* drifted broadside on the rocks between Mouille Point and Green Point, and within another half-hour was shattered. And so the tragedy continued; 18 ocean-going vessels dragging their anchors and drifting ashore with many lives lost.

The *South African Advertiser and Mail* lamented the following day that 'dead bodies of those whom only 24 short hours ago we reckoned among our greatest friends are still drifting among the tangled seaweed or tossed in cruel sport beneath the hungry crawling foam'. The newspaper added that '110 seamen are now in the Sailors' Home, three-fourths of them being from the shipwrecked ships. Many of them are totally destitute.' When the *Stag* went down, the seven men who perished were married with children. The *Advertiser* drew attention to the fact that of all the brave fellows who died in the disaster, 'the crew of the *Stag* ranked conspicuously among the first; while of these, again, Jack Collins, Joe Myers, Frank Maker and Nicholas [no surname provided] – who have all gone – were men as gallant and undaunted as ever stormed a breach or won a Victoria Cross'.[5]

Lightfoot was a member of the Committee of the Sailors' Home located in Bo-Kaap. He knew personally many of the bereaved and their families. The Myers family, for example, who had lost their brave father, Joe, were members of his church. The parents, who had married in 1856, had four children, all of whom were baptised in St George's Cathedral in the years just prior to their father's death. Samuel William (who was born in 1858), Sarah Rachel (born in 1860), Georgina Maria (born in 1862) and the youngest, Pauline Sophia (born in 1864), lived with their parents in Buitengracht Street, close to where Hendricks resided. In due course, Hendricks would fall in love with Georgina and they would marry.

While there is no direct evidence of Hendricks's early participation in cricket games, there are numerous reports of the Malay enthusiasm for the sport, which gathered in momentum in the 1870s, and pick-up matches were staged on the streets of Bo-Kaap and neighbouring suburbs. Hendricks may have joined St Paul's Cricket Club, founded with 30 members at St Paul's School in 1871. An approach was made to the Western Province Cricket Club, then based in Wynberg, requesting the use of their facilities, but the pupils were turned down. It prompted a letter from 'Peter' to the *Cape Argus* that condemned the Western Province CC's short-sighted policy in denying players who could not afford the club's subscription the chance to play on the Wynberg field.[6]

'Cricket everywhere!' wrote one new arrival at the Cape, 'An Old Peripatetic', in the early 1870s. On sailing into the bay, he had been delighted to see 'our beloved game going on half way up "the Devil's Peak"', and then 'behind Zonnebloem, on a ledge scooped as it were from the mountain's side, we have beheld stalwart young Kafirs bowling and hitting with freedom and skill'. His pleasure did not end there: 'Fort Knokke must have been named prophetically ... for there, 11s, military and civilian, receive and distribute thumps to one another's shins' and, not far away, there are 'the cricketing glories of the Parade ... as naturally as within the precincts of York or Canterbury, cricket grows beneath the shadow of St George's Cathedral' while 'breezy Green Point Common, one of the finest natural grounds on earth, at times swarms with cricketers'.[7]

Cricketers required space, and during the 1870s they made use of the Parade. Her Majesty's servants would fire 'blank cartridge in the mornings at the Masonic Hotel, and round shot at one another in the shape of cricket balls in the evenings'. And 'skirmishing round their serried ranks on every patch of green [were] crowds of small boys of all colours playing cricket'. Yet, despite the enthusiasm for the game at the various venues, Cape Town did not have 'a decent wicket whereon to bat'.[8] The *Cape Argus* took up Old Peripatetic's argument, stating that those cricketers who for years have 'knocked about the Parade stones and spoored holes in the Green Point sand, rather than give up their favourite sport, have surely earned the consideration of the Cape Town public'.[9] There was nothing to compare with Wynberg – 'the Cape Lord's' – a ground some 14 kilometres away that belonged to the ruling class who had made their homes in the beautiful southern suburbs. There, said R.M. Ballantyne, an 1870s traveller, they 'built elegant mansions, to which they retire after the business of each day to escape the heat, dust, and smells of the town. A short line of railroad runs to these verdant spots ...'[10]

Anthony Trollope, the famous writer and cousin of William Milton's father, published an account of his travels in South Africa. As a celebrity, he attracted considerable press coverage. He worked closely with the Cape governor, Sir Henry Barkly, who helped plan the trip, and the high commissioner, Sir Bartle Frere. In a book that became a 'standard work for editorialists, parliamentarians and polemicists', Trollope made the key point that, in contrast to other parts of empire, 'South Africa is a country of black men, – and not of white men. It has been so; it is so; and it will continue to be so.' He felt confident nevertheless that, for some time to come, the white man would maintain his own ascendancy over the black population, but future development depended on efforts 'to promote the working of the coloured man'. In his travels, Trollope would endorse the idea of white supremacy and the gospel of work, 'that the white man has to be master and the black man servant ... It will be sufficient for us if we can make up our minds that at least for the next 100 years we shall not choose to be ruled by him.'[11] High Commissioner Frere considered the findings of Trollope, and spoke of developing 'legislative and other means' to ensure Africans were 'subdued and converted to habits of useful labour and civilisation [and thereby made into] the subject races of an imperial mistress'.[12]

Citizenship, wrote historian Saul Dubow, 'was not a right: it would have to be earned by individuals who could show that they were conforming to the norms and precepts of the Victorian moral economy'.[13] In the end, such conformity meant another empty promise.

Trollope's impressions of Cape Town were recorded when Hendricks was beginning his working life. Twelve hours after his arrival, Trollope wrote of Cape Town as a 'poor, niggery, yellow-faced, half-bred sort of place, with an ugly Dutch flavour about it'.[14] A walk through the streets of Cape Town, he continued, 'is sufficient to show the stranger that he has reached a place not inhabited by white men ... there is so much of the savage and so much of the oriental that the ordinary Englishman does not come out and work among them'. He said that much of the industry in the town centre was done by 'coloured persons of various races' who spoke a language that 'the Dutch in Holland will hardly condescend to recognise as their own'. Trollope thought, in terms of labour, 'the most valuable race is that of the Malays, and these are the descendants of slaves whom the early Dutch settlers introduced from Java. The Malays are so-called Mahommidans and some are to be seen flaunting about the town in turbans and flowing robes.'[15] He made no mention of their passion for cricket, which is perhaps surprising because he once published a book on 'British sports and pastimes'. The early newspapers, however, referred to the Malay involvement in cricket every week throughout the long summers. It was observed that large crowds of 'coloured persons' congregated on the Green Point Common on Sundays where they indulged from sunrise to sunset in the game of cricket; a scene repeated over many years with important rivalries played out during the festive holidays.

Numerous cricket teams played within the precincts of the city with the Malay community conspicuous in the organisation of the game. It was unfortunate, if not inevitable, that the Marlburian Milton, who began work at the Cape Colonial Office in April 1878, should choose to ignore their existence. On his arrival at the Cape, he recalled 'cricketing was not in the best form' and claimed to have accompanied Western Province CC members when they were 'trying at the George Hotel and the Masonic to make up a team'. Yet contemporary reports in the *Cape Times* indicated that there was no shortage of players as coloured cricket was thriving and, apart from the rainy winter months, was played throughout the year. Milton would almost certainly have noticed the team lists and cricket results that were published every week. Over the Easter period in April 1878, he would have seen that the Star of Hope at Cape Town travelled to Paarl to take on Fair Players, while District Six played District Seven at Blood River. The Paarl Band of Hope were entertained by the Stellenbosch Commercial CC, with the former going so far as to decorate their bats with blue ribbons and the latter red. The scores were modest, because of weak technique and poor wickets. The Commercial CC totalled 60 and was able to bowl out the Band of Hope for 9 and 21.

In May 1878, Milton might have read that Beautiful Star CC defeated Lillywhite CC by an innings and 11 runs and the following week accounted for Lady Bird CC by a similar margin. After that they were scheduled to play Champion CC of Cape Town, although no scores were published. Some clubs fielded more than one side. Milton would possibly have noticed that the Star of South Africa's first team – one of the strongest club sides – was tested by the Paarl Band of Hope while their Second XI played Silver Star of Stellenbosch. Not long afterwards, the Stellenbosch club met Alberts of Simon's Town. Also in May, there were matches involving Standard CC, Colleen Bawn, Beaufort West, Roodebloem Star, Venus CC, Kaffir College CC, Rising Star CC of Rondebosch, Union CC, Cape Town's Band of Hope and the Active CC. Cricket gave pride and identity to those immersed in a vibrant cricket culture that involved numerous clubs, all of them relatively small and including players from the different population groups.

The most important cricket day in May was always the Queen's Birthday. In the course of the year, Milton would discover cricket matches were staged during the other holiday periods – Whit Monday, Christmas and New Year. Many of the contests were played out at Green Point Common, but there were also matches at Woodstock, Klapmuts, Fort Knokke, the Market Square and Claremont. Large crowds attended the games because they were popular social occasions, often with a band in attendance. At the beginning of 1879, the Star of South Africa embarked on their traditional short tour to Paarl and Stellenbosch. Teams such as the Commercial CC of Stellenbosch, Fair Players of Paarl, Uranus CC of Stellenbosch and the Union Star of Paarl acted as hosts. Then, at Easter, the Star of South Africa entertained the country sides to a cricket tournament at Green Point Common. On such occasions, the Star of South Africa assembled a Third XI that played Beautiful Star of Stellenbosch.

These cricket teams were predominantly of mixed race or Malay backgrounds with a smattering of Europeans, although any distinction would only have been a matter of degree and gone unnoticed by the players. They reflected the liberal Cape Town society, a more complex mixture of people than indicated by the Cape census of 1875, which had divided the population into two groups: 'Europeans or whites' and those referred to as 'Other than Europeans or whites'. The Star of South Africa, always regarded as a leading Malay side, comprised the following for one of their matches in 1878: A. de Jongh, H. de Jongh, J. Williams, C. Rich, A. Prince, J. de Jongh, G. Thomas, C. Vanderdorp, W. Smith, C. Newman, E. Johnson and James Martin (umpire). They included black and white, Muslim and Christian cricketers and were prepared to play any of the sides in Cape Town and the surrounding areas. Some of their most exciting encounters were those against the various army teams that regularly played club sides at all levels, a legacy perhaps of their broader imperial role and experience elsewhere, most notably India. Fixtures were often hosted at Fort Knokke or the Garrison ground, against the Royal Artillery, the Highlanders, the Fort Knokke Army Hospital and the Royal Scots. The mixed Cape Town cricket teams were not, however, matched against the better-known establishment clubs that played in the southern suburbs. Those clubs belonged to the gentry – the white establishment – who were conscious of their power and privilege and looked to exclusionary segregation in protecting their white bourgeois status.

It was in this context of class division that Hendricks would play his cricket. He was on the other edge of the class divide to the privileged patrician Milton and, like Milton, he was endeavouring to establish himself in a career. Cape Town was enjoying unprecedented prosperity at the end of the 1870s. The discovery of diamonds in Kimberley had led to the ongoing development of the railways as well as the telegraph, with economic expansion creating employment opportunities.

The Cape government had also established the Table Bay Harbour Board, which oversaw improvements that were taking place at the docks. Hendricks was able to secure a responsible position as an engine-driver, which meant that he could take his next big step in life and ask Georgina Myers to marry him. Her circumstances had changed insofar as her mother, Sophia Wilhelmina Elizabeth (Koch) Myers, had remarried – to a messenger, Thomas Roberts – and they had moved to Roeland Street. There were two further children – a half-sister for Georgina (Sophia Margaret – born 1868) and a half-brother (William John – born 1871). William John Roberts was close to Georgina and served as a witness at the baptisms and weddings of her children. He also lived for a short period at the Hendricks' home, and became a clerk on the South African Railways.

The marriage of 22-year-old William Henry Hendricks and 17-year-old Georgina Maria Myers took place at ten o'clock on Wednesday, 2 June 1880, at St George's Cathedral. It was the only wedding in the cathedral on that day and the happy occasion was solemnised by the Reverend Lightfoot himself. Georgina's uncle granted her permission to marry. The wedding was well attended by members of the Hendricks and Myers families and their friends. The witnesses were Henry Joseph Francis Verit (a storeman in De Waterkant) and Annie Verit, both close friends of the Myers family. Their mother, Sarah Verit, had acted as a witness 20 years earlier when Georgina's sister, Sarah Rachel, was baptised at St George's Cathedral in 1860.

The next two years would be memorable but anxious for the newly married couple. Their first child, Sophia Georgina, was delivered on 7 August 1882 and was named after her grandmother and mother. Georgina's pregnancy, however, coincided with the outbreak of another serious smallpox epidemic. It appears that arrangements were made for her to leave Cape Town. Lightfoot's biography records that several ships arrived with passengers carrying the disease, adding that 'there was naturally no little alarm and excitement in phlegmatic Cape Town; those who were pecuniarily able to do so, fled to the country':

> The epidemic claimed numerous victims, white and coloured, but especially those of the latter class, whose death-rate was extremely heavy. Canon Lightfoot, who had, it may be incidentally remarked, gained invaluable experience during the spread of the smallpox of 1858, went at all hours, daily and nightly, into the slums and alleys of Cape Town and made house-to-house visitations without distinction as to creed or colour of the patients ... He went amongst that suffering humanity as if he bore a charmed life. The Malays simply worshipped him.[16]

Lightfoot saw the Malay population in a different light from those whites who lived comfortably in the suburbs. When the boom years gave way towards the end of 1881 to the onset of a severe economic depression, the Malays were criticised by the ruling class as having an immoral effect on Cape Town. The press that promoted 'Englishness', notably the *Cape Times* and *The Lantern*, were particularly inclined to use the smallpox epidemic as a stick to beat the poor, indulging in negative stereotyping and blaming the Malay community. The whole question of housing and sanitation became, for a while, the basis of political activity: 'the sooner the Malays are forced to reside in a separate district the better for all concerned'.[17] The English-speaking population united behind the 'Clean Party', which entered municipal politics and criticised the dangers of poor sanitation. Victory in the 1882 election, said historian Vivian Bickford-Smith, 'signalled the emergence of a dominant class in Cape Town that was not only white and bourgeois but also predominantly English', except for Scots and anglicised Dutch-speakers.[18]

Despite the widening class and racial divisions, it was a measure of the interrelatedness of the communities over so many years that the Malays and the English should share a common interest in the game of cricket. They played together in Bo-Kaap and neighbouring areas where the races mixed freely. They would also play cricket at grounds, sometimes hired, in the white suburbs, occasionally against 'European' teams.

Hendricks is not recorded as playing for the Star of South Africa CC until 1 January 1883 when he was 25 years old. It was the occasion of the traditional New Year's fixture against their long-standing rivals, Fairplayers of Paarl. It is difficult to know how much cricket Hendricks had played up to that stage, but he was six foot, well built and athletic, which must have made him an exciting prospect. The Star of South Africa team list again suggested that the players came from a variety of backgrounds: T. de Jongh, J. Reynolds, J. de Jongh, H. Hendricks, J. Lewis, G. Pauline, H. de Jongh, D. Bush, T. Lotts, W. Bush and W. Muller. The two best cricketers in the team were the De Jongh brothers, Thomas and

Johannes, who were bakers and, like Hendricks, attended services at St George's Cathedral. The Star of South Africa (64 and 45) defeated Fairplayers (64 and 13) by 32 runs, but Hendricks experienced a modest start, being bowled by Petersen for a duck in the first innings and bowled by Jacobs for 7 in the second. He was seemingly played for his batting, featuring at number four in the order, and did not bowl.

It was the beginning of Hendricks's relatively long and happy association with the club. He would play most of his early matches on the vast tract of open scrubland that made up the Green Point fields situated not far from his home and work. In between shifts, he attended practices at the Parade, a traditional venue for both cricket and football. Sport provided much enjoyment, but there was mounting opposition to the Malay community's presence in what were considered 'European' areas. 'Vally' wrote to the *Cape Times* in 1884:

> I have no wish to interfere with certain 'darkeys' who play what they call 'cricket' on the Parade every afternoon; but I would be glad if some arrangement could be made whereby passers-by – and especially ladies – would be protected. No matter how many or who passes, they stop for no-one ...'[19]

The Parade was South Africa's equivalent of the Bombay Maidan, which historian Ramachandra Guha described as 'an expanse of green ground at the southern end of the island of Bombay'. From the early 1830s, Parsi boys would watch and imitate the cricket played by European soldiers. Unfortunately, mishaps occurred and 'a flying ball once struck the wife of a European constable out on her evening walk. The incident caused the Parsi cricketers to be temporarily banned from the Maidan.' It was a harsh punishment because the narrow sliver of land was the only place to which they could go for exercise and recreation.[20]

At the Cape, Violets CC and Hendricks's Star of South Africa continued to publicise their practices on the Parade. Unfortunately for them, the town council and the chief of police progressively restricted cricket to a far corner near the Castle of Good Hope. By 1890, the 'cricketing glories of the Parade' were over when ball-playing was prohibited altogether. Councillor Solomon said that 'cricket was played in the Parade to such an extent as to make the crossing of same positively dangerous for pedestrians'. Councillor Woodhead claimed that 'there was not much danger if only youngsters play', but criticised club players who made use of the space for practices, referring to them as 'great hulking fellows who ought to be at work'.[21]

'A Cricketer' wrote to the *Cape Argus* to ask why the game should be stopped on the Parade and not Caledon Square. He said it was the opinion of many clubs that Green Point Common was too far to go for practice and hoped that at least part of the Parade would be granted for the game. An article in the same newspaper commented:

> The stern Town Council has decreed that little boys shan't play cricket or football on the Parade any longer. The old gentleman with the crutches and the 'bell topper' may now hobble across without fear of his 'bell topper' coming to grief, but possibly some of the youthful spirits of Cape Town, who have hitherto found cricket and football on the Parade an outlet for their exuberance, may now seek other means for letting off steam even more objectionable to the City Fathers. It is an unwise thing to place too heavy restrictions on youthful sports.[22]

It was more than simply preventing children from having fun. Attitudes were hardening as cricket became part of the discriminatory tendency of empire. The council showed the way by placing pressure on clubs that struggled to obtain access to facilities. Sport in the Cape liberal context could not last as the 1880s brought about demographic and social change. 'The mineral discoveries,' says historian Shula Marks, were 'crucial in the shaping of modern South Africa and the peculiarities of its social order.'[23]

3

Opposition to the 'MCC of the Cape Colony'

> 'To us there appears no reason whatever why the well-behaved cricketers of the Malay community should not be occasionally met by European exponents of the British national game, which our coloured neighbours show such a commendable desire to emulate.'
>
> – *Cape Times* (15 February 1891)

SEPARATION OF THE races had been largely confined to the social exclusivity of the ruling class, but there were signs of a wider movement taking place. Cricket reflected society, and a class structure was rigidly maintained through the Western Province CC's obsessive desire to be the MCC of the Cape Colony. Its aim, largely driven by Milton, was to play just a few selected elite clubs and a sprinkling of festival encounters. Every effort was made to maintain a monopoly over new arrivals from England, especially those who had a title, a military rank or were products of public schools and the ancient universities. The club's negative impact on the game in Cape Town stretched further in that it chose not to risk defeat – and the accompanying scorn – by allowing the Mother City to attend tournaments hosted by the other centres.

When Milton ignored an invitation to send a team to a tournament at the Diamond Fields in Easter 1886, there was an immediate reaction. Charles Finlason, the erudite and perceptive writer for the Kimberley-based *Daily Independent*, decided to take a side to Cape Town. He loved a challenge and generated tremendous excitement when he arranged a two-week tour of the Cape by Kimberley's Stray Klips in January 1887. The players were largely from Eclectics, the club that Finlason had founded in Kimberley, with the focal point being the game against the Western Province CC at Southey's Field, where 'the carriage enclosure was full and the fair sex turned up in great force, many of them wearing the Eclectic colours'. Kimberley's irrepressible cricketers not only captured the hearts of the Cape Town ladies, but when the battle unfolded, they were also well prepared for the defining moment of the game. Kimberley had scored 110 and the hosts were four down with 40 runs on the board when Milton mistimed a big hit and was caught by the bowler, Irvine Grimmer. 'Such a howl that arose then I have not heard for many a day,' recalled Finlason. 'No one could sit down or listen; everybody had to cheer and then talk…'[1]

The Stray Klips' tour reinforced Finlason's oft-stated view that cricket was making greater progress in Kimberley than it was at the Cape. Kimberley went on to win the Extraneous Tournament that they hosted in April 1887 and then the fourth Champion Bat Tournament at Grahamstown in December of the same year. The driving force behind their success was Finlason, who keenly anticipated an independently organised tour made by the Cape Town Wanderers to Kimberley in 1888. The visitors lost two of their three matches by an innings. Their one victory owed much to a fine eighth-wicket stand between Captain Robert Spurway and Private Beech, a partnership that did not transfer to the social side of the tour. It was reported that Private Beech was forced to travel separately from the team – third class – and, 'once there, [was] studiously and contemptuously ignored by those who had sought his aid to wrest the honours of the willow from Kimberley'.[2] Pirates Cricket Club endeavoured to make Beech's stay as pleasant as possible, but, said 'Old De Beer's' in *The Lantern*, '[b]ecause that good cricketer happens to be a mere private his co-workers have considered it infra-dig and derogatory to the sublime positions they claim on the social pedestal to have any intercourse with him away from the cricket field'.[3]

Coloured clubs were also active in building a cricket network. Tours involving the country region around Cape Town – notably Paarl, Worcester and Stellenbosch – were well established. In 1887, the Red Crescents, a powerful Kimberley club, followed in the footsteps of the Stray Klips by arranging a visit to Cape Town. They were hosted by Alberts CC and played against mixed-race sides. A year later, during the Easter period of 1888, Star of South Africa went on tour to Swellendam. The small Overberg town is the third oldest in South Africa and situated more than 200 kilometres from Cape Town. Two matches were played and won against the local sides, Guardians and Excelsiors. Hendricks had a fine tour, carrying his bat for an unbeaten 38 out of 65 in the first match and recording figures of 6-7 in four overs in the second encounter.[4]

It was at this time – late 1880s to 1890 – that the revival of the Cape Town CC presented a new powerful organisation prepared to take on Milton's Western Province CC. The amalgamation of Gardens and Leeuwenhof into a strong town club was the product of Afrikaner Bond leader 'Onze Jan' Hofmeyr's meticulous planning. The two clubs shared key posts on the new Cape Town CC committee with Hofmeyr, James Sivewright, John J. Graham, Louis Smuts, William 'Billy' Simkins and Carlo Douglas de Fenzi, all well-known personalities. There were political undertones to Hofmeyr's and Sivewright's involvement in the club as they intended to forge a place for the Afrikaner at the highest level of the game. Politically, Hofmeyr 'wanted at all costs to eliminate the imperial factor in South Africa, that is the power of the British government to interfere in South African affairs to the embarrassment of a self-governing colony';[5] and on the cricket front he wished to curtail efforts to establish a governing body in the style of the MCC. A complacent Milton did not appear to realise that Hofmeyr's involvement in the game would result in the Western Province CC's hegemony being challenged.

Conflict was inevitable. At a Cape Town CC committee meeting on 12 March 1890, there were complaints that the Western Province CC was making no effort to consult with Cape Town clubs, which was anything but a new development. Simkins called for a meeting of clubs to protest the Western Province CC's actions – on this occasion, regarding the organisation of overseas tours – but Hofmeyr prevented confrontation by declaring there was insufficient time for such an arrangement. Instead, a resolution was drawn up, distributed to members of the Cape Town CC and published. It read:

> During the past season the necessity has been frequently urged on members of your committee by members of the club and of other clubs to take some steps to wrest from the Western Province Cricket Club the apparent monopoly which they hold in regard to the administration of cricketing matters in the Western Province, and obtain equal representation for all first-class local clubs on some duly constituted board in whose hands the sole management of such matters should rest.[6]

It was a strongly worded statement of intent, but Sivewright tactfully stated that the Cape Town CC committee did not agree with many of the critical remarks that were being made about the Western Province CC at that time. The *Cape Argus* rightly argued that the 'undignified squabbles only go to emphasise the long felt want of a cricket association', but success depended on Sivewright gaining the co-operation of Milton and his committee in pursuing change.[7] There was no clear indication as to how much discussion was taking place behind the scenes, but Hofmeyr, with 'a natural gift for lobbying and for grass-roots organisation',[8] was able to make use of his vice-presidents, Sivewright (who knew Milton well) and John J. Graham (the older brother of Lynedoch), in ensuring the Western Province CC fell into line.

Towards the end of 1888, the Cape Town CC decided to occupy a ground next door to the Western Province CC. Several members of the Cape Town CC who were active within the Western Province

Rugby Football Union were able to facilitate an arrangement whereby the cricketers would sub-rent the proposed new rugby facility at Newlands during the summer. Cape Town CC effectively offered members a similar environment to that of Western Province CC. Progress was rapid and demonstrated organised, sometimes aggressive, management. For Hofmeyr, it was also a matter of bringing the English and Dutch together through creating cricket opportunities for those outside the orbit of the Western Province CC. His methods in administering cricket were consistent with his political stance, where he regarded the recruitment of Englishmen as testament to the Bond's success. Addressing the May 1888 Bond Conference, he referred to progress in securing equality between Dutch and English: 'If we shall follow this path, we shall become one volk.'[9]

A united cricket governing body in the Cape was Hofmeyr's aim, although progress was temporarily stalled by the arrival of the first English team. Milton was in charge of the enterprise, which saw the tourists travel widely through southern Africa. From the outset, Finlason was alert to the importance of fostering a South African national consciousness and championed a colonial obsession to beat the Mother Country at her own game. Early on in the 1888/89 tour, he predicted that the English would be beaten and he was proved right, albeit in matches where the tourists faced more than 11 players. It did not take Finlason long to point out that, contrary to their self-image, the English did not like losing. The dapper newspaperman saw the tourists as squealers, unable to apply the stiff upper lip that was at the heart of their public-school image. In turn, they considered his comments to be in particularly poor taste at a time when proper colonial respect was expected. But then he detested a system that had not only created an 'elite', but had also cultivated a network that assisted its members to penetrate top positions in the professions. He told readers:

> Nothing that the colony has can equal anything that the old country has; nothing that a colonial-born man can do can equal what a home-born man can do. Such are the unfortunate

> opinions which are held by many men who owe every farthing they have in the world to the colony they milk systematically in and out of season. The feeling has been intensified by men who have for the moment rendered bitter and unreasonable their oft publicly repeated prognostications as to the mincemeat the formidable English cricketers would make of the colonial cricketers and been proved woefully wrong by them.[10]

The events that unfolded in the course of the tour should have been an eye-opener for Milton, as he had previously shown little enthusiasm for, or even interest in, cricket outside that played by the privileged elite at the Western Province CC. While insight was gained into the way the game was played in various outposts – 'articulate, settled, westernised black families had emerged ... Africans established cricket clubs' – the opportunity to fully unify cricket was overlooked in favour of government policy which discouraged mixed sport.[11] The subject was discussed at the time and the English manager, Major Warton, wrote of 'as quaint a sight as ever cricketers saw at Mowbray. Two or three cricket matches were being played by Malays and Kaffirs, and hundreds of Malay women in the many coloured costumes were there to do honour to their friends'.[12] The tour captain, Aubrey Smith, spoke of the need to encourage all races to play cricket in South Africa. 'Our visit, which, from all that I can see,' he told a gathering in Port Elizabeth, 'is calculated to have so great an effect on the cricket of the Cape, not only amongst the white population, but even amongst the black [people] ... wherever you go in the colonies you will find that it is cricket which binds men together in the cause of sport and I hope it will always be so.'[13]

Milton was aware that comments were being made about those communities excluded from the tour programme. In a speech at Kimberley he publicly promoted his own achievements in building the game at the Cape. He told his audience that when he arrived, there was just 'one club in the suburbs, but now in Cape Town, cricket was played everywhere, with proper materials, or with paraffin tins and a fir cone (laughter)' and that one Saturday he counted 'the names of 420 players announced in the 'papers to play cricket that day. That showed the advance of cricket.'[14] It was astonishing that he should endeavour to take credit for the progress made given his disinterest in cricket outside of the Western Province CC. Moreover, it is difficult to comprehend that Milton should deride the efforts of the black cricketers to play the game and yet a fair percentage of the 420 names would have been players of colour. Cricket participation had increased in spite of Milton and not because of him.

Huge English victories in the Eastern Cape prompted the question of why talented black cricketers had not been included in the local teams. It was an issue that upset an African newspaper proprietor, John Tengo Jabavu, who was most interested when the tourists visited King William's Town, an area where cricket played an important role within urban black popular culture. Jabavu argued that cricket matches were calculated to make the two races 'have more mutual trust and confidence than all the coercive and repressive legislation in the world'. When the English played against the white Cape Mounted Rifles, the latter's commanding officer, Colonel Zachary Bayly, was conscious that everyone should see the cricket and arranged for the ground to be 'fenced but not screened'. As a consequence, Jabavu's *Imvo Zabantsundu* could state that there were people of all classes supporting the game, with a number of black spectators among the crowd of 2,000. The newspaper recorded that 'the sympathies of the native spectators were with the English', thereby heralding the beginning of a long tradition of black support for visiting sides.[15]

The South African team selected for the first Test at Port Elizabeth represented the various parts of the fragmented southern African political map. The first 'national' team – albeit English-speaking and white – came before there was a nation, as unification was more than 20 years away. The significance of two Test matches against a unified South African team was not lost on Rhodes and Hofmeyr. Five members of the Legislative Assembly attended a farewell dinner for the touring side, with the Honourable Frederick Schermbrucker speaking to the guests of the importance of the tour in uniting the South African states. Equally appealing to pro-unification advocates were calls for cricket associations to cater not only for the Western Cape, but also for the wider population of southern Africa, an area encompassing the British colonies, Boer republics and high-commission territories. While Milton had long been the Cape's stumbling block insofar as cricket unification was concerned, he would have to adjust his ways to accommodate the plans of Rhodes and Hofmeyr. Events dictated that the Western Province CC endeavour to embrace Afrikaans-speaking cricketers. The fixture against Stellenbosch in 1889 was thus referred to in the press as 'this annual match in which considerable interest is taken', while the regular appearance of Afrikaners Nicolaas Theunissen and Pieter de Villiers for Western Province CC suggested a change of heart in its selection policy, quite apart from an immeasurable strengthening of the bowling attack. The Western Province CC's dramatic about-turn was seen as being 'Rhodes-inspired – his alliance with the Bond was just around the corner'.[16]

Hofmeyr's Cape Town CC drove developments that led to the formation of the Western Province Cricket Union on 5 September 1890. It was agreed that Western Province CC should have four delegates to the union, Cape Town CC two, Claremont two and Sea Point one. However, the election of Milton as president and Pieter de Villiers as secretary/treasurer effectively gave Western Province CC six votes against the five of the other delegates. It was an all-white governing body and cricketers of colour were not considered. An interesting arrangement was nevertheless already in place whereby the Western Province and Cape Town cricket clubs allowed the Malay community to play on their respective grounds at Newlands. It brought in much-needed revenue as the matches attracted large crowds. An article on the January 1890 tournament, for example, referred to 'the whole Malay population [having] deserted Cape Town for the sylvan pasture' and that 'from an early hour the road was alive with a string of vehicles heavily freighted with Malays [as] every conveyance was pressed into the service'. Military bands attended the matches and a further attraction was lent by 'the arrival of many of the elite of the white population, who merged themselves upon the pavilion stand, the quiet refined costumes of the ladies throwing into greater relief the wealth of colour in the other portions of the ground'.[17]

In November 1890, Western Province CC agreed to allow the Malays to use their ground at Newlands for four successive Mondays to hold an inter-town tournament. The *Cape Times* previewed the match involving Claremont and Pirates from Kimberley and stated it 'will doubtless attract thousands of the coloured population'.[18] When Claremont played Alberts, it was observed that the Malays entered into the game with much zest. A writer in the *Cape Argus* thought 'it was very funny when a batsman had been sent back, to see the players gather round one of the wickets in a squatting position and hold a sort of "pow-wow" until another man was sent in with the bat. A good catch was hailed with yells of delight.'[19] The Malays were in fact many years ahead of their time.

Such enthusiasm for the game interested reporter Harry Cadwallader, who had virtually single-handedly formed the South African Cricket Association on 9 April 1890. Not long afterwards, he had transferred to Cape Town from Kimberley and took an interest in the cricket played by the various coloured teams. His support for them was reflected in his newspaper, the *Cape Times*, where, for example, 48 team lists representing all race groups were published on 21 January 1891. The list included the Star of South Africa XI that played against Old Rocks. Hendricks had become captain of the former, a side that also included Faber, Johnson, Amos, Solomon, Roos, Isaacs, Poggenpoel, Siljour, Leach and Sedeman. In a January report it was observed that Hendricks's batting was instrumental in leading Star of South Africa to a narrow victory over Africans at Green Point, and later, in March, he took four wickets in one over against Woodstock Standard, enabling Star of South Africa (65) to overwhelm their opponents (19) with ease. Another report notes that Ebrahim Ariefdien had joined Star of South Africa and helped them defeat Uranus by an innings and 56 runs at Green Point through returning match figures of 12-24. It earned Ariefdien a place in the Cape Town side for the third Malay tournament during March/April 1891. It was an occasion in which Ariefdien took all ten wickets in an innings for a mere 18 runs against Port Elizabeth, but Kimberley emerged champions thanks to inspirational batting from Robert Grendon.

Grendon was a Kimberley player who was well known to the Cape Town team as he had enrolled at Zonnebloem College in 1878. He was the son of Joseph Grendon, an Irishman who fought in the Indian Mutiny and later became a successful businessman, and Maria, a daughter of a prominent Herero leader, Maharero. Grendon was an outstanding all-round pupil at Zonnebloem and went on to become a famous figure in the academic world. He was also a fine cricketer and represented the College First XI for several years – a strong cricket school, it fielded four sides in the course of each week's matches. Grendon's enthusiasm was such that he also played for the St Mark's and Progress cricket sides. At a time when centuries were rare, he scored 110 out of 204 (H. Daniels 68, extras 14, no other double figures) for Progress against Royal Scots (who were dismissed for 74) at Fort Knokke in January 1886. He then made another century – 103 against the Army – in the same season.

The Malays, with Abdol Burns a vocal leader, were making every effort to promote cricket. They received support from their community when Primrose of Claremont played Morning Star of Simon's Town in a 'grand Malay cricket match' on the Cape Town CC ground at Newlands, a small charge being made for admission. To assist in preparing for the inter-town tournament at Kimberley in March/April 1891, they asked Cape Town CC for a match. Contact was made with John Heyneman who told a club meeting that he thought 'it would be only sportsmanlike to accept their wishes and arrange a game'. The committee, chaired by Joe Lodge, acceded to the request, only for the hierarchy – Hofmeyr and Sivewright – to veto the arrangement.

Four days after the meeting was held, the *Cape Times* announced on 15 February:

> ...we are authorised to state that the club have declined to play their team against the Malays...To us there appears no reason whatever why the well-behaved cricketers of the Malay community should not be occasionally met by European exponents of the British national game, which our coloured

> neighbours show such a commendable desire to emulate. The English amateurs heartily welcome the Parsees; the Eclectic Club, Kimberley, have played a couple of fixtures with the Malays of the Diamond-fields and in Natal the natives play European colonists.[20]

Cape Town CC provided the first indication of an 'official' line being taken on mixed-race cricket. At the same time, there was no consensus against implementing segregation in cricket at the Cape or anywhere else in South Africa. White players reacted by assembling a strong European XI to play against the Malay team on the arranged date. The team, which included committee members from the Western Province Cricket Union, was announced as: 'Captain T. Wright, L. Smuts, A. Richards, V. van der Byl, E. Steytler, H. Calder, Clinton, J. Forde, G. Fitzpatrick, Hearne and F. Fraustaedter'. Reports noted that Vollie van der Byl did not turn up for the game, but otherwise it was a memorable occasion. 'As might have been expected,' said the *Cape Times*, 'there was a large attendance, the greater proportion consisting of members of the Malay community, and the Malay ladies turned up in considerable strength in all their best silks and satins.'[21]

The first of a series of matches between the two teams began sensationally when the opening bowler, Ariefdien, who delivered 'a very fast ball with an apparently natural break from the off', claimed 'the hat or for him the fez trick against three formidable batsmen'. The match report recorded that 'Ariefdien yorked [Alf] Richards with the first ball of his third over. He then got a fast ball to break in a surprising manner on to [Ned] Steytler's bails and third ball clean bowled Captain Townley Wright.' Ariefdien, who was described as 'an undoubtedly fine bowler', had the impressive figures of 6-33 in 22 overs, and it required the skill and experience of Frank Hearne to guide the Europeans to victory.[22]

The fixtures were popular and the Malay community attended in large numbers. Milton did not take part, although a number of notable white players were prepared to play, including a strong nucleus from the Cape Town CC. Press reports were detailed and commented on the way the Malay cricketers conducted themselves.

In admittedly patronising mood, they praised the Malays for being 'extremely orderly' and observed that they were displaying 'many points which even members of the small European clubs would do well to study'. In addition, the Malay cricketers, with the help of Europeans, staged a benefit match for Frank Hearne who 'has been giving our Musulman neighbours a few hints on the game of cricket, from which it is clear they have profited to judge by the knowledge and exemplary behaviour they showed in their first match between the Europeans and Malays a few weeks ago'.[23]

The next Malay representative cricket was a Glover Cup fixture in Kimberley over New Year 1891/92. It involved Abdol Burns's Union team taking on Kimberley's Red Crescents. Although Hendricks played his club cricket for Star of South Africa, a Malay team closely associated with Union CC, he was selected as part of what was effectively a representative Malay side. He had batted and bowled consistently well in recent club matches, and in December was invited to two 'trial' matches, the first being played between Star of South Africa and Union. Hendricks, who captained his side, made little impression with the bat as they were bundled out for 35 and 64, but he excelled with the ball. He bowled both openers for ducks and claimed seven wickets, but was unable to prevent the Samsodiens and the captain, Ariefdien (42 not out), taking Union to 156. In the second trial match, Hendricks captured another seven wickets.

The potent opening attack of Hendricks and Ariefdien dominated the Glover Cup match in Kimberley over the 1891/92 New Year period. Despite the ill-feeling created by the Powell brothers' umpiring in the course of the visit to Kimberley, it was generally recognised that the coloured communities of the two cities could field some useful players. For the Cape Town players – plus Armien Hendricks who would join them from Kimberley – their great opportunity to play against Walter Read's English team at Newlands was still to come. The match would enable Krom Hendricks to demonstrate his immense talent as a fast bowler, albeit at 34 years old, and in the process create a conundrum that would shape the direction of South African cricket.

4

The talk of the town

'The inclusion of a Malay may cause rabid colonists to change colour.'[1]

– Harry Cadwallader

HARRY CADWALLADER, CRICKET fanatic and secretary of the South African Cricket Association, was an interested spectator at the match between the South African Malay XVIII and Walter Read's English team. He marvelled at the pace that Hendricks generated and was effusive in his praise for the bowler in the *Cape Times*. The 29-year-old Cadwallader had served a journalist apprenticeship in Brighton, England, where his parents lived. His father had been a schoolmaster who became the local preacher and then a missionary during the Eighth Frontier War in the Eastern Cape. Inspired by his father's tales, Cadwallader had travelled to South Africa in 1886 and obtained a position on the *Diamond Fields Advertiser*. He was determined to make his mark on the game of cricket at the Cape Colony and it was not long before he was absorbed by the excitement of the English tours that advanced the concept of empire.

Cadwallader's pride in the English game shone through in his writing. So keen was he to be first to meet the touring cricketers of 1888/89 that he hired a boat at two o'clock in the morning to take him out to the mail steamer when it entered Table Bay. He then clambered aboard 'to welcome Major Warton and his team on behalf of the Kimberley cricketers'. The 'scoop' was duly telegraphed to his delighted editor.[2] Yet behind such boyish enthusiasm was a fearless operator, a man of perseverance, unselfishness and stoicism. Yet when it came to writing about life in South Africa – cricket, politics, diamonds and gold, economics, the stock exchange, and so on – he more than met his match when his editor encouraged him to take on Charles Finlason, the anti-imperialist scribe from the rival *Daily Independent*. Their fight over the English tour in 1888/89 was a tempestuous affair that culminated in Cadwallader siding with the English tourists in a regrettable attempt to belittle Finlason at a Kimberley banquet. Finlason remembered 'the editor [William] Roper turned [Cadwallader] on in the *Diamond Fields Advertiser* to run against me in the *Independent*, and we had one or two little bouts in the good old early days "Kicker" style, and people were surprised to see us taking a drink together'. It was to Finlason's credit that he bore no grudges against his rival and, in looking back at a highly competitive period, he recalled the talented Afrikaans-speaking cricketer Pieter de Villiers saying about Cadwallader:

> That Caddy likes his facts. Give him facts and he is satisfied. He will go for 200 miles to get a fact that makes but a single line in the paper. But what he gets, he gets solid. He ain't no Ruskin in the way of fancy touches, he ain't a gaudy painter like you, Fin, but you can cut out his stuff and paste it in your scrapbook knowing that you've got information you can rely on.[3]

Finlason's support was to prove invaluable in raising funds when Cadwallader embarked on an ambitious scheme to organise a South African cricket tour to England. It was a project that had been discussed previously in the press, but with little progress made. In the late 1870s and early 1880s the Cape Town newspapers carried reports on the success that Australia had achieved in cricket and questioned why the Cape could not attain similar status. The

Cape Times expressed its frustration when it said, 'Merchants in Australia think nothing of giving £10 or £20 each to send home a good 11, and have their appointments still open for them when they come back. Cape Town could not send a team to Port Elizabeth.'[4] In 1881, the *Cape Argus* wrote pessimistically that 'it will be a long time before [cricket in] South Africa will attain to the pitch of perfection already reached by some of the sister colonies in the Australian group'.[5] A few months later, the same newspaper pointed to the financial success experienced by Australian touring teams and stressed that 'it is time the Colony did something to show that it is not dead to sports and manly pastimes'.[6]

William Milton responded in a letter to the *Cape Argus* on 5 July 1881, stating: 'The idea of sending a team to England capable of holding its own with a first-class English XI is, as you remark, a seeming impossibility, and a great impossibility it is, I fear, likely to remain, until a greater interest is taken in the development of cricket in South Africa by those who possess the power of giving some practical proofs of that interest.' He argued that cricket had potential at the Cape, but the lack of opportunity was causing the game to languish in comparison with progress in other colonies. He put the problem down to inadequate facilities, claiming the ground at Wynberg was 'little better than the hard road and not quite so good as a Namaqualand saltpan'.[7]

Milton did not yet share the prevailing eagerness for international competition. His desire to improve playing conditions first was a sound argument and culminated in the construction of Newlands, a grand venue for international tours. There was nevertheless interest shown in competing against teams from England and Australia, a development seized upon by sports administrator Charles Alcock in *Cricket: A Weekly Record of the Game*. When, in 1883, a South African visitor told members of the Witham Club that the Cape Colony was contemplating sending a team to England, Alcock reported enthusiastically: 'It may not be long after all before Kaffreland is able to send us as fine a specimen of native cricket as that excellent all-round player, the Australian Aboriginal, Mullagh, who made such a capital show here in 1868.'[8]

Cadwallader realised from the outset that Milton, who was the most influential figure in cricket at the Cape, might oppose his ambitions. It did not help that Cadwallader had for some time been a controversial and active critic of Milton's cricket administration. His first piece to create widespread interest concerned the arrival of the Australian cricket team at Table Bay in October 1886. The visitors had communicated with the Cape Court of the Indian and Colonial Exhibition in London in the hope of extending their stay at the Cape in order to play cricket. The communication was ignored and the Australians left the boat briefly before moving on to New Zealand for two weeks. Cadwallader was incensed by the missed opportunity and lamented the inability of Cape cricketers to 'organise something', noting 'the leading club of the Colony, the Western Province Cricket Club, should have taken some measure to accord a hearty welcome to a team of cricketers whose play is universally noted; it was certainly their place to move in the matter'.[9] Unfortunately for him, his report was inaccurate: the Australian cricketers were in fact met by Milton and members of the Western Province CC soon after nine o'clock on the day after their arrival. They were escorted around the Houses of Parliament, library and museum before returning to the vessel at noon. It emerged that Milton was not to blame for the breakdown in communication; the London officials had simply not passed on the message, telling the Australians that 'they would find no cricket worth paying attention to at the Cape'.[10]

Milton organised the relatively successful 1888/89 tour under Major Warton, and Cadwallader hoped to arrange a second English tour. When the South African Cricket Association met in April 1891, Cadwallader spoke of Lord Sheffield bringing out a team that would include W.G. Grace. He described the arrangement as 'a chance probably only to be got once in a lifetime; every nerve should be strained to secure such a visit'. He believed Lord Sheffield's team would make a stopover at the Cape either en route to Australia or during the return trip. The *Cape Times* ('Home' edition) stated that Lord Sheffield was 'very busy getting together a cricket team [for] a tour in which he intends to visit India, Australia and the Cape'.[11]

Unfortunately for Cadwallader, his plans ran into opposition because the British rugby team was visiting the country during the winter months of 1891, and it was argued at a meeting of the South African Cricket Association in Johannesburg that the relatively small white population of the colony could not cope with the costs and organisation involved in staging two major tours in the same year. The setback increased Cadwallader's resolve to make an impression and he switched his focus to an overseas tour. In doing so, he identified Monty Bowden as the important drawcard he needed to attract the necessary financial backing and fixtures for the proposed venture. Such an arrangement, however, was far from straightforward.

Bowden, who had led England in the second of the two Tests played against South Africa in 1888/89, had stayed behind in South Africa to seek his fortune on the Rand goldfields. He set up a stock-broking partnership that culminated fairly quickly in bankruptcy and then left Johannesburg in order to help Transvaal win the first Currie Cup Challenge at Kimberley. He scored 63 (out of 117) and an unbeaten 126 (out of 224 for four), gave a lively display behind the stumps, and then captured key wickets as a bowler to inspire a historic victory. *The Star* described him at the time as 'far and away the best bat in South Africa', but he was also viewed as an attractive publicity proposition for the expedition that Cecil John Rhodes was organising to occupy territory north of the Limpopo.[12] Within weeks, the 'flat-broke' Bowden was ensnared by the Chartered Company, seen by some as 'a callous business enterprise known for its carelessness of the welfare of the individual'.[13]

Milton, who had become Rhodes's private secretary – and who was Bowden's opposing captain in the Newlands Test of 1888/89 – recalled standing alongside the prime minister when he read the telegram that reported the Pioneer Column's safe arrival at Fort Salisbury. Rhodes then handed the telegram to Milton with the characteristic remark, 'My young men have got the country.'[14] Bowden's role as a pioneer added lustre to his fame as a cricketer, but his initial period in the new territory created disillusionment as Rhodes's concept of community broke down. Not long afterwards, it was agreed by the *Cape Times* that Cadwallader should travel north to update views on gold prospects, the growing impatience with the Chartered Company, the findings of an investigation by the controversial Randolph Churchill and the aftermath of the British-Portuguese conflict ... and lure Bowden back to South Africa. The South African Cricket Association was advised of the development and Milton agreed to take over the secretarial duties.

The intrepid journalist was held up at the Mozambican village of M'pandas because of a lack of transport and he spent several weeks in a tent erected haphazardly on the bank of a muddy stream. It was not a place that anyone wished to stay for long. It was dirty and dilapidated, and rats were a virtually uncontrollable feature. To Cadwallader's great surprise, Bowden suddenly arrived, sweeping dramatically into the village at the head of a convoy of 70 naked carriers. He told Cadwallader that he had 'come to fetch provisions for Europeans and forces in Manica ... they have very little left'. Food was a priority and would at least account for available space once the whisky had been loaded. The erstwhile cricketer also informed Cadwallader that he hoped to travel to Durban before the next rainy season.

Cadwallader became seriously ill with fever and, in a state of exhaustion and helplessness, was fortunate to reach Umtali on Rhodesia's border with Mozambique. Bowden was also struck down with fever and was fortuitously rescued by Rhodes near Mandigo in Mozambique. The prime minister of the Cape, in his white flannel trousers, slouch hat and old salt-and-pepper tweed jacket, was on his way to visit his new acquisition, but spent time with Bowden, providing him with whisky and a horse so that he could get to Umtali. Not long afterwards, in December 1891, Charles Finlason braved the journey to Salisbury by ox-drawn cart. He was shocked by Bowden's condition and wrote, 'The hardships that he had incurred had told severely on him and he was much weakened by the fever.' Two months later, Bowden was injured when thrown from the post cart in which he was travelling. Despite his poor state, he was on the cricket field the following day because it was the first match to be played in Umtali and quite something to have an English captain taking part. Bowden drew on his last vestige of energy to take four wickets. The effort affected his condition, which deteriorated alarmingly. He had an epileptic seizure and was conveyed to the hospital – a glorified mud hut – where he died four days later on 19 February 1892. Owing to the scarcity of wood, his coffin was made out of whisky cases.[15]

It would take Cadwallader some time to accept Bowden's death – perhaps too much rested on the cricketer's return to South Africa – but there was no thought given to abandoning the idea of a tour to England. At the next meeting of the South African Cricket Association at the Central Hotel, Kimberley, on 19 November 1892, Cadwallader placed the 'overseas tour' on the agenda. It was an issue that had been spoken about for some years, with the argument being put forward that if the Parsees could visit England (as they did in 1886 and 1888) then there appeared to be no reason why South Africa should not do the same. There was the inevitable negative opposition and, said one report, the 'idea was received with the usual ridicule'. Cadwallader had, however, prepared meticulously and, with the support of South African wicketkeeper/batsman Ernest 'Barberton' Halliwell, he presented a strong argument for the venture. Griqualand West's representative, Irvine Grimmer, who chaired the meeting, expressed his interest and it was agreed that Cadwallader should be empowered to liaise officially with authorities in England in order to arrange a tour in 1894.[16] This would prove fairly straightforward for the latter who was already in communication with Charles Alcock.

Not long after the meeting, it became obvious that the Western Province Cricket Union would be the main obstacle standing in the way of an overseas tour. Milton influenced the Cape's objection to the arrangement with an argument that 'it was premature and that South African cricket was not strong enough at present to cope with the best English players on their grounds'. He distrusted Cadwallader and was almost certainly of the opinion that if work commitments precluded his involvement in organising the visit, then he did not want his union to be part of it. The Western Province committee backed Milton at a meeting in October 1893, despite Alcock's promise that 'any South African team would receive a warm welcome from English cricketers and that everything reasonable would be done to promote the success of a tour'. Milton, who was about to resign as president, relied on Lynedoch Graham to argue his case and push through a resolution that the union 'will not have anything to do with the tour'.[17]

Cricketer and rugby player Herbert Castens showed some anxiety as to the strong line being taken and moved an amendment that 'if other unions should choose to go "Home", the Western Province Cricket Union would not in any way raise any obstacle to such an undertaking'.[18] Graham accepted the amendment as a rider to his resolution. Cadwallader was not at this stage bothered by the attitude of the Cape Town elite. He knew there was interest in the town and brushed off the Western Province Cricket Union's action as 'generally expected'. He thought Graham's arguments had little bearing on the matter under discussion, adding 'most if not all the other centres have expressed themselves favourable to the project, and in Johannesburg cricketers are red-hot on the subject'. Cadwallader cursed the inaction of the South African Cricket Association – he thought it 'may just as well be ditched'[19] – but working in his favour was the fact that he was a journalist with the *Cape Times* and soon to be appointed sports editor of the weekly publication, the *South African Review*, which had amalgamated with *The Sportsman* and *Licensed Victuallers* in 1893. He was well placed to facilitate administrative arrangements, notably through communicating details of the tour, and to counter criticism.

It is uncertain at what stage Cadwallader first gave thought to Hendricks's inclusion in the South African team for the proposed tour. It is quite possible that it occurred to him when the Malays played Read's English cricketers and became a matter of greater significance after Bowden's death. Black sportsmen and entertainers from the colonies held a special appeal for English audiences. Few in Britain had seen black people from distant lands and speculators made money through parading various 'natives' as curiosities before fascinated audiences. There was widespread interest in the tour by the Australian Aborigine side in 1868, a novel expedition that provided competitive cricket as well as displays of traditional skills in which the tourists demonstrated uncanny control over boomerangs, spears and the stock whip. There was also the odd wayward moment: at Bootle, Mullagh's boomerang sliced through a spectator's hat and at The Oval a stray dog was almost cut in half.

In 1888, a group of business entrepreneurs – 'gentlemen from England' – had been keen to arrange a black South African cricket tour to England along similar lines. They launched their plan through John Tengo Jabavu's newspaper, *Imvo Zabantsundu*, claiming that they were 'wishful to ascertain as to whether there is sufficient enthusiasm and ability among the natives in the game of cricket as to warrant them in getting up a team for a tour through Great Britain during the 1889 season'. The selection criteria imposed by the 'English gentlemen' were as follows:

1. Good character, total abstainers and generally intelligent
2. Smart and athletic, good figure with no deformity
3. Must be willing to practise incessantly during the next six months
4. All candidates to prove their proficiency before being chosen and to pass a committee of experts[20]

The offer was open to 'all the native races from which it is hoped to pick the very best men' and received widespread support. A report in *Imvo Zabantsundu* said, 'We trust the various Kafir clubs will loose [*sic*] no time in arranging for an undertaking that is fraught with momentous issues for the native races of this country.' Jabavu added his support by saying that the tour to England 'would offer our friends there the opportunity of realising the tone that European civilisation gives to the society of Africans'. Letters followed to the newspaper, one comparing South African black players with the Parsees and claiming: 'I have no doubt the natives of this country with proper coaching would thoroughly efface the best records of our friends in India.'[21]

Despite the enthusiasm in support of the project, it proved an impossible assignment. *Imvo Zabantsundu* recorded there were too many practical problems, such as an inability to arrange practices because of the vast distances between towns, lack of time and finance to organise a tournament at which the selection would be made, and no elected bodies and experienced staff to handle the administrative requirements. The last of the potential investors left the country in January 1889 and the proposed tour was subsequently forgotten.

Cadwallader did not indicate that he was giving thought to nominating a player of colour for the overseas trip that he was planning. Yet an ambiguous promise was made to Charles Alcock that he would collect 'a side which will be very nearly, if not quite representative of South African cricket'.[22] He had also written enthusiastically about the ability of Malay cricketers and had been taken with the pace bowling of Hendricks against Read's team in March 1892. Cadwallader was particularly encouraged by a comment made by Read: 'If you send a team, send Hendricks; he will be a draw-card and is to my mind the Spofforth of South Africa'.[23] The South African Cricket Association meeting in November 1892 had been too early to raise such a sensitive issue, although it is likely that there was talk about Hendricks in cricket circles. It also cannot be discounted that Milton's early reservations about the tour were linked to fears that Hendricks was indeed a fine prospect and good enough to be selected.

The cricket tour was being arranged and discussed while allegations of corruption were surfacing at the highest level of Cape politics. James Sivewright came under suspicion in late 1892 when it was revealed that he had given his friend, James Logan, an extremely lucrative contract without tenders being called, for the sale of refreshments on Cape trains and stations for the unusually long period of 18 years. This 'Logan affair' was serious enough to lead to the break-up of the government and Rhodes's resignation, but he was able to successfully exploit the indecisiveness of his opponents and resume power with a restructured cabinet. In the build-up, Rhodes reaffirmed and reinforced his relationship with the Afrikaner Bond by consulting with Hofmeyr and, at one stage, deciding to ask J.H. de Villiers, the chief justice, to head the new government. Then, crucially and seemingly accidentally, Rhodes met his leading opponent, former Cape prime minister John Gordon Sprigg, on the steps of Parliament and made a deal that brought Sprigg into the reconstituted cabinet. Ties were broken with the liberal element of the former ministry, comprising John X. Merriman, Jacobus Sauer and James Rose Innes. It left Merriman, a long-serving parliamentarian, to lament the 'Rhodes-Hofmeyr way of doing business – the lobbying, the intrigue and utterly cynical disregard of anything approaching moral principle in the conduct of public affairs'.[24]

The political realignment between imperialists and Afrikaner nationalists would have a significant impact on race and politics in South Africa. The Rhodes-Afrikaner Bond coalition that gained control of the Cape government was determined to promote white ethnicity and embarked on a process to exclude blacks from political involvement. There was support from Cape Town's establishment who argued that the exclusionary practices of the past were no longer sufficient. Large-scale immigration had brought inevitable change in the urban context and the Afrikaner Bond, with strong support from the Dutch Reformed Church, were increasingly concerned by the poor-white problem. They believed it could be controlled not only with greater government expenditure on white education, but also through social separation of whites and blacks. The ideology and practice of racial separation in Cape Town in the early 1890s was in the nature of the alliance that directed the Cape government. By virtue of their actions, wrote Saul Dubow, the politicians 'sought to foreclose on the liberal promise that colour should not of itself constitute a bar to full membership of society'.[25]

Hofmeyr had for some time during 1892 and 1893 been preoccupied with the Franchise Bill that initially 'aimed at a direct restriction of the non-tribal African vote', but he would go on to question 'whether coloureds were to be embraced as part of the "South African" dominant grouping or would join Africans in the political cold'.[26] The debate was 'long and strenuous', but thanks to co-operation between Rhodes and Hofmeyr, the Bill received the support of the Cape Parliament and, significantly, the press in England who saw it as 'a matter of policy' rather than a race question.

Hofmeyr's remarks on the debate summarised the direction he intended to take:

> ... the Bill would be the precursor of a better understanding between the two great European races, and that then they could talk of a United South Africa in its best sense. The English colonist and the Dutch colonist ... were equally faithful in their allegiance to the Crown ... There was only one other matter, which created a little suspicion in the minds of the Dutch Africanders. They feared that some Englishmen in the Colony were not clear upon the line of demarcation between barbarism and civilisation, as existed in India, in Natal, and other countries where the line of demarcation was drawn between the coloured barbarian and the civilised European.[27]

The changing nature of Cape politics occurred at a time when the sportsmen of southern Africa were in the process of forming administrative bodies and arranging international tours. The political coalition's move towards segregation naturally affected a tradition whereby black and white cricketers had been free to play with and against one another. It was a complex process as the increasingly influential Afrikaner Bond also sought to weaken imperial interference at the Cape, a development that would impact the Western Province CC's desire to keep its own little England intact. Milton's grip on the game was loosened as Hofmeyr's Cape Town CC, with Sivewright prominent, assumed an increasingly influential role. An anxious, unsettled relationship developed within cricket that ultimately saw the elite white clubs close ranks in support of segregation.

Hendricks, as an outstanding player but apparently Malay, unwittingly became a pivotal figure in forcing those who administered cricket at the Cape and further afield to reveal their positions and intentions. In this regard, Cadwallader played a key role in keeping the public aware of the progress being made in Malay cricket. If he required further evidence of Hendricks's ability, this was provided in matches that began towards the end of 1892. In late December, Hendricks was invited by the Malays to play against a European XI in preparation for an inter-town tournament. The Malay XI scored 114 (Ebrahim Ariefdien 34; Charles Mills taking 7-20), a score that a team selected largely from the Cape Town CC would have expected to overtake. It was not to be: Hendricks (5-47) and Ariefdien (4-42) bowled unchanged in a fiery display that presented problems for the likes of Louis Smuts, Arthur Seccull, J.B. Munnik and John Heyneman. It was left to the professional, Mills (61), to fight a lone battle in helping his side reach 101.

Two days later, Cadwallader joined the largest crowd that had been seen at a cricket match in the Western Province that season. It was the beginning of the Malay tournament at the Cape Town CC ground and the *Cape Times* reported: 'The attendance will probably increase daily till the New Year holidays when, weather being favourable, no doubt the most brilliant assemblage of the year as regards colour – in dress – will be seen.' The home team's fast bowlers were devastating as they tore through the Kimberley batting line-up. The talented Robert Grendon (0 and 6) made no impression as Kimberley (33 and 81) went down by eight wickets to the Capetonians' 59 (J. Sheldon 9-25) and 59 for two. Only Armien Hendricks (10* and 22) was able to withstand the onslaught of Krom Hendricks (5-9 and 6-36) and Ariefdien (5-18 and 4-42). A day or two later, Cape Town (153 and 100) outplayed Johannesburg (81 and 60) with the local pacemen again dominant. Cadwallader was impressed by Krom Hendricks's speed and stamina as he accounted for Johannesburg with a match analysis of 12-88. A cricketer who would impress English audiences had been confirmed, but Cadwallader's enthusiasm continued to be tempered by concern as to how best to convey his plan to the cricket authorities.[28]

Few whites shared Cadwallader's enthusiasm for 'Malay' cricket. Despite evidence to the contrary, they believed what they wanted to believe – that Malay players had some way to go before they could be on an equal footing with white cricketers. There was no suggestion in the press up to then that any player of colour was in line for representative selection. Names such as Grendon, Ariefdien and, in particular, Krom Hendricks were well known in cricket circles, but they were prevented from playing against the premier clubs or in showpiece representative matches such as 'Mother Country' versus 'Colonial-born'.

Hendricks signalled his ambitions by applying to become a member of Cape Town CC, but was turned down. The leading clubs were exclusively white. Any attempt by Cadwallader to include a player of colour in a 'national' cricket side to tour overseas would obviously fly in the face of political developments. The issue would not escape the attention of white politicians associated with white clubs. Many on the Western Province CC membership list – which included Cecil John Rhodes – were non-playing. They were nevertheless influential in determining the direction that the club pursued. It was also considered important to have a prominent dignitary as the patron – usually the governor – rather in the fashion of the MCC, whose committee once chose Prince Albert because 'his connection placed the club in an exalted position ... the national and manly game of cricket cannot but still rise more in public estimation under such distinguished patronage'.[29]

The white establishment was not concerned with the game played by coloured or black cricketers. When an English journalist asked Herbert Castens about clubs in Cape Town, he responded: 'There are numbers of very small ones, but only eight of them are really good, and perhaps 20 are moderate ... the difficulty is to find grounds ... there are only about six altogether, which are all in the suburbs, for nobody lives in Cape Town, because of the heat.'[30] He appeared to have no idea about cricket arrangements in the city where a good many people lived, because he never played against those sides. Castens, along with Milton and other products of the public schools, was content to live in a small class-and-cricket bubble made up of teams from the southern suburbs.

Edward 'Ned' Steytler, who had played in matches against the Malays, succeeded Milton as president of the Western Province Cricket Union in October 1893. He took over at a crucial stage in the union's history, not least because he inherited the tour issue, which had reached an unsatisfactory stage. His committee adopted the view that the overseas side could not be truly representative if they 'had nothing to do with it', but they did not foresee the excitement that the tour aroused throughout the southern African region.[31] Cadwallader furnished a flow of positive articles through his columns that claimed, 'almost every leading cricketer in the country outside the Western Province has indicated his readiness to join the team'.[32] Steytler and his committee were not bothered until news was received that a leading Western Province 'sportsman' – later identified as James Logan – had agreed to a £500 guarantee, that financier and cricketer Abe Bailey was aiming to raise £1,000, and that Natal, Port Elizabeth and Kimberley had promised contributions. The required amount of £3,000 suddenly did not appear unattainable.

Finlason taunted the Western Province Cricket Union for their decision not to support the tour. He said he had thought the 'Metropolis' 'had got out of the slough that its ancient apathy and want of enterprise had kept it [in] for many years', but that this proved not to be the case. They were the first, he said, 'to throw cold water on a scheme that if carried through would be so conducive to the best interests of South African cricket'. And once again they exaggerated the prowess of English county cricketers, allowing themselves to be 'dominated by that class of old fossil who makes a point of impressing upon South Africans the intense absurdity of ever trying conclusions with anything at Home – with a gigantic capital H'. He concluded:

> These dear old dodderers, I am afraid, are still rampant in the land, and do more to discourage South African sport than all other adverse causes put together. They are so anxious to impress the poor South Africans with their inferiority, so slow to see merit in anything South African, so eager to magnify all things English. At Cape Town there are more cricket-fussing dodderers to the square yard than anywhere else in South Africa, and they are spoilt by the foolish deference that is

> shown them. As a matter of fact, they should be listened to with respect, but they should be sat on promptly when they deserve it. Unfortunately, they never are at Cape Town. In Kimberley and Johannesburg there is more irreverence and more common sense.[33]

Cadwallader sensed the momentum was with him. He had built himself an influential position as a journalist and could count on support from the other centres. The politicians were distracted: Milton was committed to maintaining the prime minister's office as Rhodes had adjourned the Cape's Legislative Assembly and travelled north. A war loomed in Matabeleland and Rhodes hurried to an area between Marandellas and Salisbury (now Marondera and Harare) where he would make himself deliberately 'inaccessible' to the imperial government. Only when news was received that Dr Leander Starr Jameson's force was on its way to Bulawayo did Rhodes emerge and follow the action, which was effectively directed by the devastating Maxim gun. Rhodes and Jameson had established the view that it was less costly to eliminate Lobengula's power base than to defend the Mashona against the Matabele impi indefinitely. Lobengula's troops were mowed down and the battlefield was swept clear by a weapon that the Matabele described as the 'S'cockacocka ... the beast that went pooh! pooh!'[34] When Jameson's men entered Bulawayo, the town was empty; Matabeleland was under Rhodes's sway.

On 3 November 1893 – the day before Bulawayo fell – Cadwallader flirted with controversy and, with his own guns blazing, published the 16 players that 'Critic' of Johannesburg thought should tour England. The report, which Cadwallader inserted in the *South African Review*, stated:

> Here is the team for England next year, and if any of my readers thinks he can improve it, I shall be glad to entertain any suggestions. First of all, Tancred, the premier bat, then Halliwell, South Africa's ditto wicketkeeper, with Prince to take the part of the Australian Jarvis. For bowlers, Innes

> (slow), Parkin and Crage (medium) and ***Hendricks (fast), form the leading quartette, although the inclusion of the latter, a Malay, may cause rabid colonists to change colour*** [author's emphasis]. Finlason, whose experience of the game makes him invaluable in big matches, and Routledge, the Liverpool bat, are indispensable, while Sewell and Davey from Natal, are snorting willow-wielders. Taberer, Frank Hearne, Mills and Cripps form the Western Province contingent, and Fichardt, the Free Stater makes up my ideal 16 ...[35]

A couple of weeks later, Cadwallader followed up on his first controversial suggestion that Hendricks should be included in the side by making several observations. He expressed concern that little attention had been paid so far that season by the press to matches played by coloured teams and felt the 'chief points of a match or two which have been contested between European and coloured 11s lately deserve to be unearthed'. He produced what his readers might have considered a balanced piece in which he adopted a fair-minded assessment of the ability of the 'coloured cricketers' while not straying too far from those touches of superiority that a ruling class would have expected from the Cape press:

> There have been contests which show that there is abundant cricketing talent among the 'natives' and there is no reason why they should not receive encouragement, so long as they behave themselves, which they have invariably done so far. They do not at least dispute an umpire's decision. These Malay and other coloured men, when on the cricket field, know far better how to keep their places and respect their superiors than do many of their coloured brethren in Plein Street on a Saturday evening.[36]

After this introduction, Cadwallader raised his main point, which concerned Hendricks. He said that the 'coloured cricketer' had been spoken of as worth taking to England with a South African team on account of his bowling, yet nothing had been recorded about him in any paper that season. It was not a rare oversight as far as Hendricks was concerned. But on this occasion, Cadwallader was able to advise his readers that Hendricks had been before the public and through his recent performances was able to demonstrate that he continued to be in fine bowling form. In one notable outing for 'a coloured team against a strong European team got together by Mills, he quite upset the calculations of the would-be learned ones'.

Hearne and Mills began the European batting at the Cape Town CC to such good purpose that they saw three figures on the board before the partnership was ended after 90 minutes' play. Hendricks was bowling all this time under a hot sun at great pace and had 43 runs hit off him in 18 overs. He kept an excellent length and eventually dismissed both professionals. 'Hearne and Mills never played better cricket here,' said Cadwallader. The comment was partly justified by the fact that from the moment Hearne left, the game changed dramatically: 'Hendricks took 7 wickets for 16 runs, a grand performance on a perfect wicket when such batsmen as R.W. Fox, E.M. Dawson-Thomas, Major Bourcicault and Middleton were playing ... Had it not been for Middleton, the rot to Hendricks' snorters must have been terrible.'

Mills scored 50 and Hearne 42, with Hendricks taking 9-59. According to the press report, the two professionals 'both expressed the opinion that Hendricks is far and away the best fast bowler they have met in the country'.[37] It was not the news that the Cape establishment wanted to hear.

5

'Why am I termed a Malay?'

> 'To take him as an equal would from a South African point of view, be impolitic, not to say intolerable, and I would not have him on those terms if he were a better bowler than Lohmann.'[1]
>
> – A.B. Tancred

THE POSSIBLE SELECTION of Hendricks in the South African touring side was to become a fundamental political issue at the Cape during the early months of 1894. The unfolding controversy would involve the Cape government at its highest level and attract the attention of numerous prominent figures in the game. The role of Malay and coloured cricketers in the broader social context was a key battle in the ongoing war over South African identity. Cadwallader, as the tour's leading promoter, wanted the side to be the strongest possible combination and, given the available talent in black cricket, to be fully representative of the country's population groups. He was aware that Hendricks and Ariefdien – as well as the Kimberley-based Armien Hendricks – were better bowlers than those in the white clubs. He also knew that there would be opposition to his plan to include them in the touring side, but, by the end of 1893, he believed that the segregationist imperatives of the white establishment could be placated. He envisaged a compromise that included selecting 'Malay' players in a South African team, but at the same time emphasising the class role of black South Africans as servants on an unequal footing with whites.

Writing as 'Under the Bell' in the *South African Review*, Cadwallader opened with a deeply defensive statement emphasising the fact that he knew just how much opposition he was likely to face in selecting black players. 'Now I am going to drop a thunderbolt,' he said, 'which I know will shock a few prejudices.' He continued:

> There is serious talk of playing one or two coloured South Africans with the team if their cricket prowess is likely to strengthen the team, and there are two dark ones in view who might in a wonderful degree strengthen the bowling, where most weakness may be felt. If it is decided to take them, they would of course be baggage men. There is a strong feeling among English cricketers that such an introduction would of itself be an attractive novelty, and if they would make the team more representative why not take them?[2]

Cadwallader had dual responsibility as a journalist (sports editor of the *South African Review* and cricket writer for the *Cape Times*) and secretary of the South African Cricket Association and was central to all matters regarding the tour that he had been asked to organise. He published a letter that called on players to avail themselves for the venture and then asked the major centres to consider likely candidates and submit nominations from their respective areas to the national selection committee. The various unions were also asked to choose the side that they believed would be best equipped to represent South Africa on an overseas tour. In the weeks that followed there was much discussion as to the composition of the team while Cadwallader maintained 'constant communication' with Charles Alcock in England and hoped 'any player selected to represent South Africa will not be prevented from any cause from playing'.[3]

For several weeks speculation centred on whether Hendricks should be chosen. Those in favour of his selection were able to point out that he was easily the fastest bowler in South Africa. The only player who rivalled him in terms of pace was Natal's Peter Madden, who was believed by even his own cricket authority to be a 'chucker' and was not considered for selection. In the Transvaal it was the stated ambition of Abe Bailey to see South Africa become a cricket power. For him, as a representative of the mining industry, the importance of getting South Africa on to the imperial stage was far more important than the Cape's parish-pump politicking around the class status of coloured players. So if making a big splash meant the inclusion of a coloured player, so be it. In fact, the likely impact and public interest that Hendricks would bring to the tour made it important that he be selected.

Bailey's Transvaal cricket committee and, for the most part, the Johannesburg press supported him on the Hendricks issue. E.J.L. Platnauer, the sports editor of the *Standard and Diggers News*, was persuaded that Hendricks was essential to the South African touring team's success. Interest in the fast bowler grew quickly and on 10 January 1894, Reuters carried a message that was published in newspapers throughout South Africa: 'With regard to the proposed cricketing team for England, the [Transvaal] papers strongly advocate the inclusion of Hendricks, the Malay fast bowler, in the team.'[4]

The issue was essentially a showdown between the different interests of the Transvaal mining industry and the Cape. The Western Province Cricket Union had not yet accepted the necessity for them to be involved in the arrangements, thus creating an awkward situation. They were the provincial body that would be called upon to nominate Hendricks, a step that they were unlikely to take. They suggested players might object to travelling with 'a coloured man on equal social terms' and that 'men declared they would rather stay than go with him', but without providing any evidence.[5] In the *Cape Times* on 11 January, Cadwallader decided to publicly support Hendricks by reminding readers that the player would be taken as a fast bowler and baggage-man. In that inferior role, one that sacrificed Hendricks's dignity to team requirements, Cadwallader argued, 'there could be absolutely no objection to Hendricks on account of his being a Malay'.[6]

Cadwallader, while seeking to maintain the Hendricks option despite popular prejudice, made a cardinal error. There was no effort to ascertain Hendricks's own position regarding his ethnicity or interest before jumping to print. Hendricks was proud enough as a man and cricketer to resent having his status traded like a piece of meat in the national press without any consultation. He responded quickly and forcibly in the next edition of the *Cape Times* on 12 January, strongly objecting to the fact that he had been characterised as a 'Malay' and stating that no one had made any attempt to establish his views on the subject of the cricket tour, his availability or the role that he would play:

> Sir – I notice in this morning's issue of your paper, under the heading of 'Sporting Intelligence', a wire from Johannesburg with your comment thereupon, wherein reference is made to my name as a possible candidate in the proposed cricketing team for England, and I hasten to take exception to same. In the first place I must disclaim any connection with the Malay community. My father was born of Dutch parents in Cape Town, and my mother hails from St Helena – then why am I termed a Malay?
>
> Further, I note it is taken for granted that should I be selected I would go with the team, but to the present no such application has been made to me to ascertain my views on the subject and I think this was the least the committee could have done before making my name thus public.
>
> Then, Sir, as to your remark that I 'might be taken home as baggage-man' I would beg to state that if chosen I would not think of going in that capacity.
>
> Apologising for troubling on your space.
> I am &c.
> H. HENDRICKS[7]

The following day, a letter from a 'Coloured Cricketer' explained the 'difference between a Malay and a coloured man ... not one coloured man out of six would allow another to call him a Malay to his face'. The implication was that it was Hendricks's desire to distance himself from the descendants of Muslim slaves who had arrived in the Batavian era in the seventeenth and eighteenth centuries and identify himself with the 'Christian ruling class'. A 'Christian' status offered opportunities for social improvement that were important to Hendricks, despite increasing concerns that the Cape's social and political landscape under the Rhodes government was undergoing a period of rapid and fundamental social, cultural and economic change.

Hendricks's letter received a hostile reception from the white supremacist press. The *Standard and Diggers News* reacted strongly with an article on 13 January that rejected the cricketer's right to defend himself against the assumptions made in print by a journalist of the dominant European class. The critical piece appeared in the 'Sporting News' column under the heading 'Mijnheer Hendricks'. The use of the Dutch honorific – derived from *mijn* (my) and *heer* (lord) – was in this case an address directed sarcastically towards Hendricks, who the columnist thought to be speaking above his station. The writer was irritated that a player of colour should have had the temerity to question the role proposed for him – that of 'baggage-man' – in the course of a South African cricket tour to England. Hendricks's statement that if he went at all, it would not be as a baggage-man but as one of the team was considered unacceptable by the *Standard and Diggers News*. It is not known whether Platnauer, as sports editor, was involved in the vicious attack on Hendricks, but the scribe claimed that 'a revulsion of feeling has set in against the impertinence of the coloured man, even among those who hitherto followed him, and the hope is expressed that he will not be taken with the team unless he agrees to go in a subordinate capacity'.[8]

The *Standard and Diggers News* sought support for their forceful anti-Hendricks line by interviewing respected South African Test cricketer A.B. Tancred. He duly provided the answers they required in unsparing racist terms. 'Well,' replied Tancred, who was a practising lawyer in Pretoria, 'after his impudent letter to the Association, I should certainly leave [Hendricks] out. If he wants to go on the same footing as the others, I would not have him at any price.' The country's champion batsman mistakenly thought that Hendricks had written to the South African Cricket Association, but he was clear in his belief that the colour question overrode cricket matters. 'As baggage-man,' said Tancred, 'they might take him and play him in one or two of the matches when the conditions suited him. To take him as an equal would from a South African point of view, be impolitic, not to say intolerable, and I would not have him on those terms if he were a better bowler than Lohmann.'[9]

However arrogant and distasteful the comments against Hendricks, they reflected the perceived cultural superiority of Europeans of the late Victorian period. Tancred's viewpoint, harsh and illogical as it may seem, echoed that of a great number of white South Africans. One such person was the writer of a letter to *The Star* (Johannesburg):

> Sir – I notice with keen regret that there is a disposition in various quarters to consider the suggestion that Hendricks, the Malay bowler, be included in the cricket team about to visit England.
>
> I am convinced that any attempt to include a coloured player in the team will be resented by the vast majority of South Africans. I have discussed the point with numbers of cricket lovers and find that, almost without exception, the only ones who are in favour of it are those who retain certain well-intentioned but wholly impracticable views, imported with themselves quite recently, and certain others who consider that 'gate' and 'victory' cannot be too dearly bought.
>
> I do not hold with either. I look forward to a friendly tussle between the English and South African cousins and, if we cannot do better, we can at least take a licking like white men.
>
> We are in a country where whites are numerically out of it, and I submit that the most cursory glance into the future

warns us, just as the experience of America in the past and present teaches, that we must preserve the line of demarcation intact. If distinctions of colour are to be removed, the initiative need not be taken by the whites. I do not think that those who treat the matter so lightly consider what the position of the other members of the team would be, nor yet the moral effect that will survive when the tour will be over and forgotten. The subject is a distasteful one, but, if needs must, I for one should take my stand at any time and in any place, and say that, taking in view the conditions of life in South Africa, it is imperative that the line be drawn sharp, straight, and unbroken between white and coloured.

It would belittle the intelligence of your readers to illustrate the logical results of relaxing the rule; and I need only add that those who take no heed of this aspect of the question, those who consider 'gate' and 'victory at any cost' the paramount aim, I cannot recognise as South African sportsmen, even to the extent of discussing the question with them – I am &c.

SCRUTATOR[10]

Such malicious comments emerged from the Transvaal, which denied the franchise to 'non-whites' (which included Africans, coloureds and Indians) and barred them from playing a political role. Compared to its neighbours, the Cape Colony was relatively 'liberal' with a non-racial franchise based on property and educational requirements, even though in the 1890s the Rhodes administration launched a concerted attack on black political rights. Rhodes and the Afrikaner Bond were concerned that the Cape's liberal constitution not only affected co-operation with the other southern African territories, but also represented a political threat to white superiority.

The debate over Hendricks's selection took place in the context of a racial political scare in January 1894. A Muslim teacher and imam of Turkish descent, Ahmed Effendi, had stood for election to the House of Assembly, the first time a black or coloured candidate had put himself forward. The establishment feared that he might be able to benefit from a constitutional peculiarity that allowed voters four votes that could be spread across candidates or used for a single candidate. It was believed that coloured voters were more likely than whites to 'plump' their votes for a single candidate, as Effendi was their only representative. On the campaign trail, Malays, coloureds and whites demonstrated their support for Effendi, including an officer of the convict station who argued that 'the Malays live here and die here but the English come here to make money'. Furthermore, there were those in the House, including Hofmeyr, who said they would not object to sitting with a well-educated man such as Effendi, but that they opposed giving the Malays 'special' consideration in that Cape Town alone should continue to vote cumulatively. Joseph Orpen moved to abolish plumping and, with Rhodes's support, was successful in his bid to facilitate an amendment: the second reading was by 40 to 24 and the third and final reading by 30 to 15. Effendi, who told one meeting that he was a Muslim but 'his principles were European', was thus kept out of the House, defeated by 2,356 votes to 699.[11]

In the same year, a reporter from the Scottish *Dundee Advertiser* saw the city's special tradition of liberalism as being deeply flawed. He was of the opinion that although coloureds were equal in the eyes of the law, there was a 'line' between them and Europeans that was 'almost as rigidly drawn as if they were a lower range of beings'.[12] The Malays had established an organisation in order to oppose the 1892 Franchise and Ballot Act and the 1893 Constitution Amendment Act, but their efforts had proved unsuccessful. Naturally, frustration and anxiety were fostered among the coloured people while political mobilisation continued intermittently. They feared the mounting racism of the white population and the failure of the ruling class to distinguish between the relatively well-educated, more successful non-Europeans and the rest of the non-European population. A meeting of Coloured Political Associations took place in the Eastern Cape in 1894, which resolved to strengthen coloureds 'as a people', but its efforts were not sustained, and it was not until the early 1900s that a lasting national coloured political organisation was established.

It is questionable whether Cadwallader was concerned by Effendi's unsuccessful attempt to enter the House of Assembly, or whether he believed that Rhodes might extend his wide-ranging influence to the selection of a cricket side. The prime minister had recently returned to a hero's welcome, having added the Matabeleland stronghold to the empire. His biographer, Robert I. Rotberg, wrote of the period that it was not as if Rhodes lacked 'projects and compelling interests'. During the first part of 1894 he was also negotiating with Britain over the war in Matabeleland; with Britain and Germany about telegraphic extensions; with Natal, the Transvaal and the Orange Free State about tariffs and a customs union; and, more bizarrely, with the Ottoman court about goats. He was concerned about the administration of Rhodesia and the northern hinterland beyond the Zambezi, an area that encompassed the future Northern Rhodesia and Nyasaland. He was, said Rotberg, 'extending his monopoly over diamonds and recapitalising his stake in gold, reconstructing and refurbishing Groote Schuur and travelling extensively ... moreover, there was no shortage of contentious domestic issues upon which his coalition regime would need to pronounce'.[13]

Despite his well-filled in-tray, cricket was one of the domestic issues in which Rhodes became involved. He was probably drawn into the question of the tour by Hofmeyr, who wielded great authority in the fateful decisions that were made in the 1890s. Hofmeyr was arguably the power behind the Cape government and Western Province cricket. He had been instrumental in setting up Rhodes and Milton in their respective positions and no doubt found it convenient that they should 'share' the same office. Hofmeyr communicated regularly with Rhodes: they were early risers, and it was usual for the two men, often joined by James Sivewright, to take a ride on horseback together before the town was astir. In late 1893, Hofmeyr had told guests at a celebratory banquet that 'the sporting associations of this country, which for the most part represent combinations of sportsmen throughout the various states ... have set an example which politicians are all too slow to follow in the aim for a United South Africa'.[14] Like Rhodes, however, he did not wish sport to lead the way through coloured representation at a national level, and he would have been disturbed by the prominent press coverage that surrounded the selection of Hendricks for the overseas cricket tour. At a crucial stage, it was decided that Milton should reassume a key role in Western Province cricket and thereafter structure the direction that the game would take.

For several months, a Milton-less Western Province Cricket Union had been in some disarray over the tour. If anything, it came as a relief when the union decided to become part of the project, although they entered on the proviso that their involvement was dependent on the guarantees being secured. To maximise the publicity surrounding their entrance, Rhodes was drawn into chairing the first public meeting at the Commercial Exchange in early February 1894. Parliamentarians Sir Thomas Upington, Thomas Fuller MLA and James Rose Innes MLA, and cricketers William Milton, H.H. Castens, Alf Richards, Ned Steytler, Louis Smuts, Godfrey Cripps and Billy Simkins were in attendance. Rhodes told his audience that he thought the overseas trip was 'a plucky thing to undertake', but warned organisers against favouritism and to 'take the best team whoever they were and wherever they might reside (hear, hear)'.[15] In terms of a united team, Rhodes possibly hoped the selectors would cast their net as far afield as the land that would become officially known as Rhodesia, but his key concern would have been the inclusion of Afrikaners in a touring team that reflected white unity as part of the Bond compact.

Milton was in the process of setting up the Prime Minister's Department, of which he would be appointed permanent head from April 1894. He was also immersed in work that Rhodes had assigned him with regard to settling prickly issues in 'native affairs'. It was 'impossible for him to go to England', although Finlason had earlier pointed out: 'He's as fit as a fiddle now, and oils his bat every morning though there are months of dreary football yet, before the delightful wickets are struck up at Newlands.'[16] Cadwallader, who had feared the possibility of Milton returning to stamp his authority on proceedings, chose to flatter the country's incumbent cricket captain. 'Papers all over the country are filled with problematic South African XIs,' he wrote, 'but everybody seems to forget that a team on tour requires a good captain.' He continued:

> As there is only one real captain in South Africa, a gentleman whose name is W.H. Milton and as a good captain essential to a touring 11, ought not he be one of the chosen. Some people seem to think that 'Joey' as his friends call him, is no good now, but if he were to get into practice, I don't think there would be many to equal him even now and he would set his team such a fine example in the field: besides a South African XI without him would be like an England XI without 'W.G.'.[17]

Unfortunately for Cadwallader and, indeed, the entire tour project, confrontation became inevitable. It was the Hendricks question that had seen Milton return to the fore as chairman of the Western Province Cricket Union selection committee. It would be his task to ensure that the imposition of the Cape government's segregationist policy was not obstructed by the individual advancement of a coloured cricketer. But, as Milton soon gathered, it was not a simple task. The ongoing press debate, public interest and the backing of at least Abe Bailey's Transvaal ensured an awkward situation. Hendricks was also attracting attention on the cricket field. The inaugural winners of the new Western Province league, Cape Town CC, were keen to see Hendricks again and fielded a powerful side against City CC at Newlands. The hosts were bowled out for 123 with Hendricks taking seven wickets, including both professionals, Charles Mills and James 'Bonnor' Middleton.

It was to Milton's advantage that he was able to discuss the situation with Rhodes, who later claimed: 'They wanted me to send a black fellow called Hendricks to England ... but I would not have it. They would have expected him to throw boomerangs during the luncheon interval.'[18] The assertion referred to the 1868 Aboriginal tour, where the team were expected to provide cultural demonstrations in addition to playing cricket. By characterising Hendricks as the South African equivalent of an Australian 'Aboriginal', Rhodes justified himself in retrospect by claiming the high moral ground against Britain's thrill-seekers.

Pelham Warner later recalled an occasion in March 1895 when Rhodes and Dr Jameson stayed at Oxford with the provost of Oriel College, Dr Munro. On a Sunday morning, some eight to ten undergraduates were asked to breakfast to meet them. 'I was fortunate enough,' recalled Warner, 'to sit next to Rhodes, and the conversation turned on the first visit, during the previous summer, of a South African team to England. Rhodes had a good deal to do with the financing of this side ...' The discussion then focused on Hendricks with Warner saying, 'I had heard that he was a good bowler,' and Rhodes responding with his explanation that Hendricks would not have been treated appropriately in England. However, any attempt by the prime minister to come across as being sensitive to the coloured man's well-being was crushed in the course of their conversation as recalled by Warner. The latter was surprised but accepted that 'this great man and great Empire-maker felt like this [because it] shows how far he was looking ahead'. Rhodes put it down to the instinct of self-preservation: 'In South Africa we have perhaps a million or two whites, and many millions more of black people.'[19]

Rhodes's decision to reject Hendricks was discreetly communicated to protect the prime minister from being implicated in any further discussion on the subject. Milton, of course, knew that the rejection of Hendricks was a great deal more complex. The Cape was shifting its colonial policy from a strategy of amalgamation to one of segregation. The movement culminated in the 'momentous and complicated' Glen Grey Act of 1894, which regulated the lives of black landowners in the Eastern Cape. Rotberg said it had been 'conceived by Rhodes ... drafted by Milton'. There had been 'extensive consultations' with Hofmeyr, an assertion supported by the biographers of the Afrikaner Bond leader who go so far as to state that 'the ideals embodied are those of Hofmeyr rather than those of Rhodes'. The Glen Grey Act therefore appears to have evolved as a collective effort, one that promised 'to extend the Cape's net of ever-tightening segregation'. It reduced Africans' access to land tenure, forcing many into the labour force for the mines. Existing African smallholders were unable to further develop their relatively successful operations and to compete with white producers. By reducing access to land ownership, Glen Grey also significantly reduced African access to the property-based Cape franchise. The Act was 'freighted with political symbolism ... a decisive native policy that was broadly attractive to whites would facilitate the creation of a united white nation capable of expanding ...'[20] Rhodes presented it as 'a Native Bill for Africa' and, despite efforts from J.W. Sauer, John X. Merriman and James Rose Innes, among others, to attack 'both the principle and the details of the bill', the prime minister carried the day.[21]

Milton, as he liked to do, worked behind the scenes and said little, but interest in Hendricks would not go away. The disparaging comments made by A.B. Tancred in the *Standard and Diggers News* upset the cricketer, who sought help from Cadwallader in his capacity as secretary of the South African Cricket Association. In what was becoming a most sensitive issue, Cadwallader advised Hendricks to back down for the sake of gaining acceptance. It was a questionable approach, but Cadwallader appeared to be concerned with the bigger picture and the importance of taking Hendricks on tour – not only as a drawcard for economic purposes, but also because South Africa needed him. Shortly before the selection committee met, Cadwallader sent a carefully considered but desperate letter to the *Cape Times*:

> Sir
> Hendricks the coloured cricketer, having made representation to me as the secretary of the South African Cricket Association, with the request that I should make them public, I beg to do so. A short time ago there appeared a paragraph in your paper referring to Hendricks as a Malay and stating there was an idea that he should play for the South African cricket team and go in the capacity of 'baggage man'. He wrote in return denying that he is Malay or Mohammedan and objecting to his name being mentioned as baggage man. It appears Mr A.B. Tancred

> in an interview in Johannesburg referred to this letter (to you) as an 'impudent letter to the association'. This was clearly an error on Mr Tancred's part, as no communication had taken place between Hendricks and the Association.
>
> I learn from Hendricks who seems to be an unassuming man and bears an excellent character for a number of years from his employers, that he would be pleased to go to England if required, on certain low terms for services rendered, and would not for a moment expect to be 'classed' with the rest of the team. Hearne and Mills speak of Hendricks as quite the best fast bowler in the country and Mr George Lohmann (he is an amateur with us here) says (this has reached England first from Lohmann himself): 'By all means take him Home' (for various reasons). Strong advices have come from other parts of the country in favour of this man's inclusion, but that question is, of course, a South African one for the consideration of the Final Selection Committee, and approval of guarantors ...
>
> H.G. Cadwallader
> Hon Secretary: South African Cricket Association[22]

By drawing on the respected opinions of the two English professionals in Cape Town, Frank Hearne and Charles Mills, as well as the support of the great English bowler George Lohmann, Cadwallader was able to present a strong case in favour of Hendricks. While it placed the Western Province Cricket Union in an awkward position, it was welcomed by the Transvaal Cricket Union, which met shortly afterwards. Perhaps a little tongue-in-cheek, *The Globe* complained that the intervention of the professionals was not cricket. 'It is a hard thing,' the newspaper pointed out, 'when an English county cricketer spends his holiday in discovering demon bowlers for the discomfiture of his compatriots.' It reported that in a private letter from Lohmann, who was wintering at the Cape, he had said that he 'advised the inclusion of a Malay in the South African team which is to visit England in May'. *The Globe* concluded that 'an "extremely fast" Malay is at any time likely to be an object sufficiently terrible to the batsman and the umpire who dares to no-ball him; but if he shares his countryman's habits of running "amok" cricket will this year assume defensive features undreamed of by [late English professional Richard] Nyren in his worst nightmares'.[23]

The *Standard and Diggers News* alerted their readers to Cadwallader's letter in a report headed 'Hendricks climbs down'. They appeared genuinely satisfied with Cadwallader's explanation and the Transvaal Cricket Union acted on it when Abe Bailey chaired a meeting with Soames, Halliwell, Tancred and Fred Smith in attendance. The question of the tour was discussed at length on the basis that 'irrespective of persons, towns, or contributions to the guarantee, the best possible team was to be picked. The whole details were fully gone into, and the merits of each proposed man and then the 15 as a whole were analysed.' They were restricted to nominating players from their own area, but included Hendricks in their '15'. The *Standard and Diggers News* reported that the selection of Hendricks was unanimous:

> The prejudice against him disappearing on the understanding that he is willing to go as baggage-man and servant. Without a doubt the Western Province must also name him, he being the only 'Spofforth' in South Africa … Hendricks is acknowledged to be a red-hot trundler, and Halliwell who will have to 'stand up' to him, is the gentleman who particularly insists on the inclusion of this dusky unit.[24]

The *South African Review* thought it was an unusual situation in that the 'liberal' Cape's 'discriminatory attitude towards Hendricks was opposed by the Transvaal where, curiously enough the greatest antipathy to mixing with the coloured race in ***social*** [author's emphasis] life prevails'.[25]

The *Standard and Diggers News* admitted 'a great prejudice' existed against Hendricks, but 'if "colour" is not an insuperable barrier, he can't be left out … there is not a white man in the country who can be designated a really fast bowler'.[26] Hendricks might have been the solution to a key problem, but he was expected to accept humiliating conditions in order to assist the white players. For him, capitulation over the 'baggage-man and servant' issue had a much deeper significance than simply securing a place in a cricket side. Hendricks was attempting to come to grips with the changing realities of his situation. The unfolding tragedy for the cricketer was a microcosm of that of thousands of black South Africans at the time. Many believed that their behaviour and attainments would allow them to pass across class lines. Cricket and Christianity were the passports to a better life on the other side of the divide.

It seemed to be a class issue rather than a race issue, and there was no shared definition across the whole population (aside from the Malay designation) of what defined a person as coloured or European at the Cape at the time. Hendricks was from a working-class mixed community with no significant divide between poor Europeans and coloureds. In 1894, he saw his status as an Anglican churchgoer as sufficient to differentiate himself from the Muslim Malays and define him in the same ideological category as Europeans – he had been married by the famous Lightfoot after all. The furore when he initially refused to take on board the baggage-man role and his subsequent acquiescence (when advised by Cadwallader) demonstrate the confusion from his perspective. But from the cricket establishment's viewpoint, he played for the Malays, came from Bo-Kaap and had a predominantly Malay name, and was therefore coloured, and that sealed his fate. There was no longer any room at the Cape for the liberal tradition. The door was shut and remained locked despite efforts by Hendricks and his supporters to chisel it open.

Charles Finlason, who had become editor of *The Press*, entered the fray. He supported the selection of Hendricks and would have selected him and the young Jimmy Sinclair in his best 11. His main concern, however, was that the issue over a coloured player had obscured the fact that those of 'Dutch descent' were not being considered. He said that the tour had been commented upon in 'every leading paper in England and Australia and is regarded as an event not only of sporting importance but of political importance as well'. It is 'a business', he argued, 'in which the honour of all South

Africa is involved'. In calling for a representative team – a 'United South African Affair' – he optimistically noted that several players who were likely to be selected were of Dutch descent. He did not name anyone, but might have taken into account Charles Fichardt (Orange Free State) who had batted well against the formidable array of bowlers that the English had on their 1891/92 tour; Pieter de Villiers, a highly respected bowler; and Frederick Kuys, a promising young player who had represented Stellenbosch before joining the ranks of Cape Town CC.

In stressing that the tour should 'assume its true importance as a national affair', Finlason used his powers of persuasion to call upon South African leaders to set an example by supporting the guarantee fund. He thought Sir John Robinson, the Natal prime minister, had been the first South African of eminence to recognise the importance of the issues involved, but, as Finlason explained, 'We can fancy the conservative old voortrekkers asking wondrously or contemptuously, "What have we to do with the English game called cricket?"' He answered his own question by calling on President Kruger to contribute towards the tour funds. 'The enlightened President,' he stressed, 'will not be slow to see the magnificent opportunity afforded him of showing the *uitlanders* that he sympathises with their old national game ... a game which will do more to merge Boer and *uitlander* into good Transvaalers than any elaborate political measure that can be devised by the *Volksraad*. Boers and *uitlanders* must not only work together, but play together ...' Finlason thought the political effect of such 'a gracious act would be altogether out of proportion to the amount subscribed'. It is not known whether Kruger responded to the editorial, but his advisor, General Joubert, was reported to have headed the list of Transvaal subscribers.[27]

The tour captured the interest of almost every white English-speaking southern African, with a few notable exceptions. Barney Barnato, a colourful Randlord who had made a fortune in diamonds and gold, said that he had no idea as to South Africa's chances of impressing overseas and, for all he cared, they 'might as well send a team of washer-women "Home"'. He contributed £100 to the guarantee fund nevertheless. Charles Rudd, Rhodes's astute business partner who secured an agreement to the mineral rights of Matabeleland and Mashonaland from Lobengula – the Rudd Concession – expressed the opinion that the time was not ripe for sending a team 'Home', but contributed likewise up to three figures.[28]

The last few days before the selection meeting were highly charged as cricket authorities and journalists grappled with the selection dilemma. In the absence of a national competition, it was particularly difficult to assess ability and form in the context of self-contained centres. Cadwallader assembled information, but much had changed from his original request. He had asked for a maximum of six nominations in order of merit from each union. The nominations were to be accompanied with averages and remarks on all-round form. The centres were also asked to choose the side that they believed would be best equipped to represent South Africa on an overseas tour. The final selection committee would consist of one delegate from each centre – perhaps consulting with Lohmann, Hearne and Mills – and was scheduled to meet in Cape Town over Easter. And, in preparation, Cadwallader hoped to arrange a practice for likely tour members under Lohmann at Matjiesfontein or Newlands. Everything did not go as planned, however, partly because an increasing number of key players became unavailable as the selection day approached, notably Milton, Tancred, Irvine Grimmer, Henry Taberer, the Wimble brothers, Charles Vintcent, Alf Richards, Charlie Fichardt and Charles Boyes. Without such players, South Africa's hopes of making a favourable impression in England were adversely affected; and, to an extent, the selectors would be forced to rely on players whose claims to being South African were a little dubious.

There was relief for Cadwallader in that his organisation was generally praised, and he was especially pleased to report that 'a rather more pretentious programme than we ever aspired for [was being arranged overseas] ... good payable gates may be confidently expected with such a class of matches'. Cadwallader had probably resigned himself to the fact that the Cape government would block

Hendricks's selection. There was further anxiety as rumours circulated that events, of which the Hendricks controversy was most conspicuous, had impacted negatively on Cadwallader's hopes to manage the side, a position he clearly coveted and seemed certain to fill. At the eleventh hour, the organisation of the tour was taken out of his hands by Milton, who took it upon himself to contact the other cricket bodies in preparation for the final selection meeting. An 'engrosser of power and reluctant to delegate', Milton believed strongly in reaching private agreement beforehand to expedite the conduct of business. This was done where possible, while he was happy to organise the meeting's agenda and then govern its discussions.[29]

There were obviously problematic areas for Milton to address at the meeting, namely Hendricks's nomination as a player, Cadwallader's application to manage the side and the inclusion of players with an Afrikaner background. The press keenly awaited the decision over Hendricks, but apparently feared a process that had Milton at the helm. A last-minute plea from 'African Sport' in Johannesburg stated, 'I suppose everyone will say that [Hendricks] ought not to go under the circumstances, but we want a good machine-bowler and he is one.'[30] And Barberton Halliwell was quoted in the *Cape Times* as saying that 'in pure justice Mr Cadwallader should be appointed as manager'.[31] There is no evidence to suggest that Hofmeyr pushed for players of Dutch descent. He had not been actively involved in cricket affairs for some weeks. The election period and its aftermath were not only time-consuming for him, but were also particularly unpleasant in that he suffered 'internal upheavals in the Bond and personal attacks'. Two weeks before the side to tour England was announced, he wrote that he wished to leave politics: 'I am dead tired of the whole business.'[32]

The final selection committee meeting was held on 25 February 1894 at De Aar, a town that had developed as a key railway junction because of its central location and importance as a distribution focus for the Great Karoo. Hopes that were held for Hendricks and for 'Dutch' representation were quickly dashed. The alienation of groups other than English-speaking whites was a feature of the gathering that Milton chaired and dominated. The men who met with him were Messrs Grimmer (Griqualand West), Dunell (Eastern Province), Halliwell (Transvaal), Yule (Orange Free State) and Cadwallader (hon. secretary representing Natal). Newspaper reports recall that in deliberations lasting more than five hours, Milton had his way on virtually every issue, most notably in the rejection of Hendricks, who became the first South African to be denied selection for his country on account of his colour. The team chosen for the tour was as follows: Herbert Castens (captain), Godfrey Cripps, Darnton Davey, George Glover, Ernest Halliwell, Frank Hearne, Clement Johnson, George Kempis, Bonnor Middleton, Dante Parkin, Thomas Routledge, George Rowe, Arthur Seccull, Cyril Sewell and Vollie van der Byl.

Van der Byl subsequently dropped out of the team and was replaced by Charles Mills.

6

'Courting a disaster for the sake of prejudice'

> 'It was not absolutely necessary to lift a coloured man up on account of the moral effect it might have on the whole coloured population.'[1]
>
> – Abe Bailey

IN THE LIGHT of the number of players who were unavailable for the tour, it was generally considered reprehensible that no place could be found for Hendricks, particularly so because the team's greatest need was for a fast bowler. A Reuters telegram sent from Kimberley stated, 'It is the almost general opinion here that the Western Province Cricket Union has, by its high-handed action regarding various matters in connection with the team for England, muddled the whole concern.'[2] The *Standard and Diggers News* said that the feeling among leading players with regard to Hendricks's exclusion was that a great mistake had been made: 'It seems like courting a disaster for the sake of prejudice.'[3] Further criticism came from a frustrated 'Rough Colt' in the *South African Review*, who exclaimed: 'There will be some surprise at their colour, coming from South Africa, and there will be a guffaw from one end of the country to the other that they left their only coloured player behind because he was coloured!'[4]

In England, *The Cricket Field* provided advice: 'On some of our crumbling wickets Hendricks would perhaps be highly effective. It is not unlikely that our visitors will regret before the end of the season that they were so particular as to the colour of their men.'[5] *Cricket: A Weekly Record of the Game* added that Hendricks's omission was 'from a cricketing point of view hardly wise policy ... as a fast bowler Mills declares him to be considerably above the average'.[6] The committee saw fit to drop him, reported Cadwallader, 'but I fancy they will have reason to wish before the tour is half over they had dropped sentiment and taken Hendricks, on the unanimous advice from the Transvaal'.[7]

The whole affair must have been doubly galling for Hendricks, who had been required politically to swallow his pride and accept a menial status and was even then unceremoniously rejected. It is hard to imagine a more bitter cricketing blow. Several newspapers did not accept that the team had been finalised and there were post–De Aar calls for Hendricks to be included. The *Natal Mercury* said that he was still being pushed as deserving of a place. 'As caste distinctions have been arranged,' said the report, 'it would undoubtedly strengthen our team. Blackham the captain of the last Australian team in England says that with a fast bowler in their 11 they would have come out a lot better than they did ... I sincerely hope Hendricks will still get in.'[8] The *Standard and Diggers News* made several attempts to persuade the selection committee – effectively Milton – to see reason. In one piece, the writer asked: 'How can we ignore the earnest exhortations of men like Lohmann and Hearne on no account to leave him out, or their statements that we might as well go without a wicketkeeper as without a fast bowler?' He continued: 'I therefore make an appeal to the selection committee to re-consider and send Hendricks, and also to the Unions in the different centres to urge on the committee the absolute necessity of doing so.'[9]

'It is a South African team,' commented the *Bloemfontein Express*, 'with but few South Africans in it.'[10] The *Standard and Diggers News* commented on Clement 'Boy' Johnson, who had arrived in South Africa four months previously. 'It is a solemn fact,' they argued, 'that throughout the whole country there is not a white man who can by any stretch of the imagination be called a *bona fide* fast bowler.' If there was one, it would be Johnson, 'but although the Irishman is certainly able to send down a "snorter", it would only be for an over or two, he being essentially only an above average trundler'.[11] One report asked why Lohmann had not been considered, because he 'has been out here longer than Johnson, and it is a sort of open secret that South Africa will be his future home'.[12] Another queried the selection of Glover, pointing out that he is 'a good all-round cricketer but has a suspicious delivery in bowling that has been a bone of contention among cricketers for a long time. Even Glover himself admits that he throws occasionally.'[13]

So suspicious were people of the manner in which the whole process had been conducted that Milton was forced to release a copy of the minutes. They were sketchy and, if anything, prolonged the dispute. With regard to Hendricks, they simply read, 'Halliwell proposed Hendricks be added to list – not seconded.'[14] According to Finlason, Hendricks 'was proposed strongly', while Platnauer stated that Halliwell's support for Hendricks was received 'with cold indifference that showed an appalling want of regard for the analytical components of the team'. He claimed that the Australians had failed in England during the previous year because of the absence of a fast bowler and that it would be 'absolutely criminal to send our team away without a fast bowler when we have Hendricks, standing 6 feet 2 inches high, who takes three or four strides to the wicket and sends down lightning deliveries all day without tiring'. Platnauer, like Abe Bailey and his committee, was desperately keen for South Africa to do well. 'The coloured race,' he tried to explain, 'should be kept in their proper sphere in this country, but in this particular instance it would be a very great mistake to allow any such abstract consideration to stand in the way of success.'[15]

Having made a strong appeal to good sense, the *Standard and Diggers News* complained that the manner in which the cricket authorities had ignored their pleas was inexcusable. The writer was prepared to accept that naive colonial men who had never been in England 'may be pardoned if they do not clearly see the importance of the matter'. However, the same could not be said of the English cricketers, and especially those who were accompanying the team, if they did not record 'their emphatic protest at the way in which the chances of a successful tour are to be jeopardised, if not entirely sacrificed, for the sake of a stolid and unbreakable prejudice against colour'.[16] It was a radical assessment of a situation that went much further than a cricket tour and would in time impact on the future of the game in southern Africa.

A letter to the *Cape Times* asked:

> Why has Hendricks not been chosen? All praise to the Transvaal for upholding his claim. Without doubt the best fast bowler in South Africa, a good field and not the worst bat in the team, but because he has a little dark blood in his veins, he is black-balled.[17]

The writer went on to ask how many people were aware that 'P.C. Charlton, a member of the Australian team of 1890, is very much darker than Hendricks, the Australian's mother being a New Zealand Maori, and his father an off-coloured man; yet he was welcomed on English cricket grounds and so would Hendricks'. Not long afterwards, the *Cape Argus* referred to Charlton being 'half Maori',[18] prompting a response from the Melbourne newspaper, *Table Talk*:

> A paper in Cape Town whose knowledge of Australian cricketers is palpably deficient, acquaints its readers with the intelligence that Percy Charlton, the Sydney cricketer, is a half-caste Maori. It is well that Cape Town is a trifle inaccessible or the genial Percy might bring a libel action against the paper, sounding in damages unlimited.[19]

With the cricket tour generating endless debate, it was a demanding period for Milton. Not even the tightest of cricket contests could have prepared him for the off-the-field tension he faced and, characteristically, he said little as he contemplated his next move. Milton liked to weigh up his options carefully and played for time over the question of tour manager. His claim that guarantors had to be consulted did not create suspicion as Cadwallader was the only candidate and it seemed a formality that he would be chosen. The other unions were not initially aware that Milton opposed the appointment and that he needed time to choose and then promote another candidate. The *Cape Argus* was the first to express its surprise that 'Western Province' should treat Cadwallader so shabbily as he had done more than anyone to put South African cricket on its feet. 'It is whispered,' said the report, 'that the Western Province Cricket Union committee after having opposed the scheme at the outset, having got a majority of selections in the team, a Western Province man as skipper [Herbert H. Castens], and the Western Province CC colours adopted for the tour, want also to dictate about the managership and are nominating a "special" of their own fancy.'[20] Further scorn was poured on Milton by the *South African Review*: 'First the Western Province would have nothing to do with the scheme, then they wanted to take it to their unmanly bosoms and suckle it as their own offspring, give it their wet-nurse, appoint their own bear-leader for it and attire it in their own raiment.'[21]

Cadwallader responded to the rumours circulating by publishing an open letter in which he appealed to the guarantors of the English tour not 'to throw him overboard, after working so hard in bringing the negotiations to a successful conclusion'. He said that he was being overlooked in favour of Billy Simkins 'in consequence of the machinations of a clique about whose actions I could "a tale unfold"'. Cadwallader might well have known the full story of Rhodes's involvement in the drama. He was probably afraid to mention the prime minister, but spoke out bravely against Milton, who, he said, had 'privately exerted influence to induce other unions for that gentleman [Simkins] against myself'. The *South African Review*, with an obvious vested interest in the matter, argued that nothing tangible had been urged against Cadwallader, whose rejection seemed unnatural and unjust. But, as he was determined to bring the matter to an issue, they hoped they might eventually be able to judge whether there were adequate reasons, or whether 'it was merely at the instance of the clique and the somewhat snobbish spirit which certain circles in Capetown have the most unenviable reputation of possessing, that he was deprived of the position he so much covets, and which all things being equal, he had fully earned'.[22]

'Umpire' in the *Natal Mercury* could not understand why Cadwallader was being overlooked and put the rumours down to 'just tittle-tattle' until they could be substantiated. 'Mr Cadwallader,' said the report, 'is very anxious to have the appointment (I think many others would like it too) but the Western Province object to him strongly and even go so far as to say they will not join the team if he is manager.' According to Umpire, 'Transvaal object to Simkins requiring £25 a month as well as travelling expenses, whereas Mr Cadwallader offered to go on the guarantee of his expenses alone.'[23] The *Standard and Diggers News* thought the vexed question of manager might easily develop into a perfect 'Apple of Discord'. The reporter argued that Cadwallader 'should certainly be chosen ... I have, however, heard one or two very unjust reasons advanced, and in one case, an absolutely stupid reason why he should not be given the post'.[24]

The *South African Review*'s investigations subsequently claimed Milton and his fellow cricket administrators had insisted on the choice of manager being 'a man of some social standing, address and be able to make a respectable after-dinner speech'. It was therefore a case of demanding that 'Mr Social-standing Simkins be manager in place of Mr Hard-working Cadwallader because [the latter] takes his cricket without champagne; and Simkins as every Anglo-Indian knows is the very name for that intoxicant itself.' One other objection openly provided was that Cadwallader had 'never been connected with any large financial job. Mr Simkins has'. Again, the *South African Review* was to the fore in defence of their sports editor. 'Ahem!' they argued. 'Mr Simkins was the President of the South African Rugby Football Board. That body had financial jobs.' According to the paper, the minutes and accounts of that board were found to be in an incomplete state as books and records had been lost during the amalgamation of the Central and De Beers Diamond Companies, and because the former secretary, Harry Boyes, had been killed in a railway accident. Said the newspaper, '[The board] got so tangled over [their administration] that Mr Cadwallader had to be brought in to straighten them out ... No Mr Cadwallader has never had to do with financial jobs. Except to separate the finance from the job ...'[25]

The 'clique' that Cadwallader had condemned in 1894 remained firmly in control of cricket and rugby until the First World War. Two of the hard-line cricket leaders, Simkins and Smuts, were also the dominant influences in Western Province rugby for more than 20 years. When Simkins was elected president of the South African Rugby Football Board in July 1893, Cadwallader was elected secretary/treasurer. They were the only office-bearers on a committee that was made up of two representatives from 'each state, colony or province'. The year they were in office together was regarded as productive with the newly designated South African Rugby Football Board proceeding towards a new constitution and adopting the rules of the English Rugby Football Union. Cadwallader was praised for getting the board into shape, financial and otherwise, but there was no reward for him. He was not nominated again and effectively paid the price for instigating the Hendricks affair.

Having been successful in orchestrating a process that culminated in the non-selection of Hendricks for the overseas tour, it was not surprising that Milton was cautious over the choice of manager. He realised that whoever was appointed would be expected to provide satisfactory answers to questions that the English would almost certainly ask concerning the role of the colour question in team selection. Milton believed Cadwallader had not only championed Hendricks, but had also repeatedly criticised the Cape government's interference in cricket. Simkins would be pleased to offer the explanations that suited Milton, specifically the claim that Hendricks was overrated. It was precisely the answer that would be given to the English press by both Castens and Simkins.

Simkins was officially nominated by the Western Province Cricket Union to stand against Cadwallader. The national votes for the two candidates were divided equally, but Cadwallader withdrew, stressing that he did not care to identify himself with the candidature for the management unless he received unanimous, or almost unanimous, support. He was later paid £50 and reimbursed out-of-pocket expenses to conclude another unfortunate episode.

An editorial in the *Cape Times* attributed the 'regrettable controversies' to a certain anarchy in the moral world that was a feature of the time and a reflection of other disorders more practical and obvious. The unpleasantness over Hendricks and Cadwallader 'ought not to have happened of course, but we are passing through an era of squalls in which influenza and Laboucheres and explosive bombs must play their part to remind the world that the reign of peace is not yet'. The editor's explanation concluded with the wish that 'the movement had been spared the slur of murky surroundings at a time when it needed all favouring auspices … For there are good souls among us, antiquated perhaps and unschooled in modern ways, that grow pensive over the excitement and enthusiasm attaching to youthful pastimes.'[26]

Politician, railway catering concessionaire and cricket benefactor James Logan, who had enjoyed a 'magnificent majority at the poll due to the coloured vote', said he was 'strongly in favour of the best team that South Africa can send of whatever class or colour, as most likely to ensure a successful tour'. Taking the advice of George Lohmann, he believed that Hendricks should have been selected 'to ensure greater success for the tour'. He therefore announced that he was withdrawing his guarantee of £500 because the arrangement had been made with Cadwallader – and not the new establishment – on the understanding that the best team would be selected to tour England. 'Hendricks ought to have been included in the team,' he argued, as 'he was their finest bowler but they would not have him because he was a coloured man … whether a man is white, black or yellow makes no difference to me, nor does his particular trade or profession. What I want to see is the crack player and the crack sportsman.'[27]

It was hoped that the influential Abe Bailey would speak out on the question of sending Hendricks, but he reserved a final decision on the matter until he had met with Milton at the Currie Cup tournament towards the end of March. He learnt of

Rhodes's involvement and, on his return to Johannesburg, a reporter from the *Standard and Diggers News* asked him whether the trip had encouraged him to change his views on Hendricks. He replied:

> That is a rather ticklish business. As you know when I went down, I was strongly in favour of sending him, but I have yielded somewhat to the very good argument that, after all, our men were going to England to learn rather than with the hope of achieving any great glory. Under these circumstances, it was argued, it was not absolutely necessary to lift a coloured man up on account of the moral effect it might have on the whole coloured population ... Under these circumstances, I waived the point as I did not wish to upset things and force it. All the same, it is a great pity there is no fast bowler in the team and I wouldn't say a word against Hendricks were he to be sent after all.[28]

The argument that the team was going to learn and not for glory was later ridiculed by Lohmann, who remarked: 'That's all very well but they would learn a great deal more during a successful tour than an unsuccessful one.'[29] The *Cape Argus* thought objections about the effect the success of a coloured cricketer might have 'upon his fellows in this country may be regarded as puerile'.[30] But a *Standard and Diggers News* reporter did not push Bailey on the matter; instead, he moved on to a subject that was known to irk the mining magnate, the controversial issue of team manager:

> What about the manage–?
> A steely glance stopped the intended question.[31]

Milton did not attend the meeting of the South African Cricket Association, which was held during the Currie Cup tournament in March. Rhodes had orchestrated the annexation of Pondoland and wished to put his stamp on the endeavour. Milton accompanied him on what Merriman was to call Rhodes's 'scamper through the

Transkei'. It was 'a triumphant journey that echoed the processions of Roman Caesars' and they travelled 'in great state in a fancy coach drawn by eight cream-coloured horses, and accompanied by 100 men of the Cape Mounted Rifles ...'[32] Parts of the journey were considered rash and dangerous, but Rhodes was firm and dominant, maintaining his belief that it would only be a question of time before the Transkei was self-supporting.

Castens represented Milton at the cricket gathering and was well briefed on the innumerable problems that had arisen in the aftermath of the De Aar discussion. An important development to occur at the meeting of the South African Cricket Association was the ruling that, in future, the administration of the national body 'should be managed by a committee of three members of the union holding the Currie Cup'.[33] As Western Province emerged triumphant in the 1894 tournament, they formed a new committee that comprised Milton, Smuts and Steytler. It was clear that Castens had pushed all the right buttons and most notably secured the removal of Cadwallader as secretary of the South African Cricket Association. The game was effectively in the hands of Milton and the Cape government, although it was reliant on the Western Province side winning the Currie Cup.

In early April, a match was arranged for the South African touring team against an All-Comers XI at Newlands. It sought to provide practice prior to the side's departure and to raise funds for the professionals. The *Cape Times* announced on 30 March that the All-Comers XI would include Hendricks and Lohmann. The *Cape Argus* welcomed the selection of Hendricks as it contradicted the view that no man of colour should be selected for a representative team. Under the heading 'Wanted: a fast bowler', the report stated that the one remaining objection 'to this man being taken to England is that there is no precedent for playing coloured men in the same team with men in South Africa'. It then argued: 'Isn't there indeed? We have seen many such matches ourselves from week to week, and hitherto the practice has not created any terrible racial hatred ... with Hendricks playing for the European All-Comers there will be a distinct and prominent precedent set up.'[34]

The idea of the official side having a 'warm time of it' with Hendricks and Lohmann operating in tandem was appealing. Then, on 31 March, Vollie van der Byl withdrew from the touring squad and, with the familiar cruel insensitivity to Hendricks's position, was immediately 'given a place in the All-Comers team in place of Hendricks'. Two days later, Lohmann wrote a letter to the *Cape Times* to announce his withdrawal and a special committee (Alf Richards, Castens and Steytler) was deemed necessary 'to fill up vacancies for the All-Comers team'. On the day of the match, Van der Byl 'for some reason or other failed to put in an appearance'.[35] One report said that he 'did not turn up, as a player at any rate', while 'many of those who did play rolled up in penny numbers, by reason of which the match, which could easily have been commenced at 11 o'clock did not begin until 12.15'.[36]

The *South African Review* had its say, commenting that, 'for reasons which can be understood, Mr G. Lohmann declined to play, and for other reasons which cannot be so easily understood, Hendricks was shunted'.[37] Earlier, Lohmann had criticised the South African selectors for not including Hendricks in their touring side 'because he is coloured'. The great English bowler was generally critical of the game's administration at the Cape and the circumstances of his withdrawal related to resentment of 'much that takes place in the Western Province under the guise of sport which is devoid of every sportsman-like feature'. In a letter to the *Cape Times*, Lohmann explained 'it is the first time in my life that I have ever refused to assist brother professionals but under the present circumstances I think I am perfectly justified in the course I have adopted'.[38]

Criticism mounted against the Western Province Cricket Union and, to Milton's immense chagrin, the *South African Review* teamed up with other newspapers to send Cadwallader overseas as their press representative on the tour. In response to this development, the South African captain was misguidedly instructed to ignore the press, a foolish decision when bold advertisement was essential to the success of the tour. Barberton Halliwell revealed that, when the team arrived in England, they took up quarters for practice at

Catford where 'a great blunder of tactics was made'. Instead of taking the press into their confidence, he said, 'the authorities chose to adopt a spirit of haughty exclusiveness that is galling under any circumstances but particularly when assumed by swaggers'. Castens carried the can and the powerful London press was said to have been alienated through 'the fatuous behaviour of an individual swollen with an exaggerated and erroneous notion of his own importance, a course of conduct which certainly showed scant consideration for the interests of those who have to pay the piper'.[39]

Cadwallader summed up the state of affairs under the tour captain:

> All attempts to draw the chief of the team into a statement as to their programme were met by a chilling snub. Practice was conducted with as much mystery as if some vital secret had to be guarded until the opening day. There may have been good reason for this policy: anyhow the Press failed either to recognise or sympathise with it. Spiteful paragraphs got into circulation ridiculing the team ... instead of starting with a boom, the team went to the wickets in their first match without exciting the slightest interest or curiosity. It was a fatal blunder.[40]

Castens, a Rugby School and Oxford product, was forthright in his comments when interviewed by *The Cricket Field* in the course of the tour. He appeared keen to discuss the colour question. When asked whether he found the spectators in England impartial, he commented ruefully that English crowds, 'even among highly educated people ... have been disappointed with us because we are none of us black'. He recalled the touring party leaving their hotel at Chatham when a working man said to another, 'Why, Bill, they ain't even coffee-coloured!' The interviewer wanted to know if the reaction of the English people had been caused by the report that Hendricks was coming. Castens replied in the affirmative – 'It is very likely' – but hurriedly defended the South African stance: '... we have been misjudged with regard to our reasons for not including him in the team. In England the colour question never crops up – with us it is always doing so. I don't defend it, but merely say what is a fact.' Castens was surprisingly frank in explaining the non-selection of Hendricks. 'I can assure you,' he continued, 'that when it was proposed to bring [Hendricks] with the team the greatest pressure was put upon us by those in high authority in the Cape Colony to leave him out, because it was feared that trouble might ensue.'[41]

In a modern interview, Castens's explanation might have been scrutinised with ruthless, probing questions, but *The Cricket Field* was a conservative publication read primarily by public-school 'old boys'. It refrained from entering into a discussion over the 'trouble' that the Cape officials envisaged. The magazine probably knew as well as Castens that the publicity Hendricks might have attracted would certainly have rendered a more than passing dent in the segregationist policies that Rhodes was implementing. Moreover, it would have been awkward for both the Cape government and the cricket administration had Hendricks been successful, as it would have made it very difficult to leave him and other coloured players out of future South African teams.

Castens offered other, less convincing reasons for the non-selection of Hendricks. He pointed out that the fast bowler had gained his reputation by 'getting a great many wickets against the English team which visited us'. He attempted to downplay the effort, claiming that the match was the last staged during the tour, when the tourists 'were all tired, and perhaps too, they treated the Malays too lightly'. Castens was surprisingly ill-informed over wickets taken and unintentionally yet deservedly complimentary over the standard of Malay cricket. The most significant point, which was abundantly clear to everyone except Castens, was the pace that Hendricks was able to generate. He had caused alarm among Read's team and those players would not have agreed with Castens's rehearsed view that 'we think his powers have been over-rated, and that on wickets in England he would not have been of much use'. Then, perhaps unwittingly, Castens disclosed the impact of social segregation and revealed the hypocrisy of the Cape's dominant class in adding: 'Another reason – the most important of all – for leaving him out of our team is that he never plays in any local European teams, and hardly ever against them.'[42]

Simkins, as might have been expected, also put across the view that Hendricks had been omitted for cricket reasons. He echoed Castens when he told *St Paul's Magazine* in an interview that was reprinted in an edition of *Cricket: A Weekly Record of the Game*: 'I think he has been over-rated here.'[43] A different view was taken by Derbyshire and England opening batsman Bill Chatterton, who had toured South Africa with Read's team in 1891/92. He was 'certain that if the colour line had been less sharply drawn, and Hendricks had been selected to visit England, his bowling would have been a revelation to us'.[44]

The former Australian captain Billy Murdoch, who had also toured with Read's team, expressed disappointment with the South African performance in England. 'As to Hendricks,' he said, 'I think myself he would have been of immense value to you, and in any case would have been a very great draw. I feel sure he would have knocked some of us and our pegs about on hard wickets.'[45] The fact was quickly seized upon by Cadwallader, who had been conscious from the moment he began planning the tour of the need to include players who could draw the crowds. He observed:

> Certainly everywhere we went we were asked why we didn't bring Hendricks with us. It was surprising how the general public had got to know about his reputation. We had to explain as well as we could the reason he was not brought, but the public, who are used to seeing on the cricket field coloured men like Messrs P.J.T. Henery and K.S. Ranjitsinhji playing in their universities and county 11s, could not quite understand it. They could not comprehend the difference of classes in the social, or rather sporting, kaleidoscope at this end and the Cape end.[46]

There were conflicting reports about Castens on the tour. The *Standard and Diggers News* thought he had 'an anxious and worrying time – the financial difficulties could not have eased his mind'. Under the circumstances, 'it was perhaps only a little natural that he should have failed on all occasions to maintain evenness of temper'.[47] Few would have understood the pressure he was under from higher authorities and sympathy might have been accorded him in such unusual circumstances. The *South African Review* mentioned that they were in receipt of a number of letters from England, 'detailing with personal and painful matters dealing with the team'. They did not publish them, so they said, as there were tales that might present 'other and more acceptable sides'. They did nevertheless reproduce a letter from a team member who said:

> We are all pulling together nicely, with the exception of Castens, who is disliked by all of us, with the exception of Johnson, who is the only friend he has amongst us ... never before have we played under such a captain as Castens, who has done nothing, but says he is going to play in every match, as he has made runs and he will play until he does so again. His average now is about 8. He is dead nuts against Kempis and says he is no d----d good ... Castens simply hates him like poison ... Cripps is the most popular man we have ... Davey was another one that hadn't a show, as Castens said that *he* was no d----d good. Simkins ... of course can't get on with Castens, who always tries his best to pick holes in Simkins' work.[48]

Simkins was a leading figure in the Cape Town CC, devoted to Hofmeyr, while Castens was an emerging influence in the Western Province CC. Both were probably a little uncomfortable with the arrangement that they should receive their instructions from Milton. The tour proved a financial failure, but not simply because of Castens's behaviour and the subsequent meagre advertising. Cadwallader wrote of the dreadful weather and the ruinous effect it had on the 'gates'. The largest attendance they had at any time was a crowd of 4,000 on the first day of the first Warwickshire match. Most of the gates fell far short of that, and 'now and again', Cadwallader said, 'the spectators have almost been limited to two blind men and a boy, as my friend, Mr Sympathetic Simkins, has frequently remarked, or, as one London paper described the attendance once, to "two ladies and a spotted dog"'. Its collapse was only avoided through assistance received from steamship companies and South African businessmen in England. Yet, despite the difficulties, the team's record was encouraging, and Cadwallader was convinced that the South Africans could have 'given all the first-class counties a "tying-up" if we only had a really good fast trundle or two'. He concluded, 'We only felt we had to live to learn.'[49]

The highlight was to play at Lord's against W.G. Grace's MCC XI. The opening day of the match was washed out and on the second morning Grace put the South Africans in to bat. The game's most famous cricketer was in splendid form on a day of low scores and proceeded to bowl the South Africans out twice, returning match figures of 12-93. In an action-packed contest, the MCC were left to score 84 runs in their second innings to win the match. They seemed assured of victory, but time was running out. They lost their third wicket at 63 and therefore needed 21 runs with seven wickets in hand. As close of play was fast approaching, Grace came on to the field and asked Castens if he was prepared to complete the match. The South African captain agreed and, 'as the MCC wickets began to fall', said George Glover, 'our fielding became phenomenal; nothing within yards of us got past'. When Halliwell brought the innings to an end with a brilliant stumping, it meant the last eight wickets had fallen for 9 runs. The MCC were all out for 72, enabling the South Africans to win in dramatic fashion by 11 runs.

'It is rare indeed,' wrote Cadwallader, 'that a first-class match should see four innings completed in one day.' Although the South African matches were not granted first-class status, Cadwallader was perhaps right to claim that the match under question was even more remarkable than the 1878 Australia versus MCC match at Lord's when the hosts (33 and 19) were well beaten by the visitors (41 and 12 for one). 'The MCC last Tuesday,' he wrote of the South African encounter, 'were not dismissed for such low scores as in May 1878, but there is no telling what might have happened had we had the Demon Hendricks with us. All the papers have lamented his absence ...'[50]

Cadwallader made frequent references to Hendricks during the tour, but he did not ignore the other players. He praised their efforts and thought it had been 'universally conceded that despite scanty patronage and unfavourable weather, over which they had no control, our boys acquitted themselves right well'. He could not resist a dig at those who had opposed the tour, pointing out how well the team had done and recalling how 'many "all wise" ones at the Cape' had prophesied that they would not win a single match. They won 12 out of 24 and only lost five. He took pleasure in the fact that no less than five members of the team had scored centuries and 'C.O. Sewell has made himself renowned as one of the leading batsmen in the world; Halliwell is acknowledged to be unexcelled as a wicketkeeper; and Rowe has established himself as a first-class bowler, while the 11, as a whole, has earned praise on leading British grounds for brilliancy in the field'.[51]

Halliwell attracted attention throughout the tour. When wickets fell so quickly against Gloucestershire and he was unable to get his pads on in the allotted time, he had arrived at the wicket at least a minute overdue. W.G. Grace met him and informed Halliwell that he was under the impression the South Africans had come to England to learn the game: 'Did he not know that he could claim his wicket for taking over two minutes to arrive?' Halliwell went on to make 110. To annoy Grace further, he employed the 'switch-hit', which Kevin Pietersen would make famous more than 100 years later. According to one report, 'Halliwell did a twist-about of this kind to Grace's bowling during the tour ... it is not generally considered good form or safe cricket to go in for clowning'. The correspondent then made a point of confirming that it was perfectly legal for a batsman to be 'able to change his position whilst a ball is in transit'.[52]

Cadwallader said he was not at all surprised that some members of the team, especially the colonial-born players, were anxious to hurry back to South Africa at great speed after the last match against Warwickshire was drawn. 'They left shivering, if not pretty wet,' he said, 'and they are likely to look back at their tour in England as a dreadfully chilly affair.'[53] At the same time, it was a great learning experience as George Glover, George Kempis and Dante Parkin acknowledged in an interview on their return. They were shocked by London's slums, stating, 'there is nothing to compare with them in the colonies. The poverty and the bare footedness is very painful to a colonial born, especially when seen side by side with wealth and luxury.'[54] The cricketers would fill their pockets with coppers and throw the halfpennies to small, ragged boys. It was also noted that pre-tour indignation at the Cape over the idea of Hendricks accompanying the side did not stop the South Africans from playing against black cricketers overseas. They met the legendary Kumar Shri Ranjitsinhji and rated him the finest batsman that they had come across; he scored 53 and 146 not out for C.W. Wright's XI against the South Africans at Portsmouth: 'A prettier bat all round the wickets it would be impossible to imagine.'[55]

Although he was not there, Hendricks was a central figure hovering over the tour. For the next few years, his influence continued to have an impact and affect all the major playmakers in South African cricket, and as such he was pivotal to the decisions they made. 'By leaving Hendricks out of their team,' said *The Cricket Field*, 'the South Africans by no means settled the colour question.'[56]

7

The Hendricks controversy comes home

> 'The races are best socially apart, each good in their way, but a terribly bad mixture.'
>
> – *Cape Argus* (30 March 1894)

TWO MONTHS AFTER the South African tour of England concluded, the Western Province Cricket Union were given a chance for second thoughts on Hendricks. They had to select the teams for the 'Colonial-born' versus 'Mother Country' contest in Cape Town, the highlight of the season. It was an occasion that defined imperial solidarity and gathered the ruling class at Newlands in a mini Lord's-like display of social ostentation. During the first part of the 1894/95 season, Hendricks had played for United Services CC in the 'white' Cape Town First Cup competition and bowled so well that he should have been an automatic choice for the Colonial-born team. His successful participation in the white league again raised the possibility of his involvement in representative cricket. The question was whether the authorities were prepared to see Hendricks attacking the best Cape Town batsmen on this most 'imperial' of occasions.

Only five members turned up to the meeting of the Western Province Cricket Union tasked with selecting the teams in October 1894, with Milton a notable absentee. Ned Steytler suggested that because Hendricks had played for United Services in a competition recognised by the union, he failed to see how he could be excluded from the representative match. Louis Smuts drew attention to the fact that 'it would be very awkward if Hendricks were chosen and the opposing team refused to play', even though there was no indication this would be the case. Thomas Lawton, an attorney, was in favour of including Hendricks, stating 'there was nothing in Hendricks's demeanour on the field that was in the least objectionable ... it had always been the boast of cricket that the peer and the ploughman could meet together in the same field'. He conceded, however, that the committee 'could not be blind to the fact that there was strong opposition to Hendricks in certain quarters'. Maynard Nash – who was secretary of the Civil Servants Club and a Milton disciple – reminded the committee that it was 'a wider issue than the mere admittance of Hendricks'. It was 'decided' that the problem should be deferred until a further meeting four days later. They needed to consult William Milton, coincidentally the best batsman in the Mother Country side and, if Hendricks was selected, a likely recipient of his thunderbolts.[1]

Members then unanimously agreed that four Australians were eligible for the Colonial-born team, before discussion moved swiftly to Godfrey Cripps, a committee member who was born in India. The committee had no difficulty in supporting their colleague's credentials and were happy to revise the constitution to allow the Colonial-born XI to include players born in 'the British colonies or in India', but were undecided in the case of the South African–born Hendricks. The outcome of the meeting disappointed Advocate Shepstone Giddy, who was representing Hendricks's United Services.[2]

After the meeting, the *Cape Times* hoped the question of Hendricks's eligibility for future teams would be carefully considered before it was 'finally disposed of one way or the other'. There were many things to be urged 'for and against', which further stressed the need for the committee to provide 'reasons' in order to ensure the relevant issues were debated. 'It seems to us,' said the *Cape Times*, 'that there are two "gates" for "coloureds" to the cricket field – the first being exceptionally good at cricket, and the next exceptionally good and appropriate behaviour, and the main question is – does Hendricks fulfil these qualifications?'[3] Given that Hendricks clearly strolled comfortably through both 'gates', it begged the question as to why there were any gates for him at all.

The selectors, however, did not abide by the committee's decision to wait for a second meeting before announcing a Colonial-born team that did not include Hendricks. They were apparently puppets acting under Milton's direction. The *Cape Times* was sympathetic to the Hendricks case, an indication that Milton was still out on a limb as regards public opinion:

> The Colonial team will not include Hendricks. This announcement may seem superfluous to those who remember how the very idea of the fast bowler's inclusion was tabooed owing to the difficulty of 'colour' but it is explained by the fact that, at a recent meeting of the Western Province Cricket Union, the question of his eligibility to play for the Colonials was described in an amicable manner, and without the loss, as far as could be entertained, of a single hair of any of the assembled delegates. To put the matter in a nutshell, we have a respectable and well-behaved coloured man in Hendricks, who in the opinion of Lohmann, backed up by that of many other leading cricketers, and by the still more potent testimony of a phenomenally low average, is one of the finest extra-fast bowlers in the world; who was not, for reasons apart from his ability as a cricketer, sent to England, nor is he to play in the match under review.[4]

Platnauer, from the Transvaal perspective, was more forceful in the *Standard and Diggers News*, criticising the Western Province Cricket Union for excluding Hendricks, 'who has been doing marvellous bowling this season', from a Colonial-born team. 'The Western Province would indeed be stultifying themselves,' said Platnauer, 'after their strenuous and successful objection to Hendricks' inclusion in the South African team to England, where race distinctions are unknown, should they include the coloured bowler in representative cricket at the Cape, where snobocracy reigns.'[5]

When the committee reassembled, Cripps tried some classic legal sophistry by suggesting that they shelve the problem until Hendricks was actually chosen for a representative team, but without indicating who then would choose him. Murray Bisset 'concurred' with this. The chairman, Lawton, was forced to remind them that selectors 'would wish to know if Hendricks was eligible'. Milton's opinion was keenly anticipated, but as usual he was not interested in discussing the matter and moved that the meeting pass on to the next business. He pointed out that he 'had been in the Western Province for 17 years and many good players had been available under the same conditions as Hendricks and the question had never been brought up'. Milton's irrelevant argument annoyed Giddy, who informed delegates that the question of whether Hendricks was eligible for selection should be settled 'once and for all'.[6] It was to no avail; Milton and his cabal – Cripps, Bisset, Smuts, etc. – were not to be shifted. Smuts seconded Milton, the motion was carried, and *The Cricket Field* stated with typical establishment lack of transparency that Milton had 'disposed of the difficulty for the present'.[7]

There was widespread and genuine sympathy for Hendricks. He had every right to play for the Colonial-born team, but not one member of the Western Province Cricket Union committee was prepared to stand up to Milton. 'In the principal Cape papers, the *Cape Argus* and the *Cape Times*,' wrote Professor Ian Goldin, 'the ethnic identification of coloureds as the dangerous elements of society continued to feed the prejudices of whites and their fears of non-Europeans.' It resulted in an ideology of the social separation of the races being 'widely articulated by English-speaking journalists and politicians in Cape Town'.[8] There was a call for stringent regulations in the 'non-white' communities where, according to historian Vivian Bickford-Smith, 'the coloured artisan and educated class, who previously had not borne the brunt of ethnic discrimination, began to suffer from the impact of the reconstruction of ethnic boundaries'.[9] But, in spite of the campaign unleashed against coloured people, there was still a happy non-racially stratified community living in areas such as Woodstock and Districts One and Six. A Grahamstown journalist visiting Cape Town, and more attuned to the rigid racial separation on the frontier, was concerned that white people were 'not by any means careful to avoid intermarriage with the mixed blood', creating a situation where 'a fusion of races is going on here, from which every other community in South Africa would shrink'.[10]

During this period of increasing uncertainty, Hendricks continued to impress on the cricket field for United Services CC, a side for whom he qualified as a railwayman. The day after the Western Province Cricket Union met for the second time, he bowled through the innings against the South African College to take 5-21 in 20 overs. It enabled United Services (105) to secure a comfortable victory over their opponents (66). On the day of the Mother Country versus Colonial-born match, he recorded impressive figures of 6-31 off 24 overs against Claremont (188). A few days later, United Services journeyed to Wynberg to meet Garrison CC. The military side won the toss and batted, only to find Hendricks in supreme form, securing 8-16. Garrison were disposed of for 65 and United Services registered another victory with Hendricks scoring a breezy undefeated 37, which included one six hit out of the ground. In the course of the destruction that Hendricks inflicted on various teams during November, the question surfaced again as to how he would perform against good batsmen on a good wicket. Cape Town CC was able to amass 242 for nine against United Services with Hendricks again bowling through the innings. His figures of 5-78 off 25 overs evinced some negative comment, but might be put into perspective in that 164 runs were struck off the 25 overs bowled from the other end for the loss of four wickets.

The treatment of Hendricks was just one example of the autocratic, hapless and ham-fisted administration of cricket by the Western Province Cricket Union not just in relation to its own affairs, but also to those of the South African Cricket Association for which, as Currie Cup holders, it was responsible. By early 1895, Harry Cadwallader had been squeezed out of his position as secretary of the national body in the fallout over Hendricks's possible involvement in the tour to England, and no successor had apparently been found. The *Natal Mercury* considered that this 'of course suits the Western Province down to the ground and lets in such bleating sportsmen as Advocate Graham, W.H. Milton and one or two other beauties in Cape Town to work their own sweet way'.[11]

In expressing dissatisfaction over developments in local cricket, the *South African Review* also complained that the daily papers had failed to notice a match played some time earlier between Western Province CC and United Services CC. It was a game that Western Province won with relatively few problems, but the writer suspected the daily press had deliberately overlooked the match because of their reluctance to acknowledge another fine bowling display by Hendricks. This accusation of not printing results or scores from Hendricks's games surfaced more than once over the years and was significant given the evident interest by cricket followers in his performances. In the match in question, Western Province scored 168 in the course of which Hendricks secured nine wickets (all bowled) for 49 runs off 17 overs, including Alf Richards, who would captain South Africa that season, and Western Province player Vollie van der Byl. This performance gave Hendricks the commendable analysis of 14-127 in his two matches against Cape Town's elite clubs, a particularly noteworthy achievement as his supporting cast was conspicuously limited. The Western Province CC innings was as follows:

Lt Andrews	run out	66
Davidson	b Hendricks	2
Van der Byl	b Hendricks	5
Dawson-Thomas	b Hendricks	32
A Richards	b Hendricks	7
F Moore	b Hendricks	7
Watermeyer	b Hendricks	0
T Ward	b Hendricks	11
Harrington	not out	14

W Welch	b Hendricks	0
Ponsford	b Hendricks	3
Extras		21
Total		168[12]

Several months later, a letter to the *Cape Times* criticised the newspaper for not publicising Hendricks's feats:

> Sir
>
> Allow me to draw your attention to the fact that, putting aside his many wonderful performances, Hendricks the crack fast bowler, in a match for the United Services against a 'first class team' of the Western Province CC last season secured nine wickets for about 40 runs. The performance is all the more meritorious when its understood that the opposition made 178 [*sic*]. I should like to point out, Mr Editor that this match was never published, though nearly every two-penny-halfpenny match was reported in your valuable paper. Was this an oversight? This is only one match out of hundreds I think but is sufficient to know I think that the man in question has played in 'first-class cricket' and has not received the recognition to which every good cricketer is entitled. I am sure that if he is selected, he will know how to conduct himself against the English team and that is something gained in 'so-called first-class cricket'... The only time so called 'first-class cricket' was shown this season was during a luncheon interval.
>
> Spectator[13]

There was no rebuttal from the *Cape Times*.

Hendricks was not considered for the next possible representative opportunity, the 1895 Currie Cup tournament hosted in Durban. Natal fielded Charles 'Buck' Llewellyn, the all-rounder who would later be considered 'coloured'. While the tournament was under way, Hendricks appeared as a 'celebrity' in a match organised by white ladies before a sizeable crowd of white holidaymakers. The men fielded and batted left-handed and could only walk after the ball, but it did not prevent the eager Hendricks from making an impression. He took a hat-trick and captured 5-8 as Mrs Potter's team of 13 ladies totalled 37 all out.[14] It was a farcical moment – Cape society ladies running in where their male counterparts refused to tread. The invitation was apparently the result of the ladies' curiosity to meet the handsome engine-driver who bowled with awesome destructive power and was at the centre of a raging controversy in their city. It also reflected public defiance of the union and sympathy for his treatment.

In Durban, Transvaal won the Currie Cup, defeating a Western Province side that included three professionals. The latter on their return claimed that they were beaten by the umpire, and not by their opponents. Relinquishing the Currie Cup was more than inconvenient for the Western Province Cricket Union because it meant the administration of the South African Cricket Association would transfer to the Transvaal. Milton was determined to delay the transition until the last possible opportunity and in the meantime organised the itinerary and handled contentious issues for Lord Hawke's forthcoming tour of the colony.

The question of colour arose again in the lead-up to Hawke's 1895/96 tour, but not, for once, with regard to Hendricks. The *Cape Times* noted that 'the Indian prince with the impossible name [Ranjitsinhji]' was being considered for the touring team.[15] This too was unacceptable to Milton, who was firmly in control of preparations and confident that he would receive sympathy from the cricket establishment in England. Lord Harris, who had taken over as president of the MCC and was destined to become chairman of Consolidated Goldfields, had previously led an administration in India that supported 'blatant segregation'.[16] Lord's, home of the MCC, was not so different from Cape Town in the virulence of its colour prejudice. Sir Home Gordon, in a famous quote in *Wisden*, explained that 'there was so much prejudice against "a nigger showing us how to play cricket"'.[17]

Hawke secured C.B. Fry as a replacement for Ranjitsinhji, with details surrounding the selection only coming to light some years later. 'Ranji would have been unwelcome in South Africa,' wrote Iain Wilton in his biography of Fry, and therefore 'he took the opportunity to urge Lord Hawke to select his friend and Sussex team-mate instead'. Fry wrote a particularly vivid and succinct description of his selection: 'There was the temporarily dispossessed Heir Apparent of an Indian State who had become a fantastic success as a batsman, and who with Rajput love of honour and glory desired to see Sussex champion county. There was a recent addition to the Sussex county 11 in whom the Rajput Heir Apparent saw possibilities.'[18]

It was 'another imperial duty', wrote Derek Birley in a reference to Lord Hawke's team that included ten amateur gentlemen (out of 14 players) who, 'with just one exception ... were all Oxford or Cambridge Blues'.[19] They were heading for the subcontinent where the storm clouds were gathering as Kruger's republic resisted the demands of the *uitlanders* (primarily British Randlords who controlled the mining industry and their supporters). The empire needed to show solidarity and commitment, and the presence of Lord Hawke and Sir Timothy O'Brien did much to reinforce relations between the British ruling class and the emerging South African capital.

The South African establishment wanted pageantry and panache, and players like Fry, George Lohmann and Sammy Woods provided personal stardust in a team renowned for its splash of multicoloured blazers, belts and hat ribbons. But others looked beyond imperial display and attacked 'their unsportsmanlike behaviour, lack of concern for locals, their complaints about pitches, unpleasant sledging and the occasional clamouring for money'.[20] The *Natal Mercury* admitted 'there is no disguising that this team is not to be compared with its two predecessors. Those who came into contact with Warton's and Read's teams found them very good fellows, the reverse is true with Lord Hawke's combination'.[21]

In November 1895, the *Cape Times* included Hendricks in its choice of a representative South African team to meet the tourists, along with Halliwell, Prince, Richards, Rowe, Routledge, Sinclair, Tancred, Seccull, Bisset and Cripps. But the Western Province

Cricket Union's attitude hardened against Hendricks with each progressive refusal to select him for representative teams. He would be forced to rely on external support for selection, but stood no chance as Milton and his acolytes, Smuts and Steytler, were appointed the selectors for all provincial and Test matches to be played against the tourists at Newlands. The committee was aware of Hendricks's form. He took 6-30, including Steytler's wicket, when playing for the mixed-race City XI against Western Province CC in an early mid-week fixture at Newlands. He was again not considered for the Colonial-born versus Mother Country match at the weekend, but claimed 6-54 for United Services against Diocesan College (Bishops) at the college ground. All his victims were clean bowled, including Western Province batsman Biddy Anderson, who would later captain South Africa, and William Short, a future Western Province player. Hendricks followed this with figures of 8-31 against Woodstock and 7-6 in his destruction of the army side, Castle, at Fort Knokke.

The fast bowler became the centre of another intense press debate prior to the selection of the Western Province XV to play the first tour match against Lord Hawke's team in late December 1895. The *Cape Times* published nine contributions on 17, 18 and 19 December, each member of the public naming a side. The majority did not include Hendricks, possibly because they did not see him as being eligible for selection. On 20 December, there were six further teams chosen, all including Hendricks. 'VFML' was one of the contributors who commented on the selection process, claiming that Hendricks 'is undoubtedly the best fast bowler here and a better bat than Kuys or Willoughby, the other fast bowlers considered'. He went on to argue optimistically that the objection to Hendricks on the score of colour, which had applied 'when he was not selected for the tour Home [in 1894] will hardly be raised here'.[22] On 21 December, 'VV' stated that he had batted and bowled against Hendricks and that the player 'is not worth a place in the team'. The writer, who was almost certainly Vollie van der Byl, further stressed that Hendricks had not played 'first-class' cricket. The *Cape Times* sports editor summed up the debate by stating: 'There are many, however, and I am inclined to be one of them who thinks he is well worth his place.'[23]

Hendricks's support base was weakened by the departure of Harry Cadwallader. Life had become extremely difficult for Cadwallader in Cape Town and he was transferred to the *Licensed Victualler* in Johannesburg. His replacements at both the *Cape Times* and the *South African Review* would take the pro-Milton position and were unambiguous in their condemnation of non-racial cricket. The *South African Review* outlined a new post-Cadwallader perspective on Hendricks when analysing the selection of the Western Province XV to play against Lord Hawke's team:

> Of course there will be the usual outcry at the exclusion of Hendricks. It is however quite idle to urge his selection, for the authorities have decided repeatedly, and very wisely, that they are dead against the introduction of the principle of coloured men playing in representative matches. If Hendricks were played we should soon be having the claims of half-a-dozen coloured men advanced for places in our teams, and it is well that the Union has definitely put its foot down on the practice.[24]

Western Province performed well against Lord Hawke's team, but the cricket was dramatically overshadowed by the attempted Rhodes-inspired coup to overthrow Kruger's Transvaal. The day after the second match against Western Province – 29 December – the Honourable Charles Coventry, second-in-command of the Bechuanaland Border Police, addressed another gathering of men on 'imperial duty'. Drawn from forces built up in Bechuanaland and Rhodesia, they were unaware of what had been arranged for them. Coventry, who had played for England in their overwhelming victory over Milton's South Africans at Newlands in 1888/89, announced, 'We are going straight to Johannesburg. We want you all to come. It will be a short trip; everything has been arranged.'[25] The overall commander, Dr Leander Starr Jameson, hoped the invasion force would be joined by the *uitlanders*. In Johannesburg, the *uitlanders* – led by the Reform Committee – were ill-prepared and frantic efforts were made to postpone the rising, but Jameson was not dissuaded.[26]

The Jameson Raid was a disaster from the outset. Supposedly, drunk men assigned the task cut the wrong telegraph wires and, as a result, the Boers were able to monitor the raiders' movements. Jameson, Coventry and their force were arrested at Doornkop, some 30 kilometres from Johannesburg, on 2 January 1896. Rhodes was forced to resign. The ringleaders of the Reform Committee, including Abe Bailey, were rounded up and sentenced to death (although Rhodes eventually paid £400,000 for their release); and Jameson was shipped back to England undercover for trial and sentence. Milton survived the fallout and continued as permanent secretary in the Prime Minister's Department under Sir Gordon Sprigg. The Jameson Raid destroyed long-standing friendships – notably that of Hofmeyr and Rhodes – and aroused intense pro-Kruger and anti-British sentiments among large sections of the Afrikaans-speaking population. The *Natal Mercury* commented: 'Most people recognise that a stupendous blunder was committed... amidst all our admiration for British pluck we must hold the balance of British fair play.'[27]

During this period, Milton focused on the cricket tour, notably the composition of Western Province sides to play Lord Hawke's tourists. He was not happy that Transvaal would be pulling the strings after the next South African Cricket Association meeting and, as the season panned out, he proved deliberately uncooperative. The Transvaalers were unfortunate in that their leading cricket administrator, Abe Bailey, was incarcerated as a conspirator after the Jameson Raid. Reports emanating from Johannesburg stated that Bailey had 'completely broken down in Pretoria gaol'.[28]

Barberton Halliwell became the dominant figure in Johannesburg cricket. He was the new South African captain and chairman of both the South African Cricket Association and the Transvaal selection committee. A world-class wicketkeeper whose verbal exchanges with W.G. Grace attracted publicity during the 1894 tour, he relished the opportunity to challenge Milton. Halliwell chaired the meeting of the South African Cricket Association at the Wanderers Social Club on 31 January 1895 and was determined that his administration would be no pushover.

Prior to the meeting, he launched a challenge to Milton on the latter's most sensitive point: Hendricks. Having lost the struggle over Hendricks on the 1894 tour, Halliwell was keen to provide the player with the opportunity that he deserved. His committee – consisting of E.J.L. Platnauer, Jimmy Sinclair, Tommy Routledge and Bertie Rose-Innes – lent their support. Rose-Innes communicated with Hendricks and asked him 'to come up for a fortnight so as to enable the selection committee to form an opinion as to his form' in view of his playing for South Africa in the second Test against Lord Hawke's side. A place was left open in the team, which included two other Western Province players, Frank Hearne and Bonnor Middleton. Platnauer wrote in the *Standard and Diggers News* that the action of the Transvaal Cricket Union was one 'few will find fault with', but Milton and the Western Province authorities were enraged.[29]

At a meeting of the Transvaal Cricket Union on 13 February, Halliwell said he had received 'a telegram from Hendricks saying he was willing to come up and asking for particulars'. He was desperate to play for his country. Cadwallader's replacement at the *Cape Times* described the selection of Hendricks as 'a most uncalled-for insult' to Western Province cricket. The newspaper added, 'Such slights are not calculated to foster that spirit of friendliness which should exist between the two chief centres of sport in South Africa.'[30] The relationship between the two unions had indeed broken down over the position of Hendricks, with the Cape press fuelling antagonism and their cricket officials withdrawing support for the South African captain. The *Cape Times* was critical of Halliwell, 'who apparently thinks that every cricketer and every cricketing centre is under his regal way', but the *South African Review* was even more antagonistic in an article headed 'The Rand sweet on Hendricks':

> The action of the Transvaal Cricket Union of inviting Hendricks, the Cape Town Malay fast bowler, to proceed to the Rand for a fortnight to enable the selection committee to form an opinion as to his form in view of his playing in the South African match there against the English team, will meet with almost universal disapproval in the Western Province. The coloured question, as it affects cricket, is very distasteful, and it is much to be regretted that it has again been forced upon us. But apart from the social considerations which render it, in Cape Town at least, desirable not to unduly inflate our dusky brethren with greater notions of their importance than they already possess, the invitation to Hendricks is inopportune and unnecessary ...[31]

The Cape press endeavoured to strengthen their argument by pushing the claims of Joseph Willoughby as an outstanding prospect. He had claimed six second innings wickets for 15 runs against Lord Hawke's team in the tourists' opening match and the *Cape Times* announced that he was nearly as fast as Hendricks. Lohmann said he was unimpressed with Willoughby and thought he had a great deal of luck against the English, but it could not be denied that he was effectively the alternative to Hendricks that the Cape had been seeking. In another revealing article, the *South African Review* let slip the panic that existed in Cape Town cricket circles over Hendricks. In rigidly determining that he could not be selected because of his colour, it was pointed out:

> The position of the local Union should Hendricks be played – and with anything like success – will be rendered difficult in the extreme, and they will do well to mark the disgust which the action of the Transvaal has raised in the Province by refusing to allow their men to play any part in the game. Though admitting that Willoughby has not been thoroughly tested as yet, it is still clear that no sane person could regard him as sufficiently inferior to Hendricks to necessitate so shameful a breach of etiquette as that of which the Transvaal

> Union has been guilty. There is still time for the Union – if it was the Union's work – to retrieve this fatal error, which must create the bitterest animosity, and it is hard to believe that Routledge, Seccull and Innes could have countenanced, or can countenance, so flagrant a breach of common courtesy.[32]

The Western Province Cricket Union also attacked the Transvaal Cricket Union for arbitrarily selecting two Western Province professionals contracted to Western Province clubs for the South African team. Said the *Cape Times*: 'Not content with upsetting all the rules which govern the picking of a South African XI by refusing to recognise the right of each union to nominate its own candidates, and including or professing to be anxious to include Hendricks in the team, it now appears they have actually been suborning, or at least attempting to do so, the two professionals Hearne and Middleton, who went up from here to Port Elizabeth.'[33] The writer was clearly uncertain as to the method with which the South African team should be assembled. According to an earlier report by the *Cape Times*, Halliwell had told delegates at a meeting of the South African Cricket Association on 31 January 1896 that the Transvaal would select the second-Test team 'and that the various Unions should nominate the men they considered eligible'.[34] This arrangement was agreed to at the meeting, but appeared to create some ambiguity. The Transvaal Cricket Union then 'affirmed the principle that each Union where a representative match was played had the final say in the selection of the team'.[35]

Milton, who was serving a second term as president of the Western Province Cricket Union, conceded that Hearne could play in the second Test, but Hofmeyr's Cape Town CC ordered Middleton to return immediately to take part in a club match, despite the fact that Milton's committee had earlier nominated him for selection. The committee was in effect overruled by the club, which then blamed Halliwell for not obtaining their consent in the matter. A confused Middleton returned to Cape Town where, it seems, he was promptly declared available for Test selection should a request be made. The row over Middleton was a warning to the Transvaal that

Western Province would not permit the selection of local players over their heads. If the Transvaal had the final word over team composition, this meant that Hendricks could well appear in a Test for South Africa. Milton and the Western Province Cricket Union were particularly vulnerable as their exclusion of Hendricks from meaningful domestic cricket meant they had little control over his career. Had he been selected, it would have destroyed the foundations of the racist structure of South African cricket.

The controversy over Hendricks's selection was hastily concluded and there was no further newspaper comment save for the *Cape Times* gloating: 'They have abandoned the idea of playing Hendricks it is satisfactory to state, but they would have been much better advised never to have mooted the scheme.'[36] That Milton refused to support Hendricks's selection was undoubtedly instrumental in the player eventually being blocked from travelling to Johannesburg. How Milton managed to achieve this is unclear. Halliwell was not a man to back down, particularly as his second-Test team was being placed in a greatly weakened position.

Another appalling episode in South Africa's cricket history saw the defenceless Hendricks again fall victim to the scheming of the Western Province Cricket Union. The behaviour of Milton and his committee culminated in the Transvaal selectors (Halliwell, Gordon Beves and Herbert Mosenthal) frantically searching for players to represent South Africa as late as the morning of the match. It provoked a sense of perverse satisfaction at the *Cape Times*, where it was reported that 'after a lot of trouble G.H. Shepstone and Fred Smith were obtained – these are by no means the best available men in the Transvaal, but they were the only players who could be got at the last moment. Thus, the representative nature of the team is entirely destroyed.'[37] The racist selection policy of the Cape's cricket administrators had divided the country and severely weakened the national side. In a show of solidarity, the press and clubs at the Cape had backed Milton, but to the detriment of South African cricket. The Transvaal took a different view, the *Standard and Diggers News* expressing deep disappointment in South Africa's defeat by an innings and 197 runs: 'Had Middleton and Hendricks been playing in this match, the phenomenal score [482] made by Lord Hawke's team would not have been made.'[38]

Ironically, Buck Llewellyn was selected for the South African team for the second Test at Johannesburg. Years later it would be confirmed that his mother was from St Helena and that his father was from Pembroke in Wales. He was thus in a similar situation to Hendricks, but came from respectable Pietermaritzburg and not a working-class area of Cape Town. On that basis, Llewellyn became the first South African player of colour. Although no specific reference to this was made in the 1890s, it may have been rumoured at the time as Llewellyn was dropped for the next Test at Newlands.

The campaign against Hendricks was bitter and unrelenting with the previously supportive *Cape Times* and *South African Review* looking for the slightest flaw in his performance. In early February 1896, he had kept Cape Town CC at bay to help United Services earn a draw after they had batted first and were out for 131. Hendricks took 2-34 in 16 overs, prompting the *South African Review* to write dismissively of him as a bowler 'about whom the Transvaal Cricket Union is so absurdly solicitous ... yet these are hardly the figures of the bowling "terror" Rand players had conjured up in fevered imagination'. The article concluded: 'Up there Hendricks is magnified by the flavour of distance and they have an idea that he is not fairly treated by the Western Province Cricket Union.'[39]

There was little room for optimism in a society that could accept Hendricks had been 'fairly treated'. Milton had made sure that Hendricks would not be given the chance to achieve his cricket ambitions by blocking all opportunities for him to play representative cricket. Hendricks had been denied deserved places in the Colonial-born, Western Province and South African teams. The old 'Cape liberal' notion of individual advancement, if it ever really existed, had given way to a cruel system of segregation in sport. For Hendricks there was still further disappointment when a proposed 'Players versus Gentlemen' match was cancelled, a decision made as a result of his potential involvement. It was Lord Hawke's idea to play the match, which would provide a mix of players from his touring side and local teams. The Professionals XI consisted of Lohmann, Hayward, Tyler, Butt (all Lord Hawke's XI), Smith, Street, Hearne, Middleton, Creese, Hendricks (all Western Province) and Handford (East London). According to the *Cape Times*, the match would 'prove an immense draw and give cricket lovers the opportunity of watching a better all-round cricket than they are likely to see again for some time to come'.[40] It was not until a newspaper report referred to Hendricks that those who were organising the fixture considered the risk attached to his playing and doing well. It was too much for Milton to contemplate.

It was at this time that the *South African Review* made a point of finding out a little more about Hendricks; possibly the only, and certainly the last, occasion that the press made an effort to get at the real story. The information was published under the heading: 'Hendricks, the fast bowler':

> Hendricks, the local fast bowler is not a Malay; his father was a European, and his mother was of St Helena. He is 38 years of age, and is very powerfully built, albeit modest and retiring in demeanour. He has held one situation of trust in Cape Town for upwards of 14 years.[41]

The Western Province Cricket Union's reason for 'categorising' him as coloured was never spelt out specifically, but appears to be derived from three interconnected factors. Firstly, he grew up in Bo-Kaap. While the community was effectively non-racial – but with a significant cultural 'Malay' element – the white establishment considered the area to be 'coloured'. Hendricks was thought to be Malay because of his participation in their cricket: it inspired his impassioned resistance to being labelled Malay in 1894 and led to his departure from the Star of South Africa CC after many years' service. Secondly, his description of his mother as St Helenian would have reinforced the establishment's perspective of him as 'coloured'. A third factor to consider was his appearance. No one in support of Hendricks saw reason to comment – the only references made in print appear to have been a description of him as 'swarthy' in *The*

Owl and mention of his relatively light complexion in a letter to the *Cape Times* from Grahamstown.

There was little Hendricks could do while Milton and his committee were in control. He did not wish to break his cricket link with the economically privileged European society, especially as he sought assimilation and a better life for his family. He never lost interest in the game, even when forced to resign himself to the task of being a net bowler, where he was at least appreciated by the touring side. In a prominent front-page interview in *Cricket: A Weekly Record*, W.A. Bettesworth asked Tom Hayward, the experienced England professional cricketer who had toured with Lord Hawke's side in 1895/96:

> Whom do you think the best bowler you met in South Africa?

Hayward, only the second batsman after W.G. Grace to score 100 first-class centuries, responded:

> Well, I thought that Hendricks bowled better than anybody else but as, on account of his colour, he was not played in any of the matches during the last tour ... As a practice bowler, which is all I know of him, he was certainly very good and very fast indeed.[42]

It was remarkable that Hayward remembered Hendricks's name given that he had never played against him outside the nets. Moreover, that he should even think to choose Hendricks ahead of all the Test bowlers reveals the impact the net experience had on him. It also suggests that the close ties between the touring professionals and the coloured 'net' bowlers that had started under Hearne was still an important, if previously unacknowledged, aspect of the tours.

Hendricks remained committed to United Services and, in the early months of 1896, soldiered on with extraordinary resilience. On 18 January, he picked up three wickets as United Services (135 for four) defeated Royal Engineers (94) with ease. At the end of January, Gardens, 'a very powerful combination with Bamford, Simpson and

Birbeck as a nucleus', defeated United Services by five wickets, though the latter, said one report, 'were aided by the dreaded Hendricks [who] took four wickets at a low cost'.[43] In February, Hendricks gave United Services the ascendancy in the opening overs of their match against Western Province CC. Hulton departed with a single run on the board, Marshall was out for a lucky 10 and Hughes followed fairly quickly – all were bowled by Hendricks. United Services then went to pieces, with their fielding being described in the *Cape Times* as 'probably the worst seen on the Western Province ground this season'.[44] Hendricks finished with 4-77 in 21 overs, his least impressive figures for some time. He came back with a vengeance in the United Services' next encounter against the South African College, played at Woodstock. He and Abrahams, the captain of Cape Town's Coloured XI, took all 20 wickets as United Services (44 and 23) defeated South African College (28 and 9) on a difficult wicket. After picking up six wickets in the first innings, the 'deadly Hendricks', as he was described by 'Leatherhunter' in the *South African Review*, captured another seven, including a hat-trick, in the hapless College's insignificant second innings.[45]

In the return match against Western Province CC at Newlands in March, Hendricks clean bowled the South African captain, Alf Richards, for a duck in his opening over. The *Cape Times* reported that Hendricks 'bowled extremely fast but with little judgement'. It was unfortunate that the criticism was left unexplained, because his figures of 2-33 in 16 overs did reflect a certain steadiness in the context of a match where Western Province scored 173 for 6 against the 64 of United Services. The comment might have referred to his duel with Vollie van der Byl, who was struck 'a nasty blow' by 'one of Hendricks's expresses' and forced to retire early.[46] It was an ill-starred incident in a relationship that was becoming increasingly tense. It was only two years earlier that Hendricks had been forced to concede his place to Van der Byl in an All-Comers XI, only for the latter to fail to turn up for the game. Then, in late 1895, evidence had pointed to Van der Byl having penned a letter to the *Cape Times* stating that Hendricks was not worth a place in the Western Province team.

The season concluded in early April with a match against the league champions, Cape Town CC, who won 16 and drew four of their 20 matches. United Services scored 69 against them, Hendricks opening the batting and making 33. Middleton claimed six wickets and Willoughby four. Hendricks then took the first four wickets (including Middleton and Howard Francis) as Cape Town swept to another victory.

With Hendricks fully committed to playing establishment cricket, it meant that he was unavailable for the coloured tournament – the sixth Glover Cup – which was played at Newlands in January 1896. Cricketers with whom he had played – such as Ebrahim Ariefdien, Lamarah Samsodien, Ryloen Samsodien, Kobus du Toit, Henry Abrahams, Edward Adams and Charles Leach – were engaged in the tournament, which involved teams representing Western Province, Kimberley and Transvaal. The coloured cricket tournaments were popular events with the funds generated helping the Western Province CC to complete their purchase of Newlands in early 1896. It was therefore somewhat ironic, if unsurprising, that the cricket writer at the *South African Review* should produce another racist piece, this time under the heading 'Our leisurely Malays':

> I trust I shall not be wounding the susceptibilities even of those whose solicitude for the welfare of coloured people is fanatical, by drawing attention to what is nothing short of a great public scandal. I refer to the playing of cricket by Malays on Mondays and other week-days when they ought to be at work. The fact that the Malay has a constitutional objection to work at all, and especially Mondays, is one of the greatest social curses of this Peninsula, for it demoralises the servant class generally. Of course, there is no law against it, but I suggest that all persons interested in 'letting out' suburban playing grounds should make a dead-set against the evil by refusing their use on any other day than Saturday to our dusky brethren.[47]

Milton referred to Newlands as the high point in his last annual statement to the Western Province CC. He mentioned that the club had had an uphill fight for many years but 'now, however, had a ground which was worth a great deal more than they gave for it and there was every chance of their getting on well'.[48] He was making hurried arrangements to leave the Cape and join Rhodes in Bulawayo. The revolt in Matabeleland that had followed the Jameson Raid was slowly succumbing to colonial weaponry and Milton had been called on to reorganise the civil service in Rhodesia. At the club meeting, John Reid took the opportunity to claim, with some exaggeration, that 'when Milton first came here the game of cricket was in a state of collapse, as a matter of fact almost defunct'.[49] Lynedoch Graham added that all regretted the captain was relinquishing his official connection with the club: 'In every little dorp in South Africa where the national game was played the name of W.H. Milton had become familiar and it was impossible to overrate the influence he had upon the affairs of the Western Province CC and the welfare of cricket generally throughout South Africa.'[50] Frank Reid later wrote of him as the figure 'that looms largest of all in the history of the Western Province Cricket Club ... [he] was a great cricketer, a great captain and a great man'.[51]

For more than a hundred years, histories of the game paid tribute to Milton's work in cricket at the Cape. A rare criticism was made by first-class cricketer Archie Difford, who recalled that 'in those days, Milton held a very similar position to that of W.G. Grace in English cricket in his prime ... in figure and appearance too, he was not unlike the greatest of all cricketers, except for the fact that he did not grow a beard'. The mere mention of Grace suggests a dominant but flawed personality, and Difford admitted he looked back on Milton with 'mixed feelings' as he was a '"hostile" leader with the virtues and faults of his essentially virile personality'. Milton 'hated to see the Province team beaten' and Difford recalled a game at Newlands when Claremont required 'half a dozen runs' with 15 minutes remaining. Milton suddenly 'shouted out from the field for the bell to be rung' to signal the end of play and 'proceeded to lead his team from the field'. The Claremont captain, Ned Steytler, hurried out 'and there was a somewhat heated altercation mid-way between wicket and pavilion'. But Milton triumphed and the Province men followed him into the pavilion. By the time Milton 'was convinced of his error, the light had gone and the stumps were not pitched again'.[52]

Milton might be forgiven for his behaviour on the cricket field, but not off it. He was content that he had advanced cricket through forging international links, building Newlands and greatly increasing the number of teams that played at the Cape, yet he diminished the game and blighted the potential of black cricketers for a century. Milton was an autocrat and a racist, who was easily drawn into supporting Rhodes in a government that replaced the 'limited tradition' of Cape liberalism with a clear segregationist policy, aimed at forcing out labour and ring-fencing the privileges of the white community. It did not bother Milton that the government made cricket a mechanism and Hendricks a victim of a cruel and oppressive strategy. Milton admired Rhodes deeply and was clearly led by him. Robert Rotberg's comment that Rhodes's 'lack of shame and guilt was intrinsic to his success' might have been written about Milton in his cricket administration. Ends were everything; any means whatsoever 'could be justified if it served great goals'.[53]

Rhodes gave his fatuous 'boomerang' self-rationalisation in a casual breakfast remark to Pelham Warner, but it was Milton who bore responsibility for the politically inspired decisions over Hendricks, and there is no evidence to indicate that he regretted them or felt the need to try to justify them. His legacy was one that fixed the colour bar, leaving Cape sport securely segregated.

8

'Let them look to God for justice for man has refused it'

'Someone was guilty of a grave error in having selected Hendricks for the All-Comers ... the two classes should be kept distinctly separate.'[1]

– W.V. 'Billy' Simkins

'The object of the Union is to encourage cricket and the best cricket, and the functions of the Union are not to judge a man's social position.'[2]

– Frank Robb

WOODSTOCK IS ONE of Cape Town's oldest suburbs. It lies two kilometres south-east of the city and is located between the harbour of Table Bay, the lower slopes of Devil's Peak and Salt River. The area was formerly known as Papendorp, after Pieter van Papendorp, who had settled there during the mid-eighteenth century, and developed from three farms (Zonnebloem, Letiebloem and Roodebloem) that were established on the slopes of Devil's Peak in 1692. It was still known as Papendorp on 10 January 1806 when representatives of the Batavian Republic surrendered there, near Fort Knokke, and the Cape became British for a second time. The decision to name the suburb 'Woodstock' was made in 1867 when local fishermen, who formed the majority of the inhabitants at the time, voted to make the change in honour of the public house that they frequented.

In the 1890s, Woodstock was still a village with open farmland and mountainside – a 'suburb of vineyards and vegetables'. There were 'grapes to be picked on the van der Byls' farm (Roodebloem); milk, thick with cream, from the herd of Jersey cows; and meat and vegetables from the German farmers at the early morning market in Sir Lowry Road'. It was a suburb of 'tickey-beers at the Altona Hotel, walks up the mountainside with its few isolated buildings and fynbos, picnics in Woodstock Cave, swimming and joining the coloured fishermen bringing in their catch at the Woodstock Beach, gas street-lamps, and developing industries'.[3]

The first railway line to be built at the Cape – as well as an electric tram service – ensured Woodstock became a popular beach resort. The *Woodstock Parish Magazine* commented on the 'blinding dust' at the turn of the century, but a few years later there was the 'promise of the roads mending their ways, and smooth hard roads and byways is the dream of a yet nearer future'.[4]

Trains and cars were to be a major part of the life of Frank Thomson Robb, who was born in Woodstock on 20 April 1864. He attended Zonnebloem College, which had been a joint project initiated by Sir George Grey, the high commissioner and governor of the Cape Colony, and Bishop Grey of the Anglican Church, in 1858 for the education of young princes and princesses of African chiefs from the Eastern Cape. In her study of the early years, Janet Hodgson said the college had a non-racial environment that catered for children from Baleya, Barotse, Bechuana, coloured, Fingu, Gcaleka, Marolong, Matabele, Mosutho, Pondomiso and white communities.[5] Although Zonnebloem (the 'place of sunflowers') changed over the years, it maintained its non-racial orientation until the 1930s, when the Education Department forced it to become a coloured institution no longer permitted to cater for white and African students.[6]

It was in this environment that Robb developed his love for cricket. He became a prominent player, representing Colonial-born against Mother Country and Cape Town at the Champion Bat tournament in 1887/88 and playing for a Western Province XXII against Major Warton's first English tourists in 1888/89. His leadership qualities were such that he led the Civil Service XI against Kimberley in 1884 when just 20 years old; the side included well-known personalities such as Jack van Renen, Louis Vintcent and Adriaan van der Byl. Robb would play league cricket until he was in his forties, while his interest in sport saw him serve as chairman of Woodstock CC and as a committee member of both the Western Province cricket and rugby unions. He also rose through the ranks in his chosen career, beginning work in the Cape government railway department before becoming secretary of the Harbour Board, dock manager and then district superintendent of the South African Railways. His later career would see him play a prominent role in the motorcar trade as the Austin agent.

In 1894, Frank Robb had in good faith proposed Milton as the Western Province Cricket Union representative on the national selection committee for the tour to England. The nomination meant little as Milton's appointment was a formality, but the events that followed drew Robb's attention to the shameful treatment of Hendricks. Not long afterwards, he made an important decision. Prior to the 1896/97 season, Advocate Shepstone Giddy, a strong supporter of Hendricks at the United Services Cricket Club, was appointed crown prosecutor in Kimberley. Robb immediately seized the opportunity, possibly with Giddy's encouragement, to employ the fast bowler as Woodstock's professional with the intention of using his services in the newly formed championship league, formerly the 'first league'. It was a good move. In early October, Hendricks (5-8) and Charles Bain, a young left-arm medium pace bowler (5-18), were instrumental in Woodstock dismissing Standard Bank for 37. In the return game, Woodstock (168) destroyed Standard Bank (27), with Hendricks picking up four wickets. Then, at Sea Point, Woodstock (85) comfortably defeated Green Point (30), with Bain taking 5-15 and Hendricks 5-18. October had provided a promising start to the new season for Hendricks, but he was living on borrowed cricket time.

Milton had departed for Rhodesia, but men who shared his notions of imperial and racial superiority, and who were equally committed to the systematic exclusion of Hendricks from representative cricket, carried on his work at the Western Province Cricket Union in his absence. They were headed by a new president, John Reid, a product of Diocesan College, who was the senior partner in J. & H. Reid and Nephew: Government Attorneys. Billy Simkins was his deputy. By the mid-1890s there were few liberal-minded opponents in the administration of the game at the Cape. So, when the Western Province Cricket Union was informed of Woodstock's plans to employ Hendricks, it responded quickly and ruthlessly. A resolution was passed that would form the notorious Bye-law 10. It meant Hendricks was immediately excluded from playing in the championship by virtue of his being a coloured cricketer. The resolution, which was published in the Cape press, stated:

> That this union will not object to any club employing a coloured professional in matches other than championship fixtures and no coloured professional or member shall be allowed to compete in championship matches.[7]

This was the first racially discriminatory legislation to be introduced into sport in South Africa and would have long-standing ramifications. Previous decisions that barred Hendricks from representative cricket had been made by the Western Province Cricket Union on their own, or at the behest of Milton or Rhodes. The avalanche of insult and hurt was essentially aimed at a cricketer against whom no one was personally capable of uttering a bad word as to his conduct, dignity and bearing. The union's latest decision smacked of cowardice and selfishness. They feared more coloured players coming through the ranks to challenge their exclusive dominance, but they were specifically scared of Hendricks – of his pace and power and his ability to show them up for what they really were: racists of the worst kind.

At the end of October, *The Owl* commented: 'Early to say but looks like Docks and United Services will battle for the wooden spoon in the Championship. It is doubtful that Woodstock without Hendricks will be far from the unenviable position.'[8]

In drawing up their fixture lists, clubs also arranged to play non-championship matches. These would involve all the championship sides, namely Western Province CC, Cape Town CC, Claremont, Garrison, South African College, Bishops, Woodstock, Gardens, Docks and United Services. One such encounter was played between Cape Town CC and Woodstock at Newlands in November 1896. The match was expected to be one-sided, because Cape Town was one of the city's premier clubs while Woodstock was a struggling team with no provincial contenders. On this occasion, reported the *South African Review*, Cape Town CC 'had their best 11 in the field, no doubt as a mark of respect for Hendricks, the fast bowler, who is playing for Woodstock'.[9] The *Cape Times* said the match was billed as one in which 'the two fastest bowlers in the Western Province' – Joseph Willoughby and Hendricks – were on show.[10]

Woodstock suffered a mauling at the hands of their visitors, the game being lost through a collapse in the batting department. They were 'powerless' against Willoughby, who captured 7-7 in a total of 47, of which no less than 20 were 'extras'. It placed pressure on Hendricks to perform, and he did: his 17.3 overs reaping a memorable 8-32 in Cape Town's score of 120. 'It was a remarkable performance,' said the *Cape Times*, 'considering the class of batsmen'.[11] His victims included five players – Charles Prince, Howard Francis, Stanley Horwood, Frank Hearne and Willoughby – who had represented South Africa at various times. The fact that Charles Bain, good enough to be a future Western Province player, had figures of 0-49 in 12 overs and Abrahams 1-21 in five, placed Hendricks's performance in perspective. But the most spectacular aspect of his high-class pace bowling was the fact that he hit the stumps on seven occasions, a feat that Willoughby managed twice. Only Hearne (24), Francis (31) and George Rowe (15 not out) made double figures for Cape Town and, said the *South African Review*, 'but for the stand made by the two first-named there might be a dismal tale to tell'.[12]

Such were the curious workings of the fixture list that Woodstock met Cape Town CC for a second time in a mid-week game on 15 December. Cape Town batted first on this occasion and reached 147. *The Owl* praised Hendricks's fine bowling: '…he was never collared and bowled throughout the innings without tiring'.[13] On this occasion, he captured 7-47 off 20.1 overs, with support coming from Bain (2-49 off 15 overs) and Marshall (1-22 off five). Only three of Hendricks's wickets were clean bowled, but he did dismiss two batsmen 'caught and bowled' and held another catch in the outfield. He was also in the runs, scoring 22, with Cape Town winning on the call of time by bowling out Woodstock for 120, an encouraging improvement on their previous batting performance. Victories followed against United Services (Hendricks taking three wickets) and a weakened Western Province CC team. The latter match was played on the same day as the Colonial-born versus Mother Country fixture and featured those Western Province players who were not involved in the representative match. It was an encounter that they would not easily forget. Although the game was played at Newlands, it was staged on a new secondary field and, said a report, 'on the bumpy pitch Hendricks was very dangerous'.[14] He claimed 7-19 off 12.2 overs as Western Province (61) fell short of Woodstock's 98.

Western Province CC beat Woodstock with ease in their championship fixture in December. *The Owl* was unimpressed, as their three professionals did all the work. The report went on to say that it was 'absurd to use professionals against Woodstock. It is not fair play especially when Woodstock are prevented from playing their professional'.[15] Cricket enthusiasts were becoming increasingly frustrated with the manipulation of the game by the Western Province and Cape Town CCs to suit themselves. *The Owl* had earlier produced a critical piece under the heading 'Cricket killing public interest'. In it, they argued that the 'crack clubs' – either Cape Town or Western Province – 'go in, make 169 for 4 and bowl opposition (Claremont and Bishops) out for 60 twice. And so, the game goes on year after year – Cape Town and Western Province first, rest nowhere ...'[16]

At the end of the first week of January 1897, Woodstock was again pitted against a weakened Western Province CC side. It was a bizarre situation, as the Western Province premier team was shielded from facing Hendricks and their lesser batsmen had no option but to take him on. 'With Hendricks included in their ranks, Woodstock are one team,' said *The Owl*. 'Without him they are another. The Western Province seems to stand in dread of him for he mows down their wickets like ninepins.' The report continued:

> Western Province CC were looking forward to an easy victory when Smith from Bishops took six cheap Woodstock wickets but then Hendricks came on to the scene and helped to stop the rot. Woodstock even then were able only to reach 76. But that proved quite enough, the Province tumbling out for 29 ... Hendricks bowled out five of a very decent second string for only six runs ...[17]

A few weeks later, Woodstock played Cape Town CC in a championship match. There were the usual references to the difficulties for Woodstock in going into a match against powerful opposition without Hendricks, their best bowler. 'Had he been playing,' said the *South African Review*, 'Cape Town would probably have been unable to score 200 for a couple of wickets.'[18] As if to stress a point, Mowbray decided to take advantage of the fact that Hendricks did not have a game during the weekend and invited him to play for them. On the adjacent ground to where Woodstock were hammered by Cape Town, 'Mowbray was chastising the Province second string, the visitors having the powerful aid of the great Hendricks whose electric deliveries struck terror into the hearts of the Province batsmen and sent them back, one after the other, whence they came.' Artie Bisset (who played for South Africa), H.M. Smith and A.C. Tofts managed to get into double figures, 'but extras (23) was the largest item, a significant commentary on the swiftness of Hendricks's bowling'. In 14 overs, he took 8-15 with

Mowbray posting a resounding victory by 90 runs. According to *The Owl*, 'people are quite convinced that nothing but pure funk on the part of the batsmen is responsible for the swarthy one's fine analyses'.[19]

There was the rare match when Hendricks had an off day. *The Owl* cited an example against Cape Town CC that saw their batsmen wanting to show 'that they at any rate were not all "struck of a heap" with funk when the burly one was put on against them'.[20] In that match, Biddy Anderson was in the form of his life. There was relatively little comment on the game in a season where sympathy for Woodstock existed within a larger picture that was far from satisfactory. 'It has happened very unfortunately,' said *The Owl*'s assessment, 'that in the very season in which the authorities chose to ban colour from taking part in championship matches they should find the Peninsula sadly deficient in bowling. There is no doubt whatever that Hendricks is bowling in far finer form than any of our fast bowlers and that if he had been allowed to play his services would have been most valuable to Woodstock.'[21]

The reasoned arguments put forward by *The Owl* were in sharp contrast to the prejudiced comment that had marred cricket reports published by the *Cape Times* and the *South African Review* during the previous year. *The Owl* had taken over Harry Cadwallader's role in monitoring Hendricks's cricket. They would also have been aware that while Cadwallader's departure upset followers of cricket, it had become inevitable. After being ditched as a committee member by two national sporting bodies because of his support for Hendricks and coloured cricket, Cadwallader had come to terms with the fact that he had virtually no support base at the Cape. He relocated to the Transvaal where he died in May 1897, a broken man weakened by the ill effects of the fever he had suffered during his journey to locate Bowden. In announcing Cadwallader's death, the *Cape Times* remarked on a 'case of such grievous need' that a public fund was set up to assist his family.[22]

Cadwallader's old rival, Charles Finlason, was forthright in his tribute: '"Old Caddy" deserves all the kudos that may be given him and it is no exaggeration to say that for the next 50 years and more the cricketers of this country will have cause to feel grateful to the first secretary of the South African Cricket Association.'[23] Yet, when Maurice Luckin produced the first comprehensive history of South African cricket in 1915, Cadwallader was not mentioned. It was a serious omission by Luckin, who was by then secretary of the South African Cricket Association and claimed to have produced 'a complete record of South African cricket'.[24]

The conflict over Hendricks showed no sign of abating as men from both sides came forward to replace the old protagonists, Cadwallader and Milton. The unsatisfactory state of affairs over Hendricks's position with regard to the championship during 1896/97 needed to be addressed. Frank Robb, who was desperate to secure Woodstock's competitiveness and clearly outraged by the treatment accorded Hendricks, decided to challenge the Western Province Cricket Union by placing Woodstock's case before them.

The *Cape Times* revealed Robb's intentions in mid-October 1897, reminding readers that the union had passed a resolution to prevent Hendricks playing in championship matches. The result of such action had proved counterproductive in the most recent season, because Woodstock 'made a poor show in the cup competition and quickly retired'. Hendricks had since then been re-engaged by Woodstock for the 1897/98 season and an application was forwarded to the union that he be allowed to play in championship matches. 'If the application is refused,' said the *Cape Times*, 'it is the intention of the Woodstock club to withdraw from the competition.'[25] The hearing was set for 5 November.

The Owl endeavoured to take a neutral stance in the matter and questioned Woodstock's tactics. 'What some people would like to know,' they said, 'is what did Woodstock mean by entering for the Union cup if they did not intend to play, unless Hendricks was allowed to play for them?' The club had, as the newspaper saw it, deliberately placed the union in an awkward position. They entered 'and when the fixture cards have been nicely printed and the season about to start, Woodstock blurt out, "We won't play"'.[26] The point, of course, was that this was exactly what Robb and Woodstock had intended. They aimed to force the Western Province Cricket Union to rule in Hendricks's (and their) favour or face maximum disruption and embarrassment. This was no moment for cap-in-hand pleading.

In the meantime, Cape Town's true cricket followers, as opposed to the cricket establishment, wanted to see more – not less – of Hendricks. He had just taken 6-6, including a hat-trick, in helping Woodstock (56) defeat Claremont (54) by 2 runs. The dramatic performance had served as a piquant appetiser for an important occasion the following weekend when Hendricks was chosen for an All-Comers XI to play against Western Province CC at Newlands. Helped by press reports, the game generated great interest. The *Cape Times* described it as an 'unusually attractive fixture at Newlands' and advertised further benefits for spectators, such as the band of the King's Royal Rifles and cheap rail fares. Western Province CC would be introducing their new professionals, John Holland and Walter Lees, but the star attraction was Hendricks, who 'has been such a terror in minor matches and his performance will be watched with much interest'.[27]

Two days before the match was played, a letter appeared in the *Cape Times* that served to remind the public of a major political issue underlying the relevance of the cricket match:

> Sir – What is the reason for not allowing Hendricks to play in championship matches? If the objection be on the question of colour, I think it a very poor objection as he plays in club matches against those teams who object to him playing in championship matches. If these clubs who object to Hendricks playing championship matches were honest and said that they are afraid of his bowling then more would be thought of them than if they object to him playing on the ground of being coloured. Although coloured, I think he is a very respectable coloured person, and very seldom is there a more respectable coloured person to be found.
>
> Sportsman
> Woodstock[28]

Notwithstanding the threat of rain, a large number of women graced the match with their presence amid an unusually sizeable crowd of 1,600 that surrounded the field.[29] The reference to the presence of 'ladies' was unusual and probably a development that concerned white cricket authorities, given that pre-match publicity had focused on Hendricks and that it was not long after Mrs Potter's celebrity match. A striking but reluctant hero, Hendricks was described at various times as being tall and powerfully built but retiring in demeanour. Yet his diffident exterior off the field of play masked the fierce determination of the 'demon' fast bowler who was quicker than anyone white South Africa could put into the field. Cricketers spoke of his gentlemanly ways while fearing the air of majesty and menace that accompanied him at the wicket. The 'ladies', who were unaffected by a prejudiced cricket environment, grasped the weight and meaning of the occasion. Many would have appreciated the obstacles Hendricks had overcome and they delighted in the underdog fighting to prove himself as a player at the highest level. Newlands offered a wonderfully appropriate amphitheatre for a clash that featured Hendricks versus the players who represented the privileged Western Province CC – and everyone wanted to be part of the day's action.

The *Cape Argus* correspondent was looking forward to the contest: 'The idea of getting a team composed of best players in clubs outside the two leading organisations to meet a representative 11 of the Western Province has turned out to be a capital one and the wonder is that it has taken so long in maturing.' Even 'the originators could hardly have expected so great a success as was scored on Saturday afternoon'.[30] The ground was buzzing and Hendricks did not disappoint, providing absorbing cricket for all who watched the game. 'He completely beat the batsmen with the pace of the ball,' said the *South African Review*, 'contriving at the same time to send down very few [deliveries] loose enough to be punished.' He 'was getting up yorkers' and the opposition batting line-up was soon in considerable trouble. His first wicket was that of Western Province batsman Allan Reid, bowled for 6 – 'too late for one of Hendricks's lightning shots'. He followed up by shattering the stumps of one of the country's leading batsmen, Murray Bisset, for a duck – 'bowled by a clinking good ball', said one writer in the *South African Review*.[31]

The collapse of the Province team astonished onlookers. On resuming after lunch, Hendricks at once bowled the professional, Holland. At that stage, his figures were 11-6-11-3. Vollie van der Byl was indecisive from the moment he arrived at the wicket and it was not surprising when he sparred at a Hendricks delivery and was caught. Two more batsmen – George Shakerley and William Griffiths – were clean bowled, making it five out of six to fall to Hendricks in this fashion. Bain bowled Lees for a duck, thereby striking a further blow for Woodstock's cause. But it was Hendricks who stunned the excited crowd. In 21.3 overs of sustained pace he captured 6-20, there being only one 4 and two 2s scored off him – the rest were singles. Press reports were unanimous in their praise. *The Owl* commented succinctly, 'Hendricks bowled beautifully',[32] and the *Cape Argus* offered a thoughtful analysis:

> For the All-Comers, Hendricks made his first appearance on the Province ground in a Saturday match, and it must candidly be admitted completely silenced the many critics who have held that however deadly in minor matches, he would meet with a much diminished measure of success if opposed to good batting.
>
> Now on Saturday, at all events, he bowled against the strongest 11 the Western Province club can at the present moment put into the field, so that as far as the strength of his opponents' batting was concerned he was put to a thorough test. Whether the state of the ground helped him or not was a point a good deal debated; probably it did to some extent, for though the soft wicket and the strong breeze must have diminished his pace somewhat, and militated against catches in the slips where the fast bowler generally reaps a little harvest, yet his balls did not rise over the stumps as they would be liable to on a hard ground and batsmen found great difficulty driving the ball cleanly or making it travel on the spongy turf.

> But putting all these things aside, all parties were agreed that he was most difficult either to play or make runs off and that he combined a good length with enormous pace.[33]

Western Province were bowled out for 85. In reply, the All-Comers battled against the new professional from Surrey, Walter Lees, who bowled fast-medium pace and captured 6-32 off 20 overs. The opening batsman, Edward Allen, kept the innings together in scoring an invaluable unbeaten 41. Hendricks, batting at ten, came in at a crucial stage. He began his innings with a hard drive for 3 runs to bring 70 up. He was then run out at 75: Allen tried to steal a single and changed his call, resulting in Hendricks slipping and being unable to regain his ground. The excitement mounted as the All-Comers edged towards their opponents' score. When the last wicket fell, Western Province CC claimed victory by 1 run. But, said *The Owl*, when the scorers conducted a recount, it was discovered that the All-Comers had indeed passed their target and therefore won the match.

The fixture had been most useful as an early-season exercise in enabling the selectors to consider the talent available, but it also reignited the establishment's dilemma over Hendricks. As one writer recalled: 'The cricket apart from the closeness of the finish, was interesting because on each side was a man whose performances were being keenly watched, and as it happened each was seen to great advantage.'[34] Frank Robb, the Woodstock chairman, saw it as an opportune moment to forward a letter to the *Cape Times* under a pseudonym:

> Sir – A special meeting of the Western Province Cricket Union has been called for this afternoon at 4 o'clock at the request of the Woodstock CC to consider whether Hendricks, the fast bowler, should be allowed to compete in championship matches played under the auspices of the Union. It will be remembered that this question was brought forward in 1896 when the Union decided that coloured professionals should not be allowed to play in championship fixtures. Since then,

however, the Woodstock Club maintain circumstances have altered so that even supposing the decision in that conclusion is the right one, the Union has by its own action put aside the objection to colour by admitting to affiliation and in competition in the championship clubs who number among their members coloured gentlemen.

Woodstock therefore contend that they no longer be debarred from making use of Hendricks' services. How valuable those services are may be judged by his performance in the All-Comers and Province match last Saturday. His inclusion in the All-Comers team shows that there is no objection on the part of the majority of clubs to play either with or against Hendricks so that it may reasonably be supposed that the question will be in his favour. Should this be the case Hendricks will be eligible to play for the Colonial-born team on Saturday and his bowling will no doubt be of great service to the side which without him will scarcely be a match for their powerful opponents. There is a very strong feeling, rightly or wrongly, on the part of the public that Hendricks is not receiving fair treatment at the hands of the Union and they will undoubtedly show this feeling by alienating themselves from the match should so palpably Colonial a product not be included in the Colonial-born 11. There is another side to the question, a side which probably does not concern the Woodstock Club and which therefore has not been brought forward yet. Hendricks is the best fast bowler in the country and although this Union refuses to avail itself of his services, it is believed no objection could be raised to his playing in the Currie Cup … for another province etc

FAIRPLAY[35]

The meeting of the Western Province Cricket Union at the Thatched Tavern was a representative one. Members in attendance were: J. Reid (president), W. Simkins (vice-president), M. Nash (secretary), C. Neumann Thomas, H. Hands, M. Bisset (Western Province), L.

Smuts (Cape Town), P. Solomon (United Services), W. Kingon (Green Point), F. Robb (Woodstock), P. Cloete (Bishops), J. Bell (Olympic), V. van der Byl (Claremont), M. Anthony (Simon's Town) and W. de Smidt (Gardens).

There were two questions on the table, the first of which evoked little discussion. The Transvaal proposal that a cricket team should visit England and that the Western Province should guarantee its share of the expenses met with no support whatsoever. The *Cape Argus* thought the Western Province Cricket Union 'was negative in a most emphatic way, all parties evidently agreeing that the time was not yet ripe for such a venture'.[36] It was the same argument that they had initially used in 1894, and for some the spectre of Hendricks might have hovered over them. Only a few months before, the English magazine *Cricket: A Weekly Record of the Game* had interviewed A.B. Tancred on the prospects of a tour. 'As South Africa is at present in such an unsettled state,' said Tancred, 'I doubt if we shall be able to do so, but we might be able to get a team together in 1899.' Questioned on the composition of the side, he thought the best possible team would be strong in all departments. 'Hendricks is a good fast bowler,' he accepted, 'but in the opinion of the great majority of South African cricketers it would not be advisable to send him, on account of the colour question, which in England you no doubt find difficult to understand.' He admitted that he could not tell what might happen in years to come, but that there were 'two or three native bowlers coming on well'.[37]

The second question that faced the delegates of the Western Province Cricket Union was that of Hendricks playing in the championship. The real significance of the discussion, however, was that it was going to be about a great deal more than cricket. 'It had been called the "Hendricks question",' said the *Cape Argus*, 'though it is more properly the "Coloured question".'[38]

The issues were introduced by Maynard Nash, who read the letter Robb had sent to the Western Province Cricket Union, asking it to review the decision that prevented Hendricks from playing as a professional in championship matches. Robb then spoke, stating he had been asked by Woodstock to move that the motion be rescinded.

He dealt fully with the arguments in favour of Hendricks being permitted to take part in championship matches, highlighting his presentation with the assertion that: 'With Hendricks at one end the whole of the Woodstock bowling was improved.'[39] Robb pointed out that since the resolution in question had been passed, clubs had been admitted to the championship that had coloured members in their ranks, and in this regard, he was sure it was the intention of the union to be unfair to Woodstock.

Robb reminded delegates that cricket was a cosmopolitan game and it generally conceded that the status of a man on the field was defined by his ability as a player. He stressed that as soon as they 'commenced debarring people they landed themselves in insurmountable complication'. The union, he said, did not describe colour and this placed a great onus on the managers of teams in the championship. 'The object of the Union,' he continued, 'was to encourage cricket and the best cricket, and the functions of the Union were not to judge a man's social position.'

The Western Province Cricket Union was not sympathetic. There was a reluctance to second the motion, with Harry Hands eventually doing so 'for the sake of discussion'. Billy Simkins complained that 'someone was guilty of a grave error in having selected Hendricks for the All-Comers'. He told members that they should use all means at their disposal to ensure the two classes 'be kept distinctly separate'. It was a powerful reminder of the direction that cricket at the Cape had taken. The language of official racist ideology permeated the statements of all those who spoke against Robb at the meeting. Louis Smuts pointed out that 'it was all good and well in some countries to talk of cricket as a levelling institution but here circumstances are so very different'. Maynard Nash, who had succeeded Cadwallader as the secretary of the South African Cricket Association, said that instead of encouraging cricket, the rescinding of the resolution would work the greatest harm to the game in the country: 'We must look to the future as well as the present'.

Union members were determined not to concede ground, but found it difficult to rationalise their defence of a patently unjust resolution. Smuts stated somewhat unconvincingly that he did not think it was fair to maintain that the union was legislating against Woodstock or any man in particular. 'For instance,' he said as his supporting evidence, 'Hendricks had some time ago asked to play for Cape Town but had not been accepted.' Smuts then professed to be 'very sorry the rule worked against Hendricks who was a very respectable man'. It was a dishonest response. While the decision of Cape Town CC was made before the introduction of the resolution, it still endeavoured to limit the ability of Hendricks to play alongside whites. Given his cricket prowess and personal qualities, it is difficult to imagine that racial/class prejudice was not behind that decision. The net result was Hendricks's initial exclusion from 'establishment' cricket and his differentiation from any other (white) player. Contrary to the myths of 'Cape liberalism', respectability and attachment to imperial culture were deemed insufficient to persuade a club committee to include a cricketer of colour. This was not without cost to them. They were denying themselves a rare talent to use in a competitive cricket environment.

Nash gave a more visceral insight into the real fears of the Cape establishment when he stepped in to comment on the clubs 'employing coloured groundsmen and some of these had children'. He saw the danger in sons being brought up in close contact with the game and reasoned that, in the future, it was highly probable they would supplant the English professionals.

Simkins drew attention to another problem in that white cricketers 'would now have people saying it was [Hendricks's] bowling they were afraid of…' Did he have a point? No reporter would have dared suggest the likes of Van der Byl and Bisset preferred not to face Hendricks, but this was clearly the truth and likely to be the public view of the two players. In the establishment's racist world, it was a fundamental challenge to the superiority of the white race for a coloured man to demonstrate superior abilities and demeanour and humiliate both their clubs and the system they espoused. Many years later, A.C. Parker stated in his *W.P. Cricket: 100-Not Out* that Robb had argued that 'those against the player were motivated by fear of his bowling prowess rather than colour prejudice'.[40] The two issues were connected, and while there were those scared as batsmen of Hendricks's fast-bowling skills, their individual humiliation was just one element in the larger question that exploded the myth of white supremacy. Parker, as a historian of white cricket at the Cape, whether deliberately or not, was blind to the impact of racism as a driving force in the South African game.

Another can of worms was Robb's clearly truthful statement that the union had already allowed clubs with coloured members to participate in the championship. Simkins and Smuts feigned ignorance, claiming that they did not know of any other club that was in this position. Robb named Docks and Simon's Town as having coloured players, the latter employing both white and black artisans in its dockyard. He pointed out that Simon's Town's best batsman was coloured. The Simon's Town representative denied that this was the case, stating that they would abide by union rules and not play any coloured men in championship fixtures. Robb's reply, 'Hard lines for Simon's Town,' drew laughter. He had made his point that there was not only suspicion and uncertainty over the colour question, but that cricket administrators were also being placed in a position where they were expected to make judgements on race.

Once again, the question came down to the quality of Hendricks. No one worried too much about the others. It was Hendricks who rubbed the nose of white supremacy in the dust. The better he did, the more it became imperative that a segregationist solution be found.

The resolution was put to the vote, and while Solomon of United Services – Hendricks's previous club – supported Robb, the other 12 voted against him.

Robb then asked for a special exception in Hendricks's case. 'All the clubs admired his play,' he declared, 'and it was a great pity he was debarred. He was not only a good player, but moreover a modest one.' Robb believed they would all like to see Hendricks play, 'but were afraid of the future', adding, 'still, they might try and stretch a point in that case'. The chairman interjected, maintaining that it would be the thin end of the wedge, but Robb countered that 'it would be an act of grace on their part to grant this concession' to someone who had played regularly in matches involving the clubs.

He conceded that 'it might turn out to be a dangerous precedent, but the Union was not ironbound and it would be quite in order if it made this exception'.

If Hendricks should be accepted for the championship season there was then the question of his selection for 'Colonial-born'. When it came to discussing his inclusion in the Colonial-born team for that weekend's match, Van der Byl said that if the resolution should be rescinded, then 'the gentleman who helped select the Colonial born team would put three coloured players in the team'. Robb posed the question: 'Can we then say that the Colonial-born side is representative if better players have been left out?'

Van der Byl, who had been born into a wealthy Woodstock family and attended Wellington College, responded, 'If they were chosen, the other eight would probably not play.' Whether his statement was true or not, it was a characteristic threat that reflected the racism that informed the whole colonial enterprise at the Cape. There again, Van der Byl's comments were rarely constructive. Hendricks had played for the All-Comers with no problem and if there was to be an objection, it would more than likely come from 'Mother Country' officials rather than 'Colonial-born' players. A second vote was taken on the proposal that Hendricks, as a special exception, be allowed to play in the championship. It was lost by 11 votes to three, thereby serving to confirm that Hendricks would not be selected for the Colonial-born team. Robb said he was surprised at the outcome of the vote because he thought 'the majority should have been the other way about'. His comments during the discussion seemed to indicate that he had canvassed opinions prior to the meeting. He expressed concern at one stage that delegates did not have the guidance of their clubs. Van der Byl responded by stating that Claremont left it to his discretion. It was a revealing admission. The other club delegates remained silent. The racism of the establishment as expressed in the meeting trumped the interests of the clubs.

An important outcome of the crushing defeat that Robb suffered was that the Western Province Cricket Union was forced to publicly confirm its policy of exclusivity and to stand rigidly behind a racial barrier in the form of its resolution. Perhaps conscious of public reaction to the union's rigid adherence to segregation, Simkins pronounced his 'sympathies were all with Hendricks who had been given the opportunity to prove his worth and had right well taken advantage of it'. There were other patronising contributions at a meeting characterised by a lack of tolerance and reactionary racial attitudes; the real tragedy being that coloured cricketers were henceforth barred from playing integrated sport at senior level in the Western Province. Van der Byl chose to ram home the triumphalist racist success of the meeting for the Western Province Cricket Union by stating that the outcome 'was not hard on Woodstock as they knew the bulk of the feeling was against them before the meeting and the large majority bore that out'.[41]

The English-language newspapers were no more supportive of Hendricks's position than the cricket officials, although letters to the Cape press from cricket followers who did not necessarily hold to the establishment's views tended to focus on the injustice of the treatment meted out to him. The *Cape Argus* summed up the prevailing opinion among white colonists by emphasising their approval for the racist position taken while suggesting some sympathy for Hendricks himself:

> ... the unanimity of feeling on the point was so great that it seemed scarcely worthwhile to reiterate the manifest objections to the coloured element being allowed to come in, and eventually the Union put its foot down by an overwhelming majority, and once and for ever it is to be hoped gave its decision against the principle of coloured men being allowed to play in Union fixtures. At the same time a good deal of sympathy was expressed with respect to Hendricks, and it was a source of general regret that the services of so capable a bowler should have to be wasted.[42]

It was not often at that time that a letter written by a person of colour was published on cricket matters in the press. The following was forwarded to the editor of the *Cape Argus* shortly after the meeting:

> Sir – Now Hendricks is debarred from playing on account of his being coloured, I will ask some of the committee to explain colour. Let us look up some of our best Cape families – yes, and relations of some of the speakers yesterday; and as for colour, Hendricks can give them points. No; it is nothing else but snobbery and caddishness. It is not manliness; they funk him. As for these so-called aristocracy, they are mere nobodys. What were their parents 25 or 30 years ago? They were some men in those days – no snobs. But, of course, the fathers are big bugs now and these gentlemen are the great 'I Am's'. They think because a man is a storeman or mechanic, he is not fit to associate with them. Be honest, you white families, and try to be men, for the colour is all over the world, even amongst royalty, since the world began, I am etc.
>
> SWARTHY[43]

The name 'Swarthy' was an interesting reference in the light of *The Owl*'s use of this adjective to describe Hendricks.

A predictable racist response was received by the *Cape Argus* a few days later under the heading 'Cricket & colour':

> Sir – I read with disgust the letter from 'Swarthy' in the last issue of the *Argus* this evening. Now, I myself object to coloured people mixing with white people, and think it is quite right that Hendricks should be debarred from playing for a white team. Can 'Swarthy' name any prominent Cape men who had coloured relations? No. I think not. Most of the best Cape families are folks of the 'Old Country', or at any rate children of them, born in the Colony. I think it utter nonsense for 'Swarthy' to say that colour is amongst royalty. Fancy a pure-bred Englishman, or any son of the 'British Isles' having colour in him; the idea in itself is absurd. It is not, as 'Swarthy' seems to think, a question of being a mechanic. A white man in this country, whether he is a mechanic or a man of position, is treated as a white man

> should be, but colour – never. He also writes: 'It is nothing but snobbery and caddishness'. Does he know the meaning of these words? I doubt it. A snob is a term generally applied to a boot-maker. 'Be honest, you white families': I am not aware that this was dishonesty, simply because a man is not allowed to play cricket with white people. Another bit of ignorance. 'Swarthy' should visit the States of America. In most of them the 'niggers' are not allowed to monopolise the sidewalks as they do here in an English town. In conclusion I might say the coloured people as a whole are not bad people, but they must keep their place and not be classed with any English-speaking race.
>
> I am, etc.
>
> Pure Bred[44]

The *South African Review* had little sympathy for Robb, complaining that 'one gets sick of the eternal cropping up of the Hendricks' case. It is four years ago since the fast bowler was debarred from a place in the first South African 11 to go home on the score of colour.' The cricket correspondent noted smugly that 'some of the thick and thin Woodstock partisans are very sore over the result of their application to the Union re Hendricks'. He was pleased to dismiss their claims with contempt: 'Let me tell them that they will not improve their case by imputing unsportsmanlike motives to the Union or by following in the line of "Swarthy" in Tuesday's *Argus*.' The *South African Review* writer claimed to have interviewed Hendricks with regard to Swarthy's letter and was able to state bluntly that 'the latter will I hope be as disappointed as he deserves to be when he hears that Hendricks is the reverse of grateful. He terms his letter offensive and the writer "no class".'[45] The author unfortunately provides too little information regarding the circumstances of his discussion with Hendricks to fully assess the accuracy of, or motivation behind, his quoted views. But, taking them at face value, Hendricks may have been wary of upsetting the *South African Review* readership. As previous articles had been unsympathetic towards him, he also would have known that the reporter from the *South African Review* was not to be trusted.

Of the union meeting itself, the *South African Review* thought there were two undercurrents of feeling, namely that 'the Union was solid against any tinkering with their anti-colour bar, and that they have every admiration and respect for Hendricks as a cricketer and a man'. The newspaper's cricket correspondent then addressed the apparent hypocrisy. He explained that Robb's appeal to the union that Hendricks was 'a fine cricketer and a well-behaved man' had nothing to do with the central argument because such views did not touch on the union's policy at all. 'That policy,' said the writer, 'is concerned with the question of colour, not cricket skill.' He continued:

> The crux of the whole matter is – whether the Union representing the white cricket community, is to open its doors to the coloured element and say, 'We'll all play together; cricket is a cosmopolitan sport,' or not. Remember, if you admit one you must admit all. Are the white cricketers in the Province prepared to do so? There is no need to answer such a question. Of course, the whole thing is absurd, and the support given the agitation can only be put down to blind partisanship. In my opinion the weak point in the Union's policy is its admission of clubs with coloured members. These can play in ordinary fixtures but not in championship matches. This is wrong altogether. If two classes are to be kept separate the distinction should be made throughout the game ...[46]

This, of course, was exactly the establishment position and the newspaper's remarks proved refreshing in getting some truth into the discussion.

The *Cape Times*, which was generally considered to be the most authoritative and widely circulating of the city's English-language newspapers during the 1890s, devoted considerable space to the latest Hendricks crisis. A number of letters were written in support of him and they requested a rethink about the decision made by the

Western Province Cricket Union. After witnessing Hendricks play on the Saturday, 'A Newcomer' said he was 'very sorry indeed to know that such a fine player should be excluded from championship matches ... and from what I can learn members of other teams do not object to playing against Hendricks in outside matches'. The writer took it that in debarring Hendricks from playing, local players 'consider it lowering and infra dig to play against coloured men [and yet] he is undoubtedly one of the finest, if not the best bowler in the Cape Colony'. 'WRP' was 'disgusted at the gross miscarriage of justice'. As regards the natives of South Africa, he said, 'let them look to God for justice for man has refused it'. 'Sportsman' thought the Western Province Cricket Union were lacking in true sporting spirit, unable 'to understand that a man's status in sport is nothing to do with race, social position etc ... to allow coloured men to play one Saturday against the same players and on the same ground but not the next is the height of absurd inconsistency'. He thought the less powerful clubs should act independently of the two senior clubs and not allow themselves to be led by the nose as they were doing: 'What pleasure is there in seeing the average championship match at Newlands – a procession and then a leather hunt, and yet when a less powerful team has a bowler who can put an end to the leather hunt and make the game a little less one-sided, we have this bogie of colour trotted out?' 'Observer' agreed with the general rule debarring coloured players from taking part, but could not help but wish the union had 'made their rule sufficiently elastic to admit of a special indulgence in the case of respectable coloured men of proved ability'.[47]

Apart from detailed articles in the sports pages and the subsequent letters, the editor, Edmund Garrett, produced a lengthy two-column piece on cricket's predicament. An influential figure in Cape society, Garrett – who was the editor of the *Cape Times* from mid-1895 until 1899 – was closely associated with Rhodes and the Afrikaner leaders Jan Hofmeyr and Paul Kruger. His political insight was valued and he entered Parliament in 1898 as the member for Victoria East. An outstanding journalist and persuasive speaker, he presented strong support for Rhodes and Sir Alfred Milner, the bellicose British high commissioner, in the course of advocating for a united South Africa, able to control its own affairs while operating within the British Empire. His leader article entitled 'Colour in cricket' provides absorbing context to events surrounding the Western Province Cricket Union's treatment of Hendricks:

> Are our natural prejudices about colour, speaking of our white community as a whole growing more intense and more pervading? ... We are not prepared to say that the decision of the Union to exclude colour from Union cricket matches is wrong. The subject is a difficult one, we confess. Hendricks himself is generally admitted to be a good fellow, as well as a good bowler. It is admitted that if the question touched him alone it would never have been raised. Doubtless there are others whose character and bearing entitle them to rank in the same category but that somebody poses us with the old persistent, inevitable question, 'Where are you to draw the line?' Once admit that the line has to be drawn, and it follows that it must be drawn so as to exclude even Hendricks. A good law makes hard cases, they say. Our colour friends of all shades and of various classes in life have taken to the white man's athletics with great vigour. The Malays, for instance, make sport the pretext for two or three holidays out of the six working days, and the spectacle is becoming familiar of young fellows in every shade of colour, as to their skins, ranging from the lightest of brown looks to the darkest of black ones, going forth to various open spaces of an afternoon, most strangely bedizened in the loudest-patterned jerseys. Can the English who carry their cricket and football to the uttermost parts of the earth look with disfavour on such a phenomenon? ...
>
> It is necessary to live in Cape Town or the suburbs to understand the bitterness of language which more white people will use, not so much about the aboriginal kafir, but about the brown population which comprises so much of the working class of the Peninsula. Politically we are of an equality in this British colony. Socially no such equality can exist, save

in the lowest social strata, until mankind has given up its thoroughly sound objection to miscegenation and does away with class difference to boot. Socially, therefore, a cleavage there must be, and perhaps the best way would be if both colours could recognise it frankly and without mutual rancour pursue an equal policy of mutual exclusion. Just as there are, at present, for instance, distinct places of residence and resort for the white, the brown and the black sections of population so there may be white athletic clubs and coloured athletic clubs, keeping to themselves and using different grounds. If once it was understood that both sides recognize the dividing line, and that each retains the right to consider itself the superior if it likes, but that at all hazards Olive Schreiner's 11th Commandment 'Keep Your Breeds Pure' must be observed, and its observances facilitated in all social arrangements: if once this were the accepted principle there would then be no need for such an act as the specific exclusion of Hendricks ... unhappily the reciprocity of exclusiveness is not easy to set up, and is particularly unnatural to the half-caste, who always wishes himself as nearly as possible as a white.

You can meet a man in sport on an equal footing and yet cling religiously to your social caste in any other relation of life where you may cherish it. If sport can then triumph over class, why not over colour? – we find ourselves asking wistfully.

Ranji rising to be a national British hero of the national British game but the man of colour, if he finds his chains fall off him when he touches the soul of England, feels them riveted on again the moment he lands in one of England's colonies. An Australian parliament had almost to pass a special bill to enable Prince Ranji to play in Australian cricket; and it is almost past hoping for that we shall ever be able to watch the wrist-play of the most lissom and graceful bat in the world on any pitch in South Africa.

A general free mixing of white and coloured youth in games nobody here is prepared to advocate, and though we should

> have thought that this extreme need scarcely follow on the admissions to white cricket of the few coloured players good enough to be played in Union matches, we find that those in closer touch with the practical conditions hold that it must follow, and to avoid it they must permanently deprive club matches of the services of one of the best bowlers in South Africa.
>
> Surely the painful discussion of the point might somehow have been managed in private. It is not without chance that we can fancy Hendricks and his friends and the coloured population reading that report. A man's a man for a'that, and it would be more or less than human if such reading prompted no bitter and resentful impulse, no nursing of grudges. A 'Cape boy' reads the gracious word of praise sent by the Queen to her coloured soldiers on the Indian frontier; he remembers what good service the Cape boys did nearer home in the Matoppos; and in the same paper he reads a debate as to whether he and his, though good enough to fight side by side with white men, are good enough to play side by side with them. And the answer – 'NO'! It may be objected that it is wrong to put forward these considerations, unless we are prepared to advocate the opposite answer. But we think it is just as well to show that we whites are not – many of us are not – blind to such considerations, even if we cannot in some particular matter carry them into action.[48]

The dilemma for Garrett was clear. On the one hand, he embraced the Rhodes–Milton view of the importance of the strict separation of the races, including in cricket, and in terms that would have gladdened the hearts of apartheid ideologies 50 years later. On the other hand, he felt some remorse about the treatment of a man in a less-than-human way on the basis of his colour, especially when it reflected on the hypocrisy of using such social and economic inferiors to defend the empire. It was a common late nineteenth-century conundrum and was a point of debate throughout the Anglo-Boer War and the First World War.

Garrett's views would almost certainly have reached Milton in Matabeleland where the Mfengu – black colonial soldiers from the Eastern Cape – had played a key role in quelling the Matabele revolt. Jan Grootboom, a fearless coloured scout known in derogatory colonial terms as a 'Cape boy', had ventured into the hills several times to clear the way for Rhodes to meet the Matabele and begin the process from which he would extract a promise of peace. Rhodes had been responsible for the introduction of the Mfengu before and after the rebellions. Apart from their assistance in the fighting, he hoped that they would increase the supply of labour for the mines, an ambitious arrangement that lacked support from all sides. Blacks regarded 'Cape boys' as unacceptable because of their support of the white government and their part in the suppression of the revolts. Whites objected to them because they aspired to 'colonial status' and tended to incite problems among the African population.

Milton might have viewed Rhodes's experiment with apprehension because the emigrants from the Cape not only enjoyed cricket, but also hoped their interest would gain them social acceptability. The Loben Club, composed of Mfengu and coloured cricketers, was formed in Bulawayo in 1898 and named in honour of the deposed Matabele king. Its cricket achievements were not reported in the local media, but details were forwarded to King William's Town where they were published in the black-owned newspaper, *Imvo Zabantsundu*. In 1901, the club played ten matches and won them all, according to their secretary. The Mfengu numbers reached 1,300 by 1905, and they played cricket up to the First World War, predominantly on the Old Scottish Ground. Their presence provided Milton with a second chance to encourage people of colour to play sport, but he stayed aloof, rarely if ever mixing with the black communities. His statement that if employers 'have a good player in their employ he will be a good worker as well' never extended across the colour barrier during his long period of influence in southern Africa.[49]

9

'Any club could object to any man'

'To argue with the powers that be is to batter a brick wall with a feather.'

– *The Owl* (3 March 1899)

A RACIALLY DEFINED hardening of the social and cultural distinctions between classes took place at the Cape between the censuses of 1875 and 1904. It was in part driven by the mineral revolution, which created a more diversified economy, new labour divisions and a growing focus on ethnic identity. The earlier division along class lines gave way to a white ethnic solidarity that became increasingly concerned with the 'poor-white' problem and their mixing with other races. In the lower rungs of society where the tradition of 'Cape liberalism' had once represented hope within racist South Africa, aspirations of achieving a colour-blind society were aggressively interrupted. According to Shula Marks, Cape liberalism was 'always a minority creed and a rather frail one at that'. It was increasingly challenged, she said, because of white alarm at the influx of migrant workers into the colony's towns and the influences of social Darwinism.[1]

But the changed economic environment and the myriad necessary economic support structures – including transport systems, education, food production, security, healthcare and medicine – that the advent of the mineral revolution created, underpinned this ideological process.

The theory of social Darwinism, which arose in the 1870s, had two elements – a belief in racial separation at its most extreme based on polygenesis or separate creations, and a ranking system where humanity could be systematically divided into superior and inferior races. By the turn of the century this ideology was expressed in a crude taxonomy headed by Europeans with the Anglo-Saxon seen as the superior race, black Africans as the inferior and the others distributed along the ladder. Social Darwinism was the dominant lens through which imperial officials viewed their world. Sir Alfred Milner, the high commissioner and governor of the Cape Colony, claimed his patriotism knew no geographical, but only racial, limits: 'It is not the soil of England…which is essential to arouse my patriotism, but the speech, the traditions, the spiritual heritage, the principles, the aspirations, of the British race…'[2] This kind of rhetoric was popularised in the writing of John Buchan, one of Milner's post-war 'little kindergarten show of dolls' – a group of young, inexperienced, frequently arrogant university graduates.[3] The ruling class at the Cape, obsessed with racial categories that reinforced their own position in a changing and potentially threatening world, subjected the inhabitants of the colony to increased formal separation.

By the turn of the century, social mixing between races had been restricted for the most part to District Six, Woodstock and small, working-class enclaves where whites and coloureds still happily intermingled and lived together. A leader article in the *South African News* commented on artisans – carpenters, builders, painters and other professions – in an area such as Cape Town:

> …where we have been astonished, and from the standpoint of our social prospects disheartened, to find how surprisingly large is the percentage of such settlers who marry coloured women. Let the Imperial Government take a census on this point in, say, District Six of Cape Town and the result will astonish them.[4]

Such astonishment betrayed a lamentable lack of both historical understanding and observation on behalf of the writer, but these views were an active part of a wider campaign to stimulate a racist moral panic. A strong element of this moral panic was the issue of public health and the vulnerability of Cape Town as the gateway to plague and other epidemics, as well as the sanitation issue that had preoccupied its politicians for decades. Racial division entrenched an arrangement whereby the 'reconstituted' coloured people occupied an invidious position between whites and Africans. They were defined as other than African migrants, whose economic and social interests were further undercut through forced removals to locations at the Docks and Ndabeni. The coloureds shared many Cape cultural and economic interests with urban Africans, who had been included in the community for generations and who, like poorer whites, formed part of a non-racial underclass. The sacrifice of African interests left the coloureds with a difficult choice – resist as an underclass or go along with the white definition of their intermediate position, thus retaining their political benefits. In the 1890s, with a hardening of racial political attitudes and attacks by Rhodes and the Afrikaner Bond on the racial property franchise, a separate coloured political organisation could prove counterproductive and extinguish all hope of incorporation into a common colonial society. 'Coloured people were anxious on the whole,' explained historian Stan Trapido, 'not to establish for themselves a political identity separate to the white population.'[5]

In this period prior to the Anglo-Boer War, the significance of the coloured vote encouraged mendacious promises on the hustings to the effect that equal rights would be granted to coloured people. In a political campaign in 1898, Rhodes altered his slogan from 'Equal rights for every white man south of the Zambezi' to 'Equal rights for every civilised man south of the Zambezi', and defined 'civilised' as a man, white or black, 'who has sufficient education to write his name, has some property, or works. In fact, is not a loafer.'[6] In reality, this was far from the truth. Rhodes had already amended the Cape franchise to include a stiff property test that excluded almost all Africans and many coloureds, whether educated or not. Milner was quick to match Rhodes's hypocrisy and raise him to new levels in his quest for war when he referred to the Transvaal's discrimination against blacks as a 'justification for intervention', while his ally, Joseph Chamberlain, the secretary of state for the colonies, told the British Parliament that victory would bring 'equal laws, equal liberty' to all.[7] Coloureds and Africans had little option but to take them at their word and hope for change and improved treatment in the event of a British victory. At the very least they thought they would retain the rights they had.

The Second Anglo-Boer War of 1899–1902 had been almost inevitable since the discovery of gold in 1886 on the Witwatersrand attracted a huge influx of diggers, chancers, investors and fortune-seekers to Paul Kruger's sleepy South African Republic with its population of Boer and African cattle farmers and herders. It was a war over gold and the means to exploit it. It was driven by the mining industry and Sir Alfred Milner. Once begun, it consumed the subcontinent, and the economy of the Cape was put on immediate war footing. Members of the working-class population of Cape Town were either in uniform or else employed on the railways, docks and transport supporting the troops. Krom Hendricks, as a long-term railway employee, had an important role to play and he, like his colleagues, must have hoped that a British victory would bring a new face to South Africa and a new deal for the non-white races.

A member of the Cape's non-European population, Geo Robson, wrote a letter to the *Cape Argus* that represented coloured hopes in the early part of the war, a stage when some at least accepted imperial assurances that British success guaranteed a better future:

> Who have more reasons to rejoice on Boer defeat and British victory than the coloured people of this Province? Have they forgotten, can they ever forget, the barbarous treatment their friends and blood relations have had to endure under Boer rule in the Transvaal? Do they not know themselves to be despised as *zwart goed* (black things) by many of the Dutch in this Colony? Have they not over and over again been threatened

> that when once the English were driven into the sea the Boers would compel them to return to what their forefathers once were? This war is in truth the complete emancipation of the coloured people from the spirit of slavery, and they know it.[8]

Hendricks continued to drive engines, play cricket for white clubs and further extend his family. As his brood grew, they left 16 Breakwater Cottages in 1891 and moved into two 'homes': 19 and 20 Dock Cottages. These were part of the Dockland area and 'comprised a set of houses all attached to each other of corrugated iron'. Adjacent to them were Fleming Street, Amsterdam Street and Ebenezer Road. In 1897, the family moved to 7 Cobern Street in De Waterkant, just below Bo-Kaap, an area where slaves and paupers were once buried. The Hendricks' eighth child and youngest daughter, Irene May, was born in 1897, followed by Percival Findlay in 1900 and Douglas John in 1901. By then, they had moved again within De Waterkant to 3 Jarvis Building, Jarvis Street.[9]

Family life and his work on the railways complemented Hendricks's growing status on the cricket field. He had impressed his home crowd in December 1897 when he took advantage of the prevailing south-easter at Woodstock to return match figures of 11-15 – ten bowled – against Alma. 'The bowler and the wind,' said the *Cape Times*, 'formed a sort of compact with complete mastery over every attempt at batting.'[10] It was a devastating performance, and his presence was eagerly anticipated when preparations began for non-championship cricket fixtures on neighbouring fields at Newlands in mid-January 1898. The matches provided an up-to-date window on the state of affairs in Cape Town's domestic cricket prior to the war, not least because the two leading clubs were in action. Western Province CC was conscious at the time of their inability to attract spectators to weekend games. They possessed a splendid venue, as well as one of the strongest sides, and they offered additional entertainment through the attendance of the band of the King's Royal Rifles. The *Cape Argus* reported:

> Of course, on Saturday the cricket fare provided was not – no reflection on Claremont – of the best; but surely there are a large number of people in the Peninsula who can appreciate Newlands for its surroundings and music, independent of the cricket being of the very first-class. It requires very little acumen to enable one to see that a serious loss is facing the club through the public-spirited resolve to keep the band performances a feature throughout the season.[11]

On the other side of the railway line, Cape Town CC hosted Woodstock in a match they were expected to dominate because of their strong batting line-up. It did not prevent the *Cape Argus* regarding the fixture to be of special interest. The writer referred to the capabilities of Hendricks as a first-class bowler being thoroughly tested – for the umpteenth time! – in that he would be performing against English professionals Jack Brown, Len Braund and Frank Hearne. 'This should be the means,' said the report, 'to inducing a number of people to visit the ground.'[12]

On the morning of the match, the *Cape Argus* took up the Hendricks story again; this time under the heading 'A curious position':

> The match between Cape Town and Woodstock today has additional interest imported into it owing to the fact that Hendricks is playing for the latter club. This, the Cape Town club rightly suspect will prove an additional attraction to the cricket-loving public. But is not the position somewhat inconsistent? Here is a player – we are not discussing the rights or wrongs of the question – who is debarred by the Union from playing in championship fixtures, yet whose inclusion in a team playing an ordinary fixture is seized upon to attract the public by more or less the people who refuse him full privileges. The position is certainly curious.[13]

After the weekend, it was the turn of the *Cape Times* to comment:

> Interest was imparted into the game by the fact that Hendricks was to take part, and many of the cricketing public were drawn to see how the redoubtable Brown would shape against the Woodstock crack. Their anticipations were, however, doomed to disappoint as Hendricks arriving a little late, Brown had already succumbed to Bain. [Yet] the match was far more interesting than the most sanguine expected ...[14]

When he did arrive, Hendricks relieved Jennings of the ball. In his first over, he clean bowled Braund, the Surrey and Somerset all-rounder who played 23 times for England. An over later, Frank Hearne, who had opened the batting for South Africa, was beaten 'by a yorker'. The removal of the professionals for relatively few runs earned Woodstock a draw and congratulations on their 'plucky and effective stand'. The crowd also appreciated Hendricks striking Brown for 4 and then 'lifting the succeeding ball out of the ground for 6, amidst applause', but it did not alter the fact that they wanted to see him bowl at the Yorkshireman.[15] Because of the ban that prevented Hendricks from playing in championship matches, he had to wait a year – until January 1899 – before meeting Brown again. Hendricks quickly and dramatically settled the individual contest against a player who had been good enough to compile a match-winning 140 for England in an Ashes encounter at Melbourne in 1895. At Newlands on 14 January 1899, the scoreboard read: Brown b Hendricks .... 0.

On Monday, 17 January 1898, a special meeting of the Western Province Cricket Union was held at the Thatched Tavern. The first business was the election of a new president. John Reid, who had stepped down from the position, attended the meeting at which fellow Western Province CC member Harry Hands nominated Frank Robb as the new president. James Bell, representing Olympic CC, promptly seconded the nomination and Robb, who was not at the meeting, was elected unopposed. Interest surrounded the move, which the Western Province and Cape Town clubs had clearly planned. Robb had hired Hendricks as a professional at Woodstock and unsuccessfully fought his case to enable him to play senior championship cricket. His election as president was therefore both surprising and potentially significant for Cape cricket as a whole and for Hendricks in particular.[16]

The Owl was of the opinion that, in the course of a decade in which the Western Province Cricket Union had inflicted considerable damage on South African cricket, there was a glimmer of hope when Robb 'was elected to preside over and rule the destinies of Western Province cricket'. Their cricket correspondent considered it to be 'the first and last move for improvement ... a strong man, and one in touch with all the smaller clubs was what was wanted'. The writer's great concern was that 'the jealousy of the "big Pots" was against anyone possessing the essential qualifications possessing the chair'.[17] Despite support for Robb, it was feared the controlling force behind cricket at Newlands remained in the hands of the two clubs that were based there.

Robb was conscious of the numerous issues that confronted him, not least being the lack of trust that other South African centres had in the Western Province. 'The popular belief outside the Province,' said the *Cape Times*, 'is that our sportsmen are trying to rule the South African roost. It is no use anyone at this end denying the impeachment for a denial would only feed the mistrust.'[18] On the domestic front, Robb was instrumental in the amalgamation of several clubs to form the Metropolitan CC in 1898/99. He hoped to fill a gap and build a front-rank club that would be able to challenge the Western Province and Cape Town CCs. There was criticism that Metropolitan CC had been formed hurriedly, had no funds and no professional, and was reliant on temporary use being made of the Corporation Athletic Ground. The press nevertheless registered optimism when Robb hired Hendricks as a 'ground bowler', although he did not play until late November. He represented Metropolitan against Arabian College and captured 6-14. The *Cape Times* stated that he was 'a great acquisition' for the newly formed club. He then picked up 5-15 in ten overs as Metropolitan thrashed a weakened Cape Town team.[19]

It was not long before Metropolitan were defeated and the old frustrations surfaced. 'The utility of bringing out the new club so many times to take a big drubbing at Newlands is to be doubted,' complained *The Owl*.[20] They then dwelt on the inclusion of Hendricks in the Metropolitan team for a non-championship match against Western Province CC in late February 1899. The opposition team was a powerful one, said the report, and Hendricks's bowling was little short of remarkable in its resource, stamina and accuracy – 30 overs, 12 maidens, 52 runs, 6 wickets. The Western Province total of 181 for six was made largely at the expense of the other bowlers. The *Cape Times* concurred, emphasising 'the effect of Hendricks's pace on a good batting side and on a good wicket'. Bisset 'foolishly ran himself out' in an effort to get to the other end, and Van der Byl, unable to get a bat on a yorker, was lbw to Hendricks for 2. Almost inevitably, in the case of the latter and given Van der Byl's antagonism towards Hendricks, 'the batsman thought the decision unjust, the ball hitting his foot'.[21]

'But what was to be gained,' asked *The Owl*, 'if Hendricks should perform marvellous feats, when by the rules of his local Union, his services are not to be availed of even in ordinary championship fixtures?' The newspaper slammed the attitude of the province's cricket administration, which had been notorious in its inconsistent treatment of Hendricks and obstinate in its refusal to resolve the issue: but then, 'to argue with the powers that be is to batter a brick wall with a feather'.[22]

In the last week of March, Metropolitan CC travelled to Stellenbosch. It was a festive occasion with a large crowd in attendance and proceedings enlivened by the band of the Victorian College. Stellenbosch emerged winners on the first innings (146 and 66 versus 111) of a match in which the *Cape Times* commented not only on Hendricks taking 'a very brilliant catch', but also bowling swiftly 'in fine style'.[23] Using the wind to advantage, he produced a striking match analysis of 13-54 (23-8-43-6 and 14-9-11-7), a performance that summed up a season in which he had once again proved himself the most effective bowler at the Cape but was prohibited from rescuing his struggling team in the championship. 'The Metropolitans,' said the *South African Review*, 'have not fulfilled the hue-tinted aspirations formed by the promoters of that amalgamation.' The writer added: 'What might have been if Hendricks were available for championship matches would be to no purpose to argue, and I do not want to raise the old Hendricks controversy now.' Instead, the article blindly concluded that 'if the "Mets" ever expect to realise their ambition they must try and discover a permanent recruiting ground and encourage a professional to coach the young recruits caught as well as to play for them'.[24] The real issue was deliberately ignored. Metropolitan CC had a 'professional', but he was debarred from playing for them when it mattered.

Prior to the opening of the 1899/1900 season, Robb and his committee devised a new league structure in which ten sides would compete in the opening round of the championship: Metropolitan, Alma, Cape Town 'B', Western Province 'B', South African College, Green Point, Victorians (Stellenbosch), Claremont, Gardens and Diocesan College. The winning side would then compete in a final stage against the Cape Town and Western Province CCs.

In order to accelerate the progress of Metropolitan, the club was allowed to enter a side in the Peninsula Cricket League, which formed the second tier of the Western Province cricket structure. Opposition sides were competitive as the league comprised club first teams, and in 1898/99, Observatory and Mowbray had become the joint holders of the league title. Metropolitan would therefore be fully tested when they played their first match on 14 October 1899, a Saturday when they had no championship fixture. It was questionable whether the spirit of the law was adhered to in this match as the Metropolitan 'second-string side' fielded William Creese (their new professional) and two others who were expected to play for the senior team in the championship. But this did not bother Observatory. Their concern was the inclusion of Hendricks. A protest was lodged against him prior to the start of the match. Rule 3 of the Peninsula Cricket League echoed the rules of the Western Province Cricket Union regarding championship cricket, stating that 'clubs shall be white teams of European origin'. It was a rule that had been overlooked in past seasons, but Observatory were well aware of the damage Hendricks had inflicted when he played for Mowbray against them.

The cricket writer at the *Cape Argus* appeared keen to see the league rid itself of players of colour. He pointed out that during the previous season the law was not as strictly enforced as it might have been, and complaints were numerous on the subject. The development had forced the committee to discuss the matter at a recent meeting, where a resolution was moved to give a more distinct reading to the law, 'which to say the least of it, is curiously worded'. However, said the *Argus*, 'no one could be found to express any views on the subject'. The writer could see no reason for such reticence, as the 'coloured question' had been a thorn in the side of legislators for a long time and the Peninsula Cricket League 'would find no better example to follow than that of the Western Province Cricket Union'. The report again drew attention to the wording of Rule 3 – it seemed advisable to take steps to ensure there was no room for doubt as to its interpretation. 'In this country,' the *Argus* argued, 'it is especially difficult to draw the line between white and coloured and as for the "European origin" part of the clause, well – a cart and four may be driven through it.'[25]

One positive development, said the *Argus*, was the protest lodged by Observatory CC, because now the 'coloured question' would be discussed and a decision reached. The writer accepted the view that the hearing might take no action because it would be 'a test case', but in the event of the verdict going in favour of the protesting side, the committee 'should declare the game void and order it to be replayed'. The newspaper was also conscious of the fact that the hearing would be of interest as it involved Hendricks. 'Let there be no half-hearted decision,' it advised the committee, 'let personalities be moved aside and matters thoroughly discussed by a body of sportsmen in a sportsmanlike way.'[26]

A meeting of the executive committee of the Peninsula Cricket League was held at the Standard Hotel, Mowbray, on Thursday, 19 October. Observatory explained their objection to Metropolitan playing Hendricks in the league match, as they alleged 'it was an infringement of the third rule of the League'. James Bell appeared on behalf of Metropolitan and stated that 'the player in question, Mr H. Hendricks, played under a misunderstanding'.[27] Observatory's representative asked that their club be awarded two points or that the match be replayed. Bell thought his club would be only too happy to meet Observatory again on the cricket field. The committee discussed the issue and resolved that Metropolitan be censured and that the match be replayed on a date to be approved by the committee; the fixture to be staged on the Observatory ground.

There was a second Rule 3 case on the same evening. It was stated that Mowbray had lodged a complaint against Lintens CC for having played brothers Peter and William Robertson, as well as Thomas Hering, in their league match on 14 October. The three players in question appeared and answered the few questions that were put to them. The players then withdrew while the committee 'deliberated and resolved that P. Robertson be eligible to play in the competition'.[28] In a bizarre ruling, William Robertson and Hering were declared ineligible to play. The committee did not deduct the two points from Lintens CC as it was their first offence, but they were warned that such leniency would not be shown to them in the future for similar breaches of the rules.

Hendricks did not publicly question the decision, and neither he nor Metropolitan contested the 'European origin' aspect of Rule 3. Moreover, the possibility of Hendricks playing in the Peninsula Cricket League was not raised again.

On 28 October, Mowbray played Observatory at the Rhodes Recreation Ground. According to the *Cape Argus*, the match was always 'looked forward to as a miniature Cape Town CC versus Western Province CC match for the keenness of the players and enthusiasm of the villagers, and the sportsmanlike feeling shown on both sides tend to show the good the Peninsula League has done'.[29] The newspaper's gushing praise for the two clubs and their cricket league was significant in the light of the recent protests and a reaction to further developments that had taken place. Lintens CC played Metropolitan CC on the same day and included both the Robertsons and Hering in their side. The ruling of the Peninsula Cricket League committee had been overturned. It is not known who intervened, possibly Frank Robb as president of the Western Province Cricket Union, but more likely the Honourable James

Rose Innes QC MLA, president of Mowbray CC. The petty protest could not have impressed Rose Innes, who made a point of attending his club's fixture against Observatory. Mowbray had traditionally played with and against cricketers of colour and, in recent seasons, Hendricks had represented the club with distinction on Saturdays when Woodstock or Metropolitan had championship matches. He had taken nine wickets (all bowled) and struck 76 runs without losing his wicket in guiding Mowbray to two crushing first-innings victories over Observatory; captured five wickets in an innings against both YMCA and United Services; and struck an unbeaten 72 against Melrose.

Two days after the Hendricks hearing, Metropolitan played Cape Town CC in a non-championship match. Hendricks returned figures of 6-31 in 15.3 overs. Two South African players – Howard Francis (20) and George Rowe (23) – were the only contributors of any note to the Cape Town total of 69. Hendricks accounted for past and future South African players – Godfrey Cripps (lbw) and Stanley Horwood (bowled) – before they could make an impression. The *South African Review* commented that Cape Town had 'evidently found the pace of Hendricks and the extreme contrast of Bain's slows too much for them'. The question was asked:

> What a farce this is and how long do the Union intend to play it? If – because of colour Hendricks is unfit to play cricket alongside white men, the line should be drawn clear and distinct against him; but to play him in ordinary matches and ban him from the championship is neither logical nor fair.[30]

The writer's all-or-nothing approach might well have been designed to curry favour with the union. Here, and in other articles from that time, the *South African Review* seemed to be imploring the Western Province Cricket Union to employ a tougher resolution that would dispense of Hendricks's services in white cricket. The newspaper was no longer a leader in cricket reporting, as had been the case when Harry Cadwallader was both its sports editor and secretary of the South African Cricket Association. That was an exceptional time for a small, weekly operation, and since Cadwallader's departure, the *South African Review* had struggled to cover cricket adequately. A reliance on various correspondents was unavoidable and posed a risk as they were not always competent. Nevertheless, when a report filtered through that someone called Hendricks had allegedly been called for throwing in a match involving Mowbray, the *Review*'s cricket writer became interested. It was precisely the sort of drama that would capture reader interest. The writer immediately jumped to the conclusion that this was Krom Hendricks and produced an embellished piece, patronisingly tinged with a smatter of sympathy, possibly in the belief that this would draw the curtain on Hendricks's cricket career. He wrote:

> Hendricks still sends them down very fast, but the effort now apparently indulges in a most palpable throw. It is not pleasant to accuse any man of throwing and certainly I do not think Hendricks does so intentionally, but that on average three balls per over, are to say the least of it, very doubtful ...[31]

Just as the *Review* became embroiled in their breaking news – which included an account from a local umpire – the *Cape Times* reported that there was a fast bowler by the name of Wales Hendricks who had been called for throwing. He was a young left-armer and had been taking a great number of wickets in the junior league, but there had been talk for some time about his suspect action. After a match between Wynberg and Mowbray, one spectator was of the opinion that, from 'the way [Wales Hendricks] delivered the ball ... I have not the slightest hesitation in saying that the majority of deliveries are throws'.[32] A representative from Wynberg then entered the argument through a letter, which he forwarded to the *Cape Times*. In pointing out that the accusation was unfair and that respected umpires had cleared the bowler, he effectively ended discussion on the subject.[33] It was an awkward moment for the *South African Review*, and one for which they failed to apologise.

A few months later, Krom Hendricks was in the news again with a performance that stunned Cape Town cricket. It came out of the blue during a non-championship game played by Metropolitan against Claremont at the latter's ground on 17 March 1900. The *Cape Argus* published the team lists as they did every week, advising Metropolitan that their players would be departing on the 1.35 train. They announced the team as: E. Allen, F. Robb, J.W. Duminy, J. Reid, J.B. Laidlaw, C.A. Bain, F. Louw, A. Sewell, J.L. Bell, A. Wiles and Hendricks – no initial being given to the 'demon' bowler on this occasion, possibly because he was regarded as the side's professional.[34] It was a full-strength Metropolitan XI, although Sewell, one of their leading players, dropped out at the last moment and could not be replaced.

Metropolitan batted first and scored 113, of which Western Province batsman Edward Allen made 54 and Charles Bain 26. Hendricks (3 not out) batted ninth in the ten-man side. Randolph van Reenen bowled remarkably well for Claremont and took nine wickets – all clean bowled – for 26. It was a modest total, but Metropolitan's strength was in their bowling, comprising as it did the formidable Hendricks and 21-year-old Bain, who was only a couple of years away from representing Western Province. To the Claremont batsmen, Hendricks was a terrifying sight, appearing to bowl faster with every over. After the opening batsmen had managed to hold out for a few overs, wickets fell at regular intervals. Claremont were ultimately blasted out for 21 with Hendricks achieving the incredible analysis of 9 overs, 9 maidens, 0 runs and 9 wickets.

'The performance is all the more remarkable,' marvelled the *South African Review*, 'as the wicket was one of the best seen at Claremont this season, and not at all bumpy.' The reporter added: 'A Claremont man explained their downfall to me as being due largely to funk ...'[35] Batsmen froze as Hendricks maintained his stranglehold, generating great pace with the ball lifting, seaming and flying off the wicket. Yet it was his accuracy that was to the fore once again, highlighted by his uncanny ability to consistently hit the stumps. Seven of his nine victims were clean bowled as the scorecard, reproduced in the *Cape Times*, indicates:

W.H. Impey	b Hendricks	7
A. Wood	c Bell b Hendricks	3
H. Gill	b Hendricks	0
W. van Reenen	b Bain	0
E. Smythe	b Hendricks	0
C.P. de Villiers	b Hendricks	0
R. van Reenen	b Hendricks	0
R. Gill	b Hendricks	0
J. Young	b Hendricks	5
A. Smythe	c Duminy b Hendricks	0
G. Ponsford	not out	2
Extras		4
Total		21

Bain 8/0/17/1 Hendricks 9/9/0/9[36]

The *South African Review*, perhaps mindful of their earlier error over the throwing question and anxious to make amends, correctly described it as a South African record and said they were pleased 'to hear that a movement is on foot to present the fast bowler with a silver mounted memento'. Unfortunately, the newspaper was unable to take on the responsibility of raising the finance, but said 'it would come as a graceful action were the nine victims to make Hendricks a small presentation as a token of a prowess which caused them one and all to beat so hasty and ignominious a retreat'.[37] Perhaps a trophy was made and is stored away in an attic somewhere. In all grades of cricket, Hendricks's feat of nine wickets in a completed innings without conceding a single run remained a South African all-comers' record for 50 years until Winton Edwards claimed all ten for no runs in 9.7 eight-ball overs for Queen's College against Selborne College at Queenstown in March 1950. Mention might also be made of Paul Hugo, who took nine wickets in nine balls for Smithfield against Aliwal North in February 1931, before going on to take all 10 for 2 runs.

Metropolitan fielded a formidable side when Hendricks played. Without him, they still managed a successful season in the championship. They won eight of their nine matches to tie for first place with Alma. A play-off was arranged with Alma's last pair carrying them to a thrilling one-wicket victory. The victors then tackled Cape Town CC and Western Province CC in a three-way second stage.

Robb did not seek a further term as president of the Western Province Cricket Union and Metropolitan CC participated in one further championship season. The club's demise was probably inevitable as they did not have a ground of their own and were reliant on Green Point providing facilities three times a week. When Metropolitan's full bowling attack was available – Hendricks, Bain, Volsteedt and Sewell – they were the best in the Cape. But it tended to be the same old story in the championship, where the stock line remained that Hendricks would have made a difference.

At the start of the 1900/01 season, Hendricks was bowling as well as ever. On a slow league wicket at Newlands that saw only 216 runs made in five hours of cricket, Metropolitan did well to restrict Western Province CC to 142 for seven. Hendricks took 4-41 – all bowled – and might have obtained a fifth wicket had the delivery not been no-balled because he had overstepped. The side's tactics were also questioned, as they had not taken the conditions into consideration. According to the *South African Review*:

> Hendricks had the best figures for the Metropolitan trundlers and he also bowled a long way the best. He was not very fast, having to bowl in the teeth of a very strong wind, but he kept an excellent length, and was difficult to score from. Bain was good for a few overs but soon tired ... Hendricks should have been given a chance with the wind, and Bain tried at the lower end. Slow bowling is often more effective against the wind, for, if high-tossed, the flight becomes more difficult to watch, especially if the breeze is at all gusty.[38]

Metropolitan were then dismissed for 74 to go down by 68 runs. They bounced back admirably to defeat Diocesan College and had the best of matches against lesser foes, the *South African Review* commenting: 'The Mets are not doing so badly.'[39] By mid-December, however, the same newspaper admitted: 'On paper, Metropolitan appear capable of big things but somehow they invariably fail to do the expected.'[40] Hendricks's cricket was often limited to playing against sides that were incapable of standing up to him. It was quite in order to destroy Western Province's 'second string', because the absurdity of the situation could then be forcibly relayed to the game's authorities who were directing cricket along racist lines. In March, Metropolitan thumped a weakened Western Province CC by 63 runs with Hendricks responsible for the initial damage, but in other non-championship matches – such as Ohlsson's Cape Breweries – it was a case of not bowling him because he was simply too good. One of the few fixtures in early 1901 that featured the desired 'needle' was played against Alma. They were to recruit a large number of 'Mets' players when the latter folded, and to have the better of a drawn fixture was therefore of some satisfaction. Metropolitan scored 147 and had Alma 74 for seven (Hendricks 4-25; Volsteedt 3-28) when stumps were drawn.

At the end of the 1900/01 season, a South African side selected by Logan and captained by Bisset toured England. The former, who had been outspoken against the omission of Hendricks from the team that toured in 1894, had the opportunity to right the wrong, but failed to include Hendricks or any other coloured players in his side. The team he chose was one 'the local newspapers attacked … saying that it could not, or should not be, designated "the South African team"' since it was a private enterprise and that 'only six of the 14 players would have the ghost of a chance of playing for South Africa in a representative match'.[41] Such was the insensitive manner in which the side was assembled that the outstanding Henry Taberer was invited but not taken, while Logan selected his own son, J.D. Logan (junior) – 'a passenger who could only be used in an emergency'.[42]

E.J.L. Platnauer, writing in the *Cape Times*, criticised the venture because 'the warfare is far from over, in fact instead of men coming back, men are going forward'.[43] He felt the unrepresentative team was unfair to both the English public and South African cricket. He did express some satisfaction in 'the team not going Home as "South Africa" but as "the Hon J. D. Logan's South African team", a very different thing'.[44] Unfortunately, the tour was later misguidedly granted 'South African' status.

Logan was not unexpectedly lambasted for taking a side to England during the Anglo-Boer War. His captain, Murray Bisset, meanwhile complained bitterly in an interview with the English magazine, *Cricket: A Weekly Record of the Game*, that people at the Cape were losing interest in the game. The reason he gave was that 'there was no variety – the worst of it is that one always sees the same familiar faces, because we have so few clubs'.[45] It is difficult to comprehend how Bisset, a prime mover in denying coloured cricketers the chance to play at championship level at the Cape, could make such a statement without questioning the reason why. The irony of the situation was clearly lost on a man whose rigid adherence to the Western Province Cricket Union's racist policies had given influential support to a situation whereby the game's authorities not only denied talented cricketers the opportunity to participate at a higher level, but also lost the large crowds that followed coloured teams wherever they played. Moreover, at a time when Bisset was articled to a Cape Town legal firm and then admitted as an advocate of the Supreme Court, it apparently never once crossed his mind to question the lack of fair-mindedness shown towards Hendricks and other players of colour.

The Anglo-Boer War did not end until both sides met to sign the Treaty of Vereeniging in May 1902. Kitchener and the largest British army sent overseas – 450,000 – beat the Boers in the end, wrote historian Jan Morris, 'only by ruthless and laborious methods of attrition, burning their farms, herding their women and children into detention camps, and criss-crossing the entire countryside with interconnecting blockhouses'.[46] 'Altogether 27,927 Boers (the majority of them children) died in the British camps,' wrote Niall Ferguson. 'That was 14.5 per cent of the entire Boer population and they died mainly as a result of malnourishment and poor sanitation.'[47] Promises made by the British leaders were broken and there was bitter disappointment for coloureds and Africans who suffered huge casualties and were betrayed by the 'white man's' peace. Imperial rhetoric that the war had been fought to bring equal rights was a lie. Milner claimed his mistake had been to accept Clause 8 of the agreement, which postponed a decision on the question of granting the franchise to blacks until after the introduction of self-government. However, wrote S.B. Spies, 'in the Boer accounts, Milner had told Smuts and Hertzog on the question of the franchise for blacks, "I am at one with you"'.[48] And more to the point, if Milner was at one with the Boers, he was also at one with the mining industry, which had no reason at all to look for an extension of the Cape's non-racial franchise.

The African Political (later People's) Organisation was formed in September 1902 in order to support the coloured population. It was launched reluctantly, because coloured people saw the political dangers of setting themselves up as a 'racial' grouping that would play into the hands of those who wished to deny them political rights on racial grounds. Nonetheless, it was recognised that the erosion of their rights required a focused opposition.

Hendricks was conscious of his position during a period of political turmoil. In the aftermath of the Anglo-Boer War, cricket played a less important role in his life. This was largely inevitable insofar as the Metropolitan senior side had folded, and he represented the relatively low-profile Molteno CC in the mixed-race City Cricket League. On the work front, however, there was an important promotion for him on the railways. In 1904, he was appointed foreman in the locomotive workshop at Salt River, resulting in the family setting up home in Woodstock, first at 8 Junction Road and then at 7 Albert Road.[49] Salt River had become a booming industrial centre of Cape Town, inhabited by white and coloured working-class families. It owed its success to the steel and locomotive industries that grew rapidly as a result of the expansion of the rail network in the early 1900s.

Hendricks also had family commitments. In February 1903, his youngest child, Douglas John, died at 20 months following a two-week illness. His eldest daughter, Sophia, fell pregnant later in the year and gave birth to a son in January 1904. She married the father, John Rowland Trott, an English soldier, at St Luke's Church, Salt River, in May 1904. Hendricks would have been deeply aware of his children growing up and seeking opportunities in a changing South Africa. Having endured months of misery and despair at the hands of the cricket authorities, he must have agonised over where he stood in a deeply divided society. His children had been brought up to regard themselves as European, but the uncertainty of their situation had become more acute. In an increasingly divided land, Hendricks could well be separated from his family on the basis of colour.

The 1894 census had used the catch-all term 'coloured' to refer to all 'non-European' people, but ten years later, the 1904 census divided the Cape population into whites, coloureds and Africans. The divisions that emerged were reinforced through whites addressing the plight of their poorer families and extending segregation, while the coloureds reluctantly accepted a situation where they were forced to defend their position and claim preferential treatment over Africans. According to the *Cape Times*, the 1904 census posed inevitable questions with regard to race distinctions. It referred to the 'delicate grades which join the "European or white" to the "mixed and other" of the census returns' and pointed out that it was 'left to the people to decide to what race they belong'.[50] As a consequence, there was a tendency to swell the return of the white class as against the coloured.

Hendricks might have found it reasonably straightforward to register as a European for the 1904 census. Yet his position was a great deal more complex. He had played for Malay teams in the past and had told the truth as he saw it when writing to the press: 'My father was born of Dutch parents in Cape Town, and my mother hails from St Helena.'[51] It is likely that in 1894 Hendricks had no idea that a St Helenian mother would preclude him from playing for South Africa – after all, why should it? – no one had been banned before for having a St Helenian mother or for being mixed race as the issue hadn't arisen. He had, however, been concerned about the possible effects of being classed as Malay, as opposed to Christian, hence the content of his letter to the press in 1894.

Thereafter, and no doubt to his annoyance, he was referred to as 'Hendricks the coloured' or 'the coloured demon bowler'. A.B.

Tancred, for example, would never have been referred to as 'the white opening batsman'. Hendricks reacted by distancing himself from Malay cricket and electing to play for white teams when the opportunity arose. He no doubt hoped that his involvement with United Services, Woodstock and then Metropolitan would eventually lead to his being accepted by the cricket establishment. This ultimately proved futile. The sands of Cape politics were running against him with white cricketers fearing that he would destroy the Western Province and Cape Town CCs in championship matches, thus humiliating the establishment. If he had been allowed to play in the championship and had achieved success, it would have been accompanied by still louder calls for his inclusion in the South African side. And if they included Hendricks, what about the other up-and-coming coloured cricket talent whose performances would demand recognition? It was simply unacceptable to those administering the game.

After a decade of confronting the white cricket establishment, Hendricks decided on one last throw of the dice. In October 1904, at 47 years old, he wrote to the Western Province Cricket Union, applying to be allowed to take part in senior cricket. A meeting was held in late October to consider Hendricks's application, but there was little appetite for engaging with this troublesome issue yet again. The committee postponed the matter, presumably to consider in private how to deal with the content of his letter.

The next meeting of the Western Province Cricket Union met at Hands and Shore, an accountancy firm, on 16 November, the day after Hendricks's wife, Georgina, had given birth to their eleventh and last child. All the usual members were present except for Frank Robb and Vollie van der Byl. John Reid presided with his vice-president, Billy Simkins, in attendance. The clubs were represented by M. Bisset (Western Province CC), A. Mearns (Claremont), P. Cloete (Diocesan College), W. Kingon (Green Point), S. Horwood (Cape Town CC), J. Cormack (Cape Town CC), J. Bell (Alma) and F. Midgley (hon. secretary).

Reid was the key figure in the post-Milton cricket establishment. He had presided over the November 1897 meeting where it had been decided that Hendricks was not eligible to play for Woodstock in championship cricket. Reid's consistent views on the Hendricks issue inevitably reflected the segregationist political orthodoxy in the post-Rhodes environment. As the senior partner in a firm of government attorneys, he also maintained the closest of relationships with the colonial administration, following in Milton's and Rhodes's footsteps.

The *Cape Argus* reported on the meeting:

> A lengthy application was read from Hendricks, the well-known fast bowler to play in senior cricket matches. He held that he had played in friendly games but under the rules he had been debarred from playing in championship matches. He advanced various arguments for his admission, but the chief was that he was the son of European parents.[52]

It would appear Hendricks offered the perfect opportunity for the committee to save face and admit an error in his case. But, typically, Reid began the meeting by simply ignoring Hendricks's statement regarding his parentage and stating bluntly that 'there was a resolution in effect that colour was not permitted in matches under the auspices of the Western Province Cricket Union'.

Why did it take Hendricks until 1904 to formally claim European ancestry? This is puzzling given that the issue of his racial origins was the reason for the shocking treatment he had received for more than a decade. Possible clues to the timing lay in the census, Hendricks's promotion to foreman at the Salt River workshop, and to his concern that his family might be categorised as non-European and subjected to increasing efforts by the authorities to physically segregate the population along racial lines. In the contemporary environment, and as the walls threatened to close in on his personal life, he decided on a gamble. Thanks to the press, he was already one of the highest-profile 'coloureds' in the colony, but should the Western Province Cricket Union grant him permission to play championship cricket, his status as 'European' would be acknowledged. His friends, Frank Robb and William Kingon, may have encouraged this strategy.

Kingon, a long-time representative of Green Point CC, was the lone spokesman among the assembled delegates in favour of Hendricks's application. He had been present in 1897 when Robb requested that the fast bowler be allowed to play in the championship, but did not second the motion. Seven years later, Kingon supported Hendricks's application. Conscious that the cricketer's claim to be European might not be accepted, Kingon stated that Hendricks had pointed out that the law in question had already been broken. He 'instanced the case of Docks, which club, he stated, had a player that was scarcely qualified to compete in the Championship'. Kingon then asked the killer question: 'How was the line of colour to be drawn?'

Reid ignored the question as he had ignored Hendricks's claim. He was neither interested in references to the Docks player, nor prepared to be drawn into a debate. He maintained doggedly that 'there was no question in this particular case'. Determined to conclude the discussion as quickly as possible, he added resolutely: 'The applicant was debarred under the rules.'

Murray Bisset, who had also sat on the 1897 committee that had refused to rescind the anti-Hendricks resolution, said that 'any club could object to any man it felt was not qualified under the rules'. This response was startling, opening the door to a potential raft of objections with or without grounds, which the Western Province Cricket Union would be forced to adjudicate.

The circus continued with Simkins surprisingly suggesting that the issue be postponed yet again. He noted incorrectly that Metropolitan CC had made a previous application, when it was in fact Woodstock. He recalled the meeting, no doubt aware that his union had not handled it at all well and that the editor of the *Cape Times* had felt the need to respond by writing a detailed leading article. Seven years later, Simkins, who was in the process of making a tentative entry into politics, tried to play the part of a man who could make a reasoned judgement. He began by commenting that the application 'was an important question'. He said that 'Hendricks was a well-conducted man', before observing that it was 'important to know what was actually on the records of the Union'. He, of course, knew only too well what was there – the resolution that he had helped introduce – but 'thought it would be better if the matter was deferred until a later date, when the resolution arrived at, would be before the meeting'. Simkins was ignored. A delay might have enabled the press and public to have another opportunity to debate the issue. That was the last thing Reid wanted.

Bisset again took the floor. With what had become by now routine hypocrisy, he said he 'had always found Hendricks a very gentlemanly player, but they must be governed by the rules. If exception was made in this instance it would create a dangerous precedent, and he did not think they should make any exception.'

'Then in that case,' responded Kingon, 'Prince Ranjitsinhji, if he came out here, could not play championship cricket?'

'Yes, that is so,' said Reid, 'as the rules stand, and unless a special meeting were held, otherwise the law would stand.'

At this juncture, Bisset abruptly moved that the committee did not see its way clear to grant the application. One of the subordinates on duty, Mearns from Claremont, immediately seconded him. Kingon proposed as a forlorn amendment that a special exception be made to the rules in Hendricks's case while upholding the general principle, but even this received no seconder, and the Bisset motion was carried.

The *Cape Argus* concluded their report: 'Hendricks therefore cannot be allowed to participate in "competition" cricket.'

It is not certain whether Hendricks had aspirations of furthering his cricket at championship level, or whether he simply looked to use the Western Province Cricket Union – his perennial adversary – to enable him to get the fact that he was European into the public domain. This then begs the question as to whether Kingon had acted in self-interest, with the hope that Hendricks could play for Green Point in the championship, or whether he had been asked by Hendricks – or Robb – to front the request. Either way, the union officials were not going to co-operate and hid behind their resolution.

There was one more intriguing loose end. Kingon was anxious to have the agreement of the Western Province Cricket Union to a merger of the Green Point and Sea Point clubs. The union, usually hidebound by process and inclined to refuse such requests, agreed immediately. Was this part of a deal in return for Kingon's agreement to drop the Hendricks issue? In any event, the question of Hendricks's participation in the championship would not be on the Western Province Cricket Union agenda again, but he was certainly not finished on the pitch.

The intransigence of the cricket committee might have been expected. They held the opinion that Hendricks was coloured and were not prepared to reconsider the matter as outlined in his letter. For them to accept Hendricks in the championship would have been a huge loss of face, effectively an acknowledgement that they had committed a colossal and unimaginable error. The conduct of the meeting was unsatisfactory and its conclusion unsound, with no apparent discussion of the main points that Hendricks had raised. The refusal to consider his letter was particularly frustrating for the player. But he could be satisfied that the *Cape Argus* should publish his claim that his parents were both European and, more significantly, that it had not been addressed, let alone dismissed, or even questioned.

10

'Cricket under a cloud with no silver lining'

> 'Is the Western Province Cricket Union a real live governing body?'
>
> – *Cape Times* (10 November 1904)

THE DEBATE OVER Hendricks and the 'coloured question' did not end with the vote taken by the Western Province Cricket Union in November 1904. Their high-handed approach almost inevitably led to further problems. The odd behaviour at the meeting of Billy Simkins, a leading figure in Cape Town CC, gave rise to speculation that there were issues in club cricket still to be addressed by delegates. Unpleasant letters to the press from Louis Smuts, a long-serving member of Cape Town CC, followed the meeting. It seemed that Smuts was attempting to divert attention from his club's problems. He irritated Alma by complaining about their defensive cricket when they made no attempt to chase a target that Cape Town had set for them. He also put forward a controversial scheme that would see the colleges eliminated from a restructured championship.

The *Cape Times* expressed their concern over Smuts's irrational behaviour, stating that after all the years he had spent in many branches of sport, there was a danger of his becoming 'autocratic and almost despotic'.[1]

Letters from 'Longstop' to the *Cape Times* shaped the connection with the 'coloured question'. On 20 December 1904, the writer asked: 'If L.B. Smuts is anxious that his club [Cape Town] should lead in good form, why play a coloured man?'[2] It was evidently well known that Cape Town CC was fielding a coloured player in their side, thereby flouting the union's infamous 'Hendricks resolution' (Bye-law 10).

'Cover-point' then entered the argument. He had not seen Cape Town play that season and did not know the composition of their team, but he felt there was good reason to comment. 'If they are playing a coloured man, then how is it that Hendricks is debarred from playing in championship cricket ... There is no use bringing a rule into force without it being kept to the letter, as one is just as much entitled to the privilege as the other. Perhaps someone will explain ...?'[3]

The player under question – who had not as yet been named – was then selected to represent Western Province against Eastern Province in late December. It prompted Longstop to write again to the *Cape Times*. 'Was it pique,' he asked, 'that got the man into the Western Province team?' Then, eager to provoke the union into a response, he opined: 'Shades of Western Province cricket that we cannot raise 11 white men to represent us! We should certainly play Hendricks against Transvaal.'[4]

The *Cape Times* felt obliged to explain that Longstop was an old and devoted supporter of the game. He was, in fact, a former cricket writer with the *Cape Times* who had previously attended meetings of the Western Province Cricket Union and was familiar with the way it operated. In the current debate, the newspaper might have collaborated with Longstop in order to coerce the union into making a statement. It commented that 'perhaps [Longstop] did not adopt quite the nicest method of raising the coloured question again, but at any rate he raised it in such definite shape that we cannot see how it can fail to be brought before the Union again'.[5]

Longstop's correspondence was briefly discussed at a meeting of the Western Province Cricket Union on 10 January 1905. William Kingon thought that the union should investigate the matter, but Reid, who chaired the meeting, 'ruled that this could not be done'.[6] The chairman argued that the point had been made by an 'anonymous' member of the public and had not been submitted by a club via its delegate.

On 11 February, Longstop revealed himself as W.J.A. Wheeler and, while accepting the decision made by the union not to follow up, he was surprised that 'none of the clubs playing in the championship had sufficient courage to bring forward the question of Cape Town fielding a player who should have been excluded by Bye-law 10'.[7] Wheeler then proceeded to deal with Smuts's comment on dropping the colleges from the championship and whether Cape Town CC should be allowed to field a coloured player. He was of the opinion that the colleges were an invaluable nursery for Western Province cricket and that the reason Cape Town CC wanted to omit them from the championship was so that they could make use of college players to strengthen their team. He suggested that the club would be in a better position if the championship competition was dropped altogether, as they could then play as many coloured men as they chose.

Wheeler targeted Western Province cricket's corrupt administration in his criticism, asking whether the rules of a competition were to be broken with impunity. He felt certain 'that had a smaller club played the same man, that club would have been brought to book'. He was keen to emphasise that he had no objection against a coloured man as a cricketer, going on to explain:

> I think that Hendricks in particular (for the compulsory exclusion of whom, I believe, rule 10 was specifically passed), would be of great service to local cricket, owing to the excellence of his fast bowling, of which we have none too much.[8]

Four days later, on 15 February, the *Cape Times* commented on Wheeler's letter by naming the mystery player involved – George

Whitehead – and stating 'it once again brings into prominence the question of Whitehead's eligibility to play for the Cape Town CC in championship matches'. The cricket correspondent conceded that 'everybody is well aware that the question is an awkward and uncomfortable one', but he believed it had to be settled one way or the other:

> It is all very well to say that the matter has not been brought to the notice of the Union by one of the delegates. All delegates on the Union are perfectly well aware that Whitehead's eligibility has been questioned not only in the press but also in conversations by many cricketers and even delegates themselves. We venture to say that many delegates if not a majority of them find that the Union bye-law is being broken in deed and there can be no doubt that a great deal of discredit attaches to the Union among the outside public for their inertia in the matter… Whitehead's eligibility has been clearly questioned. Yet the Union shrinks the plain and positive duty of inquiring into the matter and deciding the issue.[9]

In calling for Whitehead's eligibility to be 'squarely faced', the *Cape Times* thought it was just another excuse on the part of the union 'to say that a very large and far-reaching question would be raised'. It was the same racist language that had been used when Hendricks was prevented from participating in representative cricket. The difference in the Whitehead situation, however, was that the union hoped to support his participation in all cricket by avoiding the controversy that the Hendricks ban had created. Such hypocrisy was obvious, with Whitehead appearing to receive special treatment because he was a Cape Town CC player who had coached and played the game overseas. In a strongly worded article, the *Cape Times* reminded the union of the key question that had been raised regarding Whitehead's eligibility: 'Is he a coloured professional under bye-law 10 or is he not?'[10]

At the same time, cricketer Stanley Horwood waded into the discussion. He had voted against Hendricks in November and was clearly unable to see the irony attached to his supporting Cape Town CC's decision to include Whitehead in their side. Horwood appeared to see himself as a spokesman for the union:

> Sir
>
> Kindly allow me a line in your columns to make one or two observations regarding the valuable advice offered by 'Longstop' to the Western Province Cricket Union over the playing of an alleged coloured man in Currie Cup and championship matches. Evidently 'Longstop' does not belong to any of the clubs in the Peninsula. If that is so, may I suggest that he join one forthwith, whereby his influence might be employed to better advantage than writing in attaining the objects he has at heart and then being afforded an opportunity of having his alleged grievance brought before the committee of the Union officially! As an alternative perhaps the Union might officially legislate and permit him to attend the meetings and give expression to his views as a representative of the public. In conclusion, I find some others will join me in sympathising with 'Longstop' that for nearly three years such a calamitous irregularity as he alleged has been allowed to continue without ever a dissenting voice from the public or from the controlling body of our local cricket. I am etc.
>
> S.E. Horwood[11]

Horwood's letter offered little more than a sarcastic attack on a man who dared criticise Cape Town CC. It did, however, reveal the bureaucratic structure that surrounded and safeguarded the hierarchy of the Western Province Cricket Union. A crucial factor in this situation was that the union had – since Milton first assumed control – been run by a clique that was propped up by clubs and delegates too fearful to challenge the 'big two'. The men from the Western Province and Cape Town cricket clubs who directed the union assumed an importance in all matters of a political nature, but failed miserably to develop the game in the area under their administration.

On 10 November 1904, the *Cape Times* had asked: 'Is the Western Province Cricket Union a real live governing body?' It was argued that a large number of clubs were affiliated to the union and several competitions conducted under its auspices, yet there were 'no fixed interval meetings, inadequate and unclear representation'. Clearly, the way in which Milton had directed affairs continued to prevail after he departed and, once again, the *Cape Times* was asking whether the union possessed the confidence and respect of the clubs. It then answered its own question, declaring: 'Cricket in the Western Province is under a cloud with no silver lining.' There was no new talent and no coaching, and the game had 'turned into a dreary business that will soon cause it to become as extinct as the dodo'.[12]

Not long after Whitehead's name was linked with Bye-law 10, another embarrassing situation emerged that was openly condemned by the press. The 'coloured question' over which the union had frequently floundered was complicated by their decision to organise a match between 'Professionals' and 'Amateurs'. The game was designed to replace the annual festival encounter between 'Mother Country' and 'Colonial-born', a contest in which Hendricks had never been allowed to play. It had always been the most prestigious event in the local programme, a major social occasion hosted by the Western Province CC, but the decline in the performances of the Mother Country team had rendered it uncompetitive. The replacement fixture was planned to be equally prestigious and modelled on the annual 'Gentlemen versus Players' match staged by the MCC. Profits would go to the Somerset Hospital.

Problems began when the professionals demonstrated their contempt for the Western Province Cricket Union's decisions and named both Hendricks and Whitehead in their side. In the lead-up to the match, the union held frantic meetings behind closed doors. Typically, they reacted by trying to devalue the fixture. Bisset and Horwood immediately became unavailable. So too did several other 'amateurs'; some allegedly acquiring injuries. The union then withdrew the event from Newlands, a venue that had always offered festival matches the necessary pomp and ceremony and was attended by the great and the good of Western Province society.

Instead, the fixture was moved to the windswept, bumpy and unpicturesque Green Point track. And, while it was initially scheduled (like the Mother Country versus Colonial-born fixture) over two consecutive Saturdays, it was moved to a Monday and Tuesday, minimising the likely attendance.

The 'Professionals' team for the fixture to be played on 6 and 7 March 1905 was announced as: King, Killick, Holland, Vogler, Whitehead, Middleton, Richards, Pate, Smith, Hendricks and Light (captain). The 'Amateurs' fielded a number of players who had or would play first-class cricket, namely Douglas Davies, Harrie Coggins, Allan Reid, Mick Commaille, Sibley 'Tip' Snooke, Harold 'Paddy' Carolin (captain) and Arnold 'Saturday' Knight, with the last two named famous for their deeds as rugby Springboks. Carolin, who would be Paul Roos's vice-captain on the historic 1906/07 rugby tour to the United Kingdom, won the toss and his side made a confident start. Vogler and Middleton opened the bowling, followed by Whitehead and King.

The amateurs had reached 151 for five when, said the *Cape Times*, 'Hendricks replaced Killick at the bottom end and the high rate of scoring at once stopped, the new bowler's fast deliveries giving trouble ... with his first ball in his next over Hendricks got past O'Reilly's defences. 158-6.' The powerful Knight arrived at the wicket and, after driving Hendricks to the off boundary, he opened his shoulders in the next over from Pate smashing 4, 4, 6, 4, 4, 6 – 'as fine a piece of hitting as has yet been seen on the Green Point track'. It lifted the amateurs to 245 all out. Middleton's 4-69 in 15 overs proved to be the best bowling return; the remaining wickets being shared, with Hendricks taking 1-27 in five overs. The Professionals then made 287, of which King contributed a majestic 160, leaving the Amateurs a limited period in which to bat a second time. It gave Hendricks an opportunity to open the bowling with Middleton, but he was probably trying too hard and did not do full justice to the occasion: '10-up was long in coming, the bowling being too good to take liberties with. Hendricks was bowling fast enough but there was little variety or headwork in his deliveries ...'[13]

For Hendricks, his chance of playing in such a prestigious representative match had come too late. He was already a grandfather with a full-time job playing in a team of professional county and international players. That he was asked to play was nonetheless a huge tribute to him and his reputation, and he had his moments in the match. The real disappointment was that the contest was not the showpiece it should have been. The Western Province Cricket Union was severely criticised for its incompetence. 'Some strong comment has been made,' reported the *Cape Times*, 'on the lack of support shown for the Amateurs versus Professionals fixture … the want of support was due to the hastiness of preparation and mismanagement.' Nothing was heard of the match until three days before it was due to be played and, said the report, 'the management would have done far better if they had secured the Western Province ground'. The union had not made it clear that the proceeds were to be devoted wholly to charity, namely the Somerset Hospital. 'Further,' commented the newspaper, 'Monday and Tuesday were about the most inconvenient days for the general public … taking all into account the result is not altogether surprising.'[14]

This was not incompetence; it was deliberate sabotage. The union's fears over the 'coloured question' had clearly tipped the whole administration over the edge, a situation that had begun with the receipt of Hendricks's application to play championship cricket in November 1904. The decision to turn the match at Green Point into a low-key event was yet another step towards entrenching segregation and further emphasised how low the union was prepared to stoop in order to deal with the Hendricks factor and to keep the 'coloured question' under control. That the Somerset Hospital was to be the beneficiary did not interest Reid and his committee in the course of their decision-making.

As Hendricks made his way home to 7 Albert Road in Woodstock, he might have pondered his cricket career and his future. He had appeared on a representative stage for the first time in a decade and had been able to give a good account of himself, bowling with pace and fire. Although at an advanced age in cricket terms, he knew he was still capable of performing at a reasonably high level. But the hostility of the cricket establishment had been unrelenting. The reaction by the Western Province Cricket Union regarding his application for inclusion in the championship on the grounds of his European origins was, if anything, more aggressive than on previous occasions. They showed no interest in considering, examining or testing this new information, rather choosing to ignore it with disdain. The support of his fellow cricketers in selecting him for a representative team was gratifying, but the union's actions in undermining their own fixture suggested that the extraordinary patience Hendricks had shown for more than a decade was fundamentally misplaced. He was the victim of an ideological vendetta.

The union ignored him, but they also ignored the involvement of other coloured cricketers playing for Docks, Simon's Town and, most compelling of all, Cape Town CC. The central figure was his team-mate in the professional side – George Whitehead – who was considered by a number of observers, not least the *Cape Times*, to be coloured, and Hendricks must have wondered, perhaps bitterly, at the differential treatment he received. Whitehead was born in Cape Town in June 1882, perhaps as part of the mixed-race community of strawberry farmers at Palmboom near Newlands. He was a promising left-hand bat and a left-arm fast-medium bowler who had impressed in the Newlands nets and become a protégé of Walter Richards, the old Warwickshire professional and Western Province CC coach, in 1899.

Richards took the promising Whitehead with him to England with a view to his joining the ground staff at Warwickshire and qualifying to play county cricket. He may have taken this step, as Buck Llewellyn had done a little earlier, to avoid any awkward issues about his racial background and perhaps sidestep the possible application of Bye-law 10. Whitehead coached at King Edward's School, Birmingham, and played a single first-class game for Warwickshire against W.G. Grace's London County in 1902, scoring a single run and failing to take a wicket. He returned to Cape Town in time for the start of the 1904/05 season. He immediately signed with Cape Town CC and became a mainstay of their attack, and of Western Province in Currie Cup and representative matches against the English tourists in 1905/06. His long first-class career as an opening bowler and lower-order batsman lasted from 1904/05 to 1920/21, encompassing 29 first-class matches for Western Province and Griqualand West. He claimed five wickets in an innings seven times and ten in a match twice, taking 118 wickets at the commendable average of 18.88.

Whitehead's bowling statistics at first-class level indicate that he was an above-average cricketer. He played an important role for Western Province in the period before 1910 when the region's bowling resources were particularly thin, and his lively left-arm deliveries fizzed disconcertingly off the Newlands mat. The furore that accompanied the debate in the *Cape Times* as to Whitehead's position in the championship faded quickly. He was not subjected to a Bye-law 10 investigation, and he managed to avoid the dehumanising treatment suffered by Hendricks. The inevitable question arises as to whether Whitehead should have played for South Africa but did not because of discrimination at national as opposed to provincial level. While there is no direct evidence to suggest he was debarred from selection, calls for his inclusion in the side to play against Johnny Douglas's 1913/14 MCC tourists were not acted on by the selectors. Interestingly, Whitehead was the only player in Luckin's cricket history who remained without an initial throughout, despite the presence of many other professionals, including C.B. Llewellyn.

Whitehead's case was deemed to be different from that of Hendricks. It was essentially a matter of class. Hendricks, whatever his background, had come from the Malay community and had played for a primarily Malay team, going so far as to represent the Cape Malay XVIII. His fate was sealed, whatever the reality of his position, once the Cape began to unravel its class-based liberal tradition and reinforce the relationship between class and race. The events of the 1890s made Hendricks's cricket ostracism part of a broader political agenda.

No matter what community Whitehead might have originally come from, he had no obvious Malay ties and spent some of his formative cricket years at 'Home' under the patronage of a Western Province CC professional. On his return, he was accepted straight into Cape Town CC, one of the two big clubs and a forum through which Hofmeyr, Simkins and Smuts wielded sufficient power to deter Western Province CC or any of the smaller clubs from mounting a challenge. As Murray Bisset announced at the Western Province Cricket Union meeting in 1904, it was open to the clubs to raise concerns against individuals as to where the line of colour was to be drawn. Even then, the union's hierarchy could decide whether or not it wanted to discuss the issue, as Kingon discovered when he requested they investigate Whitehead's position. In the end, the union may have learnt that while Bye-law 10 was a safety valve and deterrent to ensure that establishment cricket remained essentially white, it was a good idea to turn a blind eye in the case of Whitehead and others. They did not need to create more Hendricks-type *cause célèbres*. Whitehead, in later years, became the groundsman at Alma CC's Rhodes Recreation Ground in Mowbray. And, in another of history's record of coincidences, he was to die like Hendricks in the same place – Mowbray – and in the same year – 1940.

By the end of March 1905, shortly after the 'Amateurs' had played the 'Professionals', it was clear that the Western Province Cricket Union was in disarray. The next meeting saw both the president (Reid) and the vice-president (Simkins) absent, despite the critical issue on the agenda of whether Diocesan College and the South African College should be dropped from the championship.[15] Godfrey Cripps was elected to the chair and Smuts from Cape Town CC provided background details to the thorny question. He claimed to have been brought in 'by certain gentlemen' to play a leading role in cricket legislation. He had since received a characteristic letter from Allan Reid, which was distinctly lacking in courtesy, followed by further letters from Paddy Carolin, a Bishops spokesman, and the South African College, where Smuts's name had been removed from several honorary positions. Smuts's motion was nevertheless carried by a vote of five to four, despite protests from Kingon that Cripps had voted as a delegate and then made the casting vote. Two long-standing sides in senior cricket were thus excluded, prompting the South African College delegate to lament 'the death of college cricket'. The colleges felt cheated by the political machinations of the union.[16] They had, after all, backed it loyally for many years, and the South African College had won the championship as recently as 1900.

Delegates from the two colleges had also been conspicuous in denying opportunities to Hendricks, perhaps partly because he had frequently made deep inroads into their batting. But in late 1905, it no longer really mattered, as Hendricks was in the last phase of his cricket career, not as fearsome as he had previously been, but still able to revel in the satisfaction of once being the fastest bowler in the land. He stood out among cricketers, both as an imposing figure physically and as a player around whom the game's authorities and the press had – wittingly or unwittingly – bestowed an aura of superhuman achievement. For the members of his community, there was also the martyrdom of his being sacrificed by the colonial authorities on the altar of white supremacy.

The crowds came to see him bowl in a way in which they would come to see no one else. He was still a huge drawcard in his twilight years, especially in Woodstock; a towering figure within a changing landscape. Cape Town in mid-decade was, like the rest of the subcontinent, mired in depression as the slow reconstruction of the mining industry and the economy as a whole stumbled over problems of inadequate investment, immigration and labour. *The Cape* reported that Woodstock had become 'a town of factories, of workmen's houses, of middle-class shops and rival church spires ... [with] ugly and irreverent surroundings'. The depression had turned its once rural character into a galvanised-iron town left to the mercy of the south-easter that has always had such an impact on the region. The magazine might have touched on the way the strong, persistent wind had once swept ominously over the cricket field, intensifying the threat of Hendricks's bowling and creating havoc among visiting batsmen. The windblown Albert Road, where Hendricks lived, was characteristic of the enveloping depression with 'its uneven and shabby houses, its dusty little huckster shops and its occasional waste spaces strewn with rubbish; the tin-roofed cottages with advertisements painted on their walls; the black mass of gas works’.[17]

Amid the changing, deteriorating environment of his community, Hendricks played on. Politically, his position was pivotal to any discussion about cricket’s ‘coloured question’. The Western Province Cricket Union might have established control over leading coloured players by describing them as professional, but, in Hendricks’s case, he had already built a reputation. He did so even while cricket writers and the public questioned the failure of the press to produce match reports covering his games. Such was his ability that he rose above the discrimination of the union and the bias of their officials in the selection of representative teams.

There were more letters to the Cape press, commentaries and leading articles on the Hendricks phenomenon than about any other issue in the game for more than a decade. Hendricks suffered an endless series of painful and humiliating rebuffs, but he kept his dignity and remained a thorn in the side of the imperialist establishment that controlled Cape cricket. Some years earlier, Frank Robb had informed the union that it was their task to encourage cricket and not to adopt the role of judging a man’s social position. They stubbornly ignored the advice, believing that a ‘resolution’ would defend them against any possibility of Hendricks infiltrating their ranks and embarrassing them and their players. And when he did, they huddled together at the Thatched Tavern to discuss ways to bolster their defence system and prevent precious products of the Western Province and Cape Town cricket clubs from being exposed to his demon deliveries. They feared him, even when he was nearly 50 years old, and they spitefully refused to consider even his claim that he was in fact European. Such uncompromising behaviour robbed them of Hendricks’s talents and set up the self-inflicted debacle over the match between the professionals and amateurs at Green Point. At every stage, an inflexible and insensitive cricket establishment revealed its obsession with power and political manipulation, as well as an inability to understand the social or cricket implications of the decisions they were making.

By March 1905, those involved in Western Province cricket were conscious of the fact that for some five months the administration of the game had reeled almost uncontrollably from one crisis to another. There was a need to stabilise the situation, for those in authority to make concessions and for the press to project a positive image of cricket to the public. It was no easy task in a period of political turmoil amid a depression, and when the strength of the game had moved to the Transvaal. In responding to the prevailing difficulties, the *Cape Argus* chose to conclude a chaotic season by projecting a sense of optimism during its coverage of the Currie Cup Final played between Western Province and Transvaal in late March 1905. The newspaper endeavoured – despite the inevitable whiff of racism – to paint a picture of an appreciative crowd at Newlands:

> To stroll around the ground when play was in progress was a liberal education, and though the attendance of ordinary matches does not support this view, it is astounding to find that such a large population of the splendid audience take such a rational interest in the king of games. From his Grace the Archbishop and the General Commanding the Forces, to the fez-crowned Malays who made the trees near the entrance their own particular pitch, it was a typical cricket gathering, a crowd that came to see cricket and that applauded every good piece of play – and the game abounded with them – with delightful impartiality. It came for a long day of cricket – close upon three thousand of all classes – it saw excellent batting, smart and accurate fielding, and bowling such as is rarely seen when there is a long day in the field.[18]

Over the next few months, the Western Province Cricket Union escaped further drama over the 'coloured question'. There were a number of factors that contributed to this state of affairs. The first was that Hendricks was no longer playing for one of their clubs. The second reason was that leading figures in cricket met behind the scenes and seemed to reach agreement on matters that might have provoked further controversy. Simkins and Robb appeared to lead negotiations that brought relief to those players of colour currently involved in the game, although there was no fair-minded long-term solution in the way the arrangement played out. Robb, who was back playing cricket for Docks, arrived at a general agreement with Simkins, whereby those cricketers who had received humiliating coverage in the press would in future be treated with the respect they deserved. The issue was possibly sealed in February 1906 when Simkins invited Robb to play for the Simkins XI against Attridge's XI at Newlands.

There was little that they could do for Hendricks. He was too high profile and the attitudes of the Western Province Cricket Union – of which Simkins continued to be a leading figure – would not go far beyond the arrangements that were made. The union would in fact continue their efforts to ensure that cricket within their jurisdiction remained exclusively white. This was evident in the selection of Bisset as president in the 1907/08 season and from 1911 to 1913, and Van der Byl from 1914 to 1927. Attitudes hardened under their direction. The bye-laws of the Western Province Cricket Union were published in an 'Official Handbook' to reveal a change from coloureds being prevented from playing in championship matches to a new ruling that stated: 'No coloured professionals or members shall be allowed to compete in any matches under the jurisdiction of the Union.'

Hendricks's cricket in the white domain had been controversial and exciting. Where there was unpleasantness, it occurred in gatherings of the union hierarchy and not on the field of play. His cricket was characterised by a mutual respect from all the population groups, everyone who played or followed the game appreciating the fact that they had witnessed an exceptional player. When J.J. 'Boerjong' Kotzé began making a name for himself as the South African opening bowler, a letter to the *Cape Times* in December 1905 prompted debate over whether he was faster than Hendricks.[19]

11

'The great and mighty Hendricks'

> 'Mr H. Hendricks in his day was probably the fastest bowler South Africa has ever produced.'
>
> – *Cape Argus* (26 March 1915)

WHEN METROPOLITAN CC withdrew from senior cricket at the end of the 1900/01 season, Krom Hendricks joined one of Cape Town's newly formed mixed-race leagues. He had little choice, because he was barred as a 'coloured' from playing in the Western Province Cricket Union's senior championship by Bye-law 10 and from the Peninsula Cricket League by Rule 3. The exclusion of such a high-profile player served as a warning to clubs in the Western Province, although Hendricks was the only cricketer ever to be barred from the establishment's competitions. Calls for Bye-law 10 to be applied in the case of George Whitehead were ignored by the Western Province Cricket Union. While Rule 3 was used in the case of William Robertson and Thomas Hering, a higher authority subsequently overturned the decision. Whitehead went on to become a key bowler for Cape Town CC and Western Province, and the Robertson brothers – with Peter often conspicuous – joined Wasps, another affiliate of the Peninsula Cricket League. It did not mean that the cricket establishment had changed its views and there was no longer discrimination against those players who were not white. Assumptions of white English moral authority still prevailed in the first part of the twentieth century, but those who directed the game feared another 'Hendricks affair'.

One other cricketer had been the subject of a resolution at the Cape during this time. South African player and Boer soldier Charles Fichardt was accepted as a member of Western Province CC in October 1900, but the decision was opposed soon afterwards. At a meeting that was hurriedly called, a committee member, Ivor Difford, objected to Fichardt's membership and proposed that 'no prisoners of war should be allowed to play cricket down here'. The *South African News* was keenly following Fichardt's story and reported that, 'to the eternal disgrace of the Western Province club, Mr Difford's proposal was carried'. It was left to the club secretary, Harry Hands, to write to Fichardt:

> ...I had spoken to Mr Chiappini, your proposer, and I had hoped he would have communicated to you what is somewhat unpleasant. When you were elected it was not known to the committee that you were here on parole and the committee have passed a resolution that no Boer prisoners on parole shall be eligible for membership of the club. The resolution was passed at the first meeting of the committee subsequent to your election.[1]

The *South African News* then chose to embarrass the club by noting it was 'common talk in cricket circles at the time that the motion did not emanate really from Mr Difford but that Mr [James] Logan was understood to be responsible for it. This was done in the name of sport – a monstrous and unheard-of thing.' The article, written by 'Dux', added: 'The result has been that one of South Africa's finest cricketers has been debarred from playing down here because he was true to his country!' Dux concluded with the taunt, 'We all know that Mr Difford has been asked to manage Mr Logan's team overseas [the 1901 tour to England].'[2]

Western Province CC members – John Reid, Murray Bisset, Vollie van der Byl and other committee luminaries – found themselves in an awkward position over passing a resolution that prevented a white cricketer from playing the game. The decision was not unanimous, which enabled a club member, Bennie Wallach, to force the committee to reconsider the resolution in Fichardt's favour. As a result, the decision was overturned. Committee members were no doubt conscious that Fichardt was influential, being a prominent anti-imperialist and successful businessman. His family had hosted Emily Hobhouse, the British pro-Boer humanitarian, during her campaign to expose the conditions of the concentration camps built to incarcerate Boer women and children. Given the situation, and with the war not yet over, it is surprising that a cricket match was subsequently arranged where Van der Byl's XI played Fichardt's XI at Newlands in February 1902. Pelham Warner, a leading figure in English cricket tours that promoted imperial solidarity, played for Van der Byl's side, and George Whitehead, who would become central to the colour controversy, was selected for Fichardt's team.[3] Whitehead, who had been outstanding for Cape Town CC during the 1901/02 season, was going up to the Rand, but had changed his mind and was about to head overseas for the purpose of qualifying for Warwickshire.[4]

Hendricks in the meantime joined Molteno CC. Despite his age, he was keen to keep playing the game competitively, and the newly formed, predominantly coloured City Cricket League, which staged matches over successive Saturdays, offered him this opportunity. He understood the workings of cricket in the Western Province better than most. He had maintained his links with cricketers in Bo-Kaap and had played whenever he could for the mixed-race City CC during the 1890s. At the same time, he often represented 'white' clubs at Newlands, where the establishment believed he posed a challenge to the government's segregationist policies. Hendricks was therefore familiar with the complex nature of a process that resulted in coloured people going their own way in establishing separate cricket structures. The development was consistent with the lead set by coloured politicians who had previously rejected ethnic organisations, fearing their chances of assimilation into European society would be affected if they did not provide support for white politicians. When it became obvious that white politicians were not going to accommodate their aspirations, they began to organise along ethnic lines 'to provide a springboard by which the group could launch its campaign for inclusion in the white society'.[5] The whole question of colour was capable of considerable fluidity subject to social priorities and perceptions at the time.

Inter-town and inter-colony tournaments had been organised by black cricketers along similar lines to the white Champion Bat and Currie Cup. The first of six 'Native' inter-town tournaments was staged in 1884/85. The first 'Malay' tournament was held in 1889/90, with Hendricks playing in the fourth (1891/92) and fifth (1892/93) competitions. By 1897/98, seven Malay tournaments had been played. At that stage, the Barnato Memorial Trophy was presented in honour of the mining entrepreneur, and a new competition superseded the African and Malay inter-town tournaments. Western Province became the inaugural champions in 1898/99, prior to the tournament being temporarily halted by the Anglo-Boer War.

The South African Coloured Cricket Board was formed in 1903, primarily to administer the provincial competitions that were being arranged. Its constitution took an important political step forward in setting out a specific non-racial agenda and stating that it did 'not recognise any distinction amongst the various sporting peoples of South Africa, whether by creed, nationality or otherwise'.[6] The Western Province Coloured Cricket Union was affiliated to the national body and renewed its involvement in the Barnato Memorial Trophy tournaments, winning three of the next four competitions – in 1903/04, 1907/08 and 1912/13 – prior to the advent of the First World War.

Hendricks continued to make himself unavailable for coloured representative teams that were selected for the Barnato tournaments. He had pursued this strategy since the 1892/93 Malay tournament in order to keep open his links with establishment cricket. This arrangement was maintained when he began playing in the non-racial City Cricket League, although the liberal environment of the league allowed him some flexibility.

Cricket was an integral part of the lives of the coloured people at the Cape, and within a short time, Western Province sub-unions were formed. The Cape District Cricket Union was the first, founded in 1900, with its sides contesting the Bailey Shield, named after the member of the Legislative Assembly for Woodstock, Amos Bailey. The union possessed splendid grounds at Mowbray, and under the grand old oaks one could hardly find a more pleasant spot to watch cricket in the whole peninsula. The City Cricket League followed in 1901 with teams having a strong Christian identification. In the first few years, the league attracted Molteno, Providence, Thistles, Nil Desperandums, Sea Point, Advance, St Augustine, Fernwood and Crusaders. Before long, there were other suburban and district sub-unions in a thriving cricket environment that saw the establishment of the Zeeman Cup as an inter-board competition.

Many of the clubs that played in the different leagues had been in existence for some years. Molteno CC was probably the oldest of the clubs that joined the City Cricket League. It had played mid-week and Saturday matches at Varney's Corner, Green Point, since the early 1890s, relying largely on the support of 'old boys' of Zonnebloem College. The club was formed by Sir James Tennant Molteno, a fine all-round sportsman who had represented Cape Town at the third Champion Bat tournament in Port Elizabeth in 1884/85. In the course of the match against Kimberley, Molteno made the second highest score of 31 and his team-mate, Frank Robb – Hendricks's prominent supporter both on and off the field – followed up by taking 4-4 to help set up a notable victory for Cape Town.

Sir James, a barrister, and his 18 siblings were an influential family that held positions of responsibility in business and government. Their father, Sir John Molteno, the first prime minister of the Cape Colony, had married three times; his first wife, the coloured daughter of a merchant colleague, died tragically in childbirth. Sir James, who became the first speaker of the South African National Assembly, entered the Cape Parliament in 1890 at 25 years old, when he sat on the backbenches with Hofmeyr. He and his siblings formed a strong anti-imperialist group that not only opposed Milner's efforts to take South Africa into the Anglo-

Boer War, but thereafter also endeavoured to expose the malpractices that took place under British martial law. In the years that followed the war, the Molteno family supported John X. Merriman in his efforts to extend the Cape's 'qualified franchise' across South Africa, but they were opposed by the Milner reconstruction administration and the alliance between the British government and the mining industry, which sacrificed the rights of the non-white population in the interests of unification and gold. With two brothers in the Cape Parliament, a sister who worked closely with Olive Schreiner and Emily Hobhouse, and Percy Molteno an active Liberal MP in Britain, the family remained deeply involved in South African politics for many years. They were closely associated with John Tengo Jabavu, editor of *Imvo Zabantsundu*, while Percy publicly supported and donated large sums of money to the fundraising activities of Sol Plaatje, John Dube and the fledgling African National Congress.

St Augustine CC is probably the most famous of the early city clubs. The Reverend Sidney Warren Lavis, who would become dean of the Diocese of Cape Town, founded it in September 1899 and named it after the theological college at which he had studied. He had suggested the formation of a cricket club because he was concerned by the lack of activities for the youth of that time. The various club meetings were held in the St Paul's schoolroom and it was there that members elected their patron, His Grace the Archbishop, and vice-patron, Archdeacon Thomas Fothergill Lightfoot.

The strongest side in the City League in its early years was usually Crusaders, but Molteno had some hard-fought encounters against them. In early 1904, Crusaders defeated Molteno by 3 runs – 65 and 62 against 64 and 60 – with Krom Hendricks picking up seven wickets across the two innings and top-scoring with 27 in the first innings. A year later, he put Molteno in a good position by taking the first six wickets to fall in the Crusaders' total of 79 and another three in their second innings. But when Molteno batted, Hendricks was dismissed for a 'pair' and his team-mates offered little resistance in a match lost outright by 71 runs. Hendricks enjoyed his cricket among the community where he felt most at home and where his efforts on the field still had considerable impact. Where match reports appeared over his two seasons with Molteno, it seemed the old bowling menace was still there. On one occasion, he returned an analysis of 8-31 playing against East End at Green Point in a non-league encounter, enabling his team to win by 12 runs.

Press coverage was sketchy for teams that included players of colour, but the *Cape Times* did provide the City Cricket League with a regular service in terms of team lists for the Saturday matches. Details of 'mixed-race' matches would appear under 'Other Games' and follow the Senior Championship, the Reserve or League Championship, the Junior Championship (suburban and town sections), the Pennant Championship, the Merchants' League and white 'Friendlies' in a definite pecking order. The details of some 40 fixtures were listed every week, most with team lists, which involved recording well over 800 names in matches on Saturdays. The information provided included details of the venue, with most sides having been allocated grounds at Green Point, as well as starting times (2.45 or 3 p.m.) and, where necessary, train departure times. In later years, the *Cape Times* listed the coloured teams within their respective leagues and under relevant headings, but there were few scores published after the weekend's cricket. Western Province CC continued to dominate the sports pages, invariably reported first and in considerable detail. Over the week, other scorecards and reports appeared, sometimes for even the most insignificant games, such as Wagon-makers versus Boilermakers, Rondebosch I Zingari versus Urban Police, and Railways Second XI versus Railways Third XI. The Merchants' League received generous attention with matches such as Stuttafords versus Jaggers or Chemists versus Cleghorns reported at length.

Through brief references allocated to the City Cricket League, it can be established that Hendricks left Molteno prior to the 1905/06 season and joined Crusaders, a club that used one of Green Point's grounds, marked '1 to 17'. It is not clear what personal or perhaps career reasons encouraged Hendricks to switch to his erstwhile rivals, but it was obvious that he would further strengthen the champion club. When Molteno played Crusaders on 10 and 17 February 1906, they fielded A. Hendricks, P. Hendricks and S. Hendricks in a match dominated by Krom Hendricks who took 12-25 in helping Crusaders to victory by five wickets.

The *Cape Times* noted that Hendricks was named captain of Crusaders in 1906/07. There were fixtures against St Augustine, Providence, Sea Point, Roslin College, East Maidens and Green Rose, with the side also travelling by train to play Robertson, a farming centre situated more than 150 kilometres inland. One incident that gained prominent coverage was when Hendricks, wittingly or otherwise, got caught up in a dispute between Crusaders and St Augustine that spilled over into the pages of the *Cape Times*. There was a lack of clarity over whether a game had to finish at 6.30 p.m. as scheduled or whether the umpires had the power to continue it for a further 15 minutes if one side had a chance of victory. 'Mickey' wrote in to complain that although the umpires had agreed to another 15 minutes, the Crusaders captain (Hendricks) had taken his team off the field at 6.30. St Augustine refused to acknowledge a draw and appealed. 'The talk of my club being unfairly treated,' said Mickey, 'is thoroughly in accordance with an impression prevalent (especially since they have been identified with this league) with the members of the Crusaders – that because they have the great and mighty Hendricks playing for them, they have the right to bully the league and that all things should be done to their way of thinking.'[7] Several other correspondents supported Mickey, and the captain of Sea Point wrote in to say that Crusaders had themselves batted on beyond 6.30 to 6.40 p.m. in their match in a bid to force victory.[8] The issue created a flood of correspondence that unfortunately was not published. Ironically, the story comes almost full circle – Hendricks's alleged offence was exactly that with which William Milton was accused in his autocratic days as captain of Western Province CC.

Hendricks played regularly for Crusaders in the City Cricket League over the next seven seasons. He was captain for a couple of seasons, although the honour was shared and thereafter given to J. Francis, F. Wilkinson, F. Elliott, J. Benting and R. Kayter, each for a season or longer. Scores were published for a fixture against Sea Point on 8 October 1907, a week before Hendricks celebrated his fiftieth birthday. It was a good match for him as he struck 20 and recorded a match analysis of 9-31 in a Crusaders victory by 34 runs (43 and 133 versus 65 and 77). Of further interest is that during the 1907/08 season, and then again a year or two later, the initial 'W' was used when referring to Hendricks in team lists. This was unusual because he had been referred to as 'H. Hendricks' over a period of nearly 30 years. This was evidence of a belated realisation that the correct form of his name was 'W.H.' Hendricks.

By the 1908/09 season, the City Cricket League comprised Crusaders, St Paul's, Molteno, St Augustine, Thistles, Sea Point and Providence, with fixtures structured on a home-and-away basis. Clubs also had 'B' teams that were engaged in a separate league. There was a strong nucleus of clubs with one or two changes occurring every so often. In 1909/10, East Ends joined the league and both Molteno and Thistles dropped out. Thistles returned in 1910/11 to re-establish a seven-team league, with the same teams participating in 1911/12. At the end of that season, Providence and St Paul's withdrew, but Surrey joined the league, which was reduced to six teams for 1912/13 and 1913/14. Naming sides after English counties was not uncommon and other coloured leagues featured Yorkshire, Derbyshire and Warwickshire. The various communities followed the English county championship, sometimes through links they had with visiting professionals. The City League also continued to stage benefit matches for professionals, and when the long-serving Bonnor Middleton died in December 1913, a fixture was played to aid the widow and family of the cricketer. On that occasion, Hendricks played for G.B. Fox's XI against Stephen Reagon's XI at the Caledon ground in Mowbray, a match which the African Political Organisation's newspaper, *APO*, said also featured 'Geo Whitehead and several other prominent cricketers'.[9]

By December 1913, the Western Province Coloured Cricket Union was flourishing, probably at the height of its power before the First World War. At its fourth annual meeting held at St Paul's School, the chairman, Robert Hoedemaker, was able to announce that the organisation encompassed the City Cricket League, the Metropolitan and Suburban Union, the Claremont and Districts

Union and the Cape District Union. Applications for affiliation were also read out and accepted from the Wednesday Cricket Union, the Stellenbosch and District Cricket Union and the Drakenstein Cricket League. The inter-union competition for the Zeeman Cup gave players from the various organisations a chance to become involved in representative cricket. With the governing body becoming increasingly significant, it was able to announce an impressive list of officials:

> Patron: Hon W.P. Schreiner [who was both active and generous]
> Vice-patrons: Advocate M. Alexander MLA, Sir John Graham K.C.M.G., Harry Hands, Rev S.W. Lavis and John Parker [mayor of Cape Town]
> President: Dr A. Abdurahman
> Vice-presidents: J. Zeeman, J. Luyt, J. Reagon, H. Smith, J. Fredericks, S.F. Geyer, H. Hendricks, H. Hartog and N.C. Karsten
> Chairman: R. Hoedemaker
> Secretary: H.B. Reagon
> Treasurer: H. Viret
> Assistant secretary: A. Reagon[10]

The election of Krom Hendricks as vice-president was well received, yet difficulties were ever-present and, at the annual meeting in November 1914, it was observed that the City Cricket League had withdrawn from the South African Coloured Cricket Board. *APO* stated sarcastically: 'We wonder why? Perhaps they have got tired of trying to get up any higher on the log [Zeeman Cup] – they ended at the bottom last year. Why not try again?'[11] The breakaway was part of ethnic and religious differences, as well as leadership tensions, within the communities. It was also an early example of a broader problem that would characterise South Africa's black cricket organisations in years to come. Not long before, *APO* had warned the South African Coloured Cricket Board that it could never be fully representative of coloured cricket until the authorities overcame 'a narrow-minded section of coloured cricketers whose grounds for objection against the establishment of the Board is based on religion and other absurd notions'.[12] It did not help that the increasing influence of the government's policy of segregation had filtered into everyday life and reinforced separate sporting organisations.

Hendricks continued as a vice-president of the Western Province Coloured Cricket Union, with further honours coming his way. At the end of the 1914/15 season, he was asked to select and play for an invitation side in a match staged at the Green Point track over two Saturdays in aid of the Central Good Hope Red Cross Society. In promoting the game, the *Cape Argus* noted that 'Mr H. Hendricks in his day was probably the fastest bowler South Africa has ever produced'.[13] According to the *Cape Times*, 'the teams were led by Mr H Hendricks (the South African fast bowler) and Mr G M Stephen of the Green Point club'.[14] The team for which Hendricks was responsible was selected from some of the best players in the City Cricket League and the Western Province Coloured Cricket Union. Stephen's side contained prominent players from the white leagues.

Stephen's XI (188 and 123) had the better of the drawn game against Hendricks's XI (75 and 57 for three), but the result was of secondary importance. The *Cape Argus* recorded the match as having been 'a most praiseworthy charity event' with play of the keenest standard between 'two representative 11s, one white and the other coloured'.[15] Hendricks did not bowl and, as opening batsman, was dismissed for a duck. 'But,' said the *Argus*, 'Hendricks, whose reputation as a fast bowler is known throughout South Africa, distinguished himself by cleverly catching Arthur Burmeister [the rugby Springbok] at short-leg.'[16] It was a key dismissal as wickets thereafter tumbled quickly – after an hour's play, six had fallen for 63 – before Charles Cawse, batting at number 11, changed the course of the match by smashing 65.

The references made by the Cape's leading newspapers to Hendricks suggest that he had, if anything, gained even greater celebrity as one of the country's most famous and formidable players. Yet, despite Hendricks's impact on the game, when Maurice W. Luckin published his supposedly comprehensive *History of South*

African Cricket in 1915, Hendricks received only one specific mention among its 848 pages. Arthur Seccull, the South African batsman, in his review of the 1894 tour noted there had been discussions over 'the inclusion of the Cape coloured boy, Hendriks [*sic*]'.[17]

Luckin's publication, compiled when he was secretary of the South African Cricket Association, became the standard reference book for the country's cricket. It is noted for its impressive detail, but, apart from a reference to the Malay XVIII versus W.W. Read's touring team in 1891/92, it ignores the history of cricketers of colour who played the game with passion in many parts of the country and throughout the period. Luckin rubber-stamped the racist view that only white cricket mattered.

A review of Luckin's publication that appeared in the *Cape Times* reflected the disregard of the game played by the coloured population. It stated:

> The book is brimful of interest to every cricketer in the country ... from the earliest days of the institution of the national game in this country down to the present time every phase of cricket in every part of the country is fully dealt with.[18]

At the time the book was being launched, the former South African captain, Murray Bisset, was standing for Parliament. *APO* was evidently taken in by his pre-election campaigning and reported that 'if the coloured people work hard his return will be assured'. They thought he was 'sound on the colour question, having promised to do what he can to remove the "colour bar" in the Act of Union'. There was no apparent recollection of the slippery Bisset having been a leading spokesman in the Western Province Cricket Union's determination to entrench the colour bar in cricket. Now on the wider political stage, he was adopting a different stance, and in the build-up to the election, he was elected as a patron of the predominantly Muslim Cape District Union. 'Mr Bisset,' said *APO*, 'has the support of such well-known men as Messrs Roberts, Reagon and Feeder, names that are a sufficient guarantee that he will get the coloured vote.'[19]

Bisset, the Unionist candidate for South Peninsula, was elected to Parliament and immediately drawn into a debate in late 1915 over the government's decision to establish the Cape Coloured Corps as part of the United Defence Force. A *Cape Times* editorial noted that critical references to the corps had come from the Nationalist benches in Parliament, but that these had been opposed by 'the new members of the Cape Peninsula'. The editorial criticised Charles Fichardt – a founder member of the National Party – but stated it could 'understand the attitudes of some Free State members in this matter [as] they have grown up in an environment which makes it difficult for anybody subjected to its influence to think of the coloured man or the native as a person who has any rights at all'. In contrast, the newspaper found it extraordinary that the member for Humansdorp, who came from a Cape family, should talk 'as if the enlistment of a corps of coloured men to assist in fighting the common enemy were intrinsically objectionable and dangerous'.[20]

Bisset argued in favour of the qualities of the corps encamped at Simon's Town. 'Every account that [he] had received had been redounded to their infinite credit,' said the *Cape Times*, 'their conduct having been exemplary and their zeal and progress, from the point of view of military efficiency, having been marvellous.' The editorial argued that instead of making the formation of a Cape Coloured Corps 'a theme for condemnation or abuse, Parliament may thank God that half a century of fair and just treatment at the Cape has brought the coloured population to a livelier appreciation of the advantages of the protection of the British flag than can be asserted of some of their fellow citizens'.[21] The editorial's assessment of British rule – with Murray Bisset singled out for praise – was absurd in terms of the segregationist policies and broken promises that people of colour had experienced and suffered in the course of the last 30 years.

Adding further irony to the situation was the appointment of Vollie van der Byl to command the Labour Battalion in France. Lieutenant-Colonel van der Byl – like Bisset, a bitter opponent of coloured cricketers playing in the white Cape league – took the highly regarded coloured cricketer C.J. Nicholls with him 'to be a batman of sorts'. During the 1905/06 English tour, Nicholls had been used to bowl to the visiting batsmen in net practice sessions and had made a favourable impression on the English captain, Pelham Warner, who later wrote: 'One young Malay with a fast left-hand action hit my middle stump nearly every other ball and Denton (the leading run-scorer on the tour) began his South African career by being caught and bowled by the first three balls and clean bowled by the next three.' Nicholls supposedly earned three gold half-sovereigns for bowling to the English over three afternoons. In France, he was engaged by Van der Byl to assist soldiers with their cricket. 'Their master-servant relationship of many years at Newlands,' wrote André Odendaal in *Divided Country*, 'was now carried over into the conflict.'[22]

The war years disrupted cricket at the Cape. Crusaders folded at the outset of the fighting and their players spread out to other clubs and different leagues. Hendricks decided on Sea Point, J. Francis and W.J. Boonzaaier played for Hand and Heart CC at Claremont, and F. Wilkinson and M. Franciscus joined East End. After one season with Sea Point, Hendricks moved across to St Augustine CC in 1915/16. In an unusual development, the City Cricket League log table was published that season. It recorded Sea Point and St Augustine sharing first place ahead of St Paul's, East End, Thistles and St Phillip's. Four of the sides had 'B' teams playing in a separate competition.

In the 1916/17 season, the Western Province Coloured Cricket Union provided sides to play in a series of matches organised by William Sewell, a former Metropolitan CC player. The games were in aid of the Sportsman's Contribution to the Governor-General's Fund and played against a Western Province XI during the Easter period. The third and final match involved the Western Province Coloured XI playing against the Western Province XI at Green Point. The *Cape Argus* observed 'the well-known fast bowler, H. Hendricks, has chosen a capital side' with several of the coloured batsmen above average. The report singled out Taliep Salie, an outstanding prospect who had successfully defied Province bowling on successive Saturdays with unbeaten innings of 61 and 25 against an attack that included Western Province players Frank Bond and George Whitehead.[23] The team that Hendricks selected and captained was chosen from the various leagues and included players from Thistles, Good Hope, Roslin College, Arabian College and Violets. The Western Province XI included Mick Commaille, the South African Test cricketer, and seven players who had represented or were about to represent Western Province, namely Frank Reid, George Whitehead, William Colson, Cecil Colman, Abel Bensimon, George Taylor and Frank Bond.

The press wrote positively of the cricket played, stating that interest never flagged for a moment from start to finish. A good crowd 'with coloured supporters predominating' arrived for the fixture, which began at 11.00 a.m.[24] A brass band composed of coloured musicians added much to the enjoyment of proceedings and A. Gamieldien managed to get the Western Province Coloured XI off to a rollicking start with a quick-fire 55, but when he was run out, the side was unable to maintain the momentum as wickets fell steadily. Salie was dismissed for the first time in the series of matches, having scored 13. The disappointing total of 144 scored in two hours was largely the result of good bowling from Taylor (5-45) and Whitehead (2-19), as well as some impulsive hitting. The batsmen, explained reports, struggled to handle a type of bowling with which they were not accustomed; Taylor's slow googlies contributed much to their undoing. Hendricks, batting down the order, was caught soon after striking a 6.

The coloured players were keenly alert in the field where, said the *Cape Times*, they 'were the superior in that department of the game, the veteran H. Hendricks in particular being frequently applauded'.[25] Gamieldien caught Mick Commaille (37) with a magnificent running catch and the *Cape Argus* recalled 'the veteran, H. Hendricks, did well to take hot returns from [Allan] Tregidga and Bensimon – he seemed particularly happy getting rid of the latter for a duck'.[26] Despite the efforts of the fielders and impressive bowling figures of 5-45 from G. Baden, the Western Province XI overhauled their opponents' total for the loss of six wickets.

The series was particularly notable for the arrival of Taliep Salie, who was playing for Violets at that time. Not only did he bat well, but he also showed promise as a skilful purveyor of the art of leg-spin. He benefited from playing against George Taylor, who also appears to have been a Western Province player of mixed-race background. Taylor's mother, Mary Lyowes, was a single parent and domestic worker from Victoria West, but George was subsequently adopted by her employers, George and Robina Taylor.[27] Perhaps it was through Taylor that Salie was able to add the googly to his bowling armoury. It helped establish him as a fine all-rounder of international class. Syd Reddy would later recall that Salie once claimed all ten wickets in an innings for a Malay XI against a European XI that included Springboks Dave Nourse, Xenophon Balaskas and Archibald Palm.

Hendricks turned 60 in the course of the 1917/18 season. He had played competitive cricket for nearly 40 years. The City Cricket League was as strong as it had ever been with Silver Crowns (formerly in the Metropolitan and Suburban Union League) and Foresters lining up alongside Sea Point, St Augustine, St Paul's, Thistles and East End. Hendricks chose to return to Sea Point and team lists referred to the inclusion of H. Hendricks 'senior' and H. Hendricks 'junior'. No firm evidence could be obtained that his son had joined him in the side, but this might well have been the case in a significant year. An interesting development was that Sea Point would name three reserves for their 'A' team during the season, possibly fulfilling an arrangement where a 'squad' could assist an older player or two.

At the end of the season, in April 1918, it was hoped that another match between the Western Province XI and the Western Province Coloured XI could be arranged at the Green Point track to aid the Governor-General's Fund. It fell through, said the *Cape Times*, because of actions on the part of clubs belonging to the 'Coloured Union'. The clubs concerned, Good Hope and Roslyns, were in the process of playing a 'knock-out' cup final, their most important match of the season.[28] They had played the first Saturday at Green Point track and objected to being relegated to a side ground for the second part of the game in order that the fundraising fixture could be accommodated. The published report was critical of the clubs in that they 'set competitive cricket above representative fixtures to the detriment of the war funds, and the Coloured Cricket Union is apparently not strong enough to overrule the ill-considered decision'.[29] Various arguments could be put forward, but the problem stemmed from the fact that white officials were not in touch with coloured cricket and only made the effort to become so when it suited them. It was a situation that would not improve and was obviously aggravated by the policy of segregation.

News from the war fronts indicated that the Cape Coloured Corps were distinguishing themselves as infantrymen in battle. In East Africa, they were commended on their outstanding record in major military operations against the Germans and, as a result, saw further service in Egypt, Palestine and Turkey. They became involved in a major offensive 'to knock the Ottoman Empire out of the war' and played their part at Square Hill and Kh Jibeit in paving the way for General Allenby to break through to Damascus.[30] The corps also excelled on the Egyptian cricket fields, winning the divisional championship, having beaten the 158 Brigade HQ and 436 Company RE in their semi-final and final respectively. Two highly rated cricketers, Sergeant Alies and Corporal Fredericks, spearheaded a series of victories for their side against an All-Comers team, with both men selected for a combined team that played in Alexandria.

Later, members of the Cape Coloured Corps who had played regularly against white soldiers in the First World War sought a match against Herbie Collins's Australian Forces team that toured South Africa in 1919. 'However,' says André Odendaal in *Divided Country*, 'they were reminded that fighting together for the King did not mean they should try playing together back home.'[31]

Hendricks, it seems, had no intention of retiring but, like so many others, faced tragedy in the latter part of 1918. His wife, Georgina, developed cancer and died in the New Somerset Hospital on 23 November. The announcement appeared in the *Cape Times*: '... my dearly beloved wife, Georgina Hendrickse, passed away, aged 56, deeply mourned.'[32] Throughout this period, the global influenza pandemic raged, arriving in South Africa in September 1918, with the country becoming the fifth hardest hit in the world. About

500,000 people would succumb in South Africa, 62 per cent of that number in the Cape. The day before Georgina died, the *Cape Times* stated that there was 'no prospect of competitive cricket being revived during the present season'.[33] When games resumed in the new year, Hendricks's team, Sea Point 'A', withdrew. St Paul's won a revived competition that involved seven sides – Armadale being a recent addition – with each team playing six matches.

Krom Hendricks survived the Spanish flu, but his long and illustrious cricket career had finally drawn to a close.

12

Hendricks and the world: An international perspective

'It appears that in the beginning the British had no intention of teaching the natives to play cricket ... the Indian might roll the pitch or serve the whisky. He might even watch cricket and (at a price) retrieve the ball or throw it for the sahibs to bat back. He was not expected to play the game. But he would.'[1]

– Ramachandra Guha

THE INTERACTION BETWEEN race and cricket was complex and significant in the evolution of empire as well as South Africa itself. Hendricks's struggle with the Western Province authorities was an extreme example of how imperialists from the 1880s to the First World War used race to create a white national identity.

By contrast, Charles Bennett 'Buck' Llewellyn, who shared a similar ancestry to Hendricks, not only managed to represent South Africa, but also became the second black cricketer to play in a Test match. Llewellyn's experience demonstrates the fluidity of racial stereotypes and categorisations in southern Africa, which enabled him to succeed in an international career while Hendricks was thwarted from representing the country of his birth.

Race was an issue in all countries where cricket was a badge of imperialism. The supposed cultural superiority of the white Anglo-Saxon race was used to rationalise the imposition of British rule over a vast empire. Imperialists generally believed that the world benefited from their domination and that they had a moral obligation to extend their influence as far as possible. The British believed that they were best equipped – as they defined themselves as the race at the top of the social pecking order – to instruct so-called inferior races in the habits of civilisation and 'fair play'.

Powerful men during this period lent their support to the expanding British influence, happy to justify their plundering of the empire's resources by subverting the narrative to embrace the specious concept of the 'white man's burden'. In their opinion, they were doing the world a favour. Cecil John Rhodes stated unequivocally: 'I contend that we are the finest race in the world and that the more of the world we inhabit the better it is for the human race.' The human casualties were ignored. Rhodes himself added considerable territory to the empire and was hardly bothered when gently reproved by Lord Rosebery for using 'swashbuckling methods more suited to the reign of Queen Elizabeth I than to the circumspect era of Queen Victoria'.[2] After all, Rosebery was part of the system. He had married Lord Rothschild's cousin, Hannah, and was aware that Rhodes was often dependent on the exceedingly wealthy banker. Moreover, Rosebery – who served as foreign secretary and as prime minister – fully shared Rhodes's imperial stance, if not his methods, and believed strongly in an all-powerful Britain, and in 1895 made Rhodes a member of the Privy Council. He would, five years later, pose a revealing rhetorical question for students at Glasgow University: 'What is Empire but the predominance of race?'[3]

'Cricket was intertwined with the Empire,' wrote historian Jack Williams in assessing a game that helped to sustain the racist British imperial project. Belief in the ethical quality of the empire, he continued, 'was based on assumptions of racial superiority, of the white English race having a natural moral capacity that made it uniquely fitted for the exercise of imperial power'.[4] Yet in sport, argued cricket historian Sir Derek Birley, the Victorians were divided, making an enormous fuss about the class distinctions between amateurs and professionals. 'The MCC,' he added, 'displayed a complacent superiority…with the help of extra-large doses of hypocrisy [which] had a lot to do with the Graces and W.G. in particular.'[5] Success was achieved in the dissemination of the imperial games around the globe, but sport under imperial administration was used to define and consolidate divisions and reinforce the superiority of the elite ruling class. Cricket, said David Frith, 'could never bring about any real fusion of species' during the latter part of the nineteenth century. 'Class distinctions held firm,' he wrote, 'in cricket as in real life.'[6] These were comments that perhaps over-simplified a process of struggle over both class and race, and the flexibility of those concepts in reality as opposed to rhetoric.

There were just three black cricketers involved in the first 172 Test matches played over a period of 51 years. This was largely because the three countries that played Test cricket – and founded the Imperial Cricket Conference (ICC) in 1909 – were Australia, England and South Africa. It was not until 1926 that the ICC allowed delegates from India, New Zealand and the West Indies to attend their gatherings for the first time. The West Indies played their inaugural Test match at Lord's in June 1928. They were followed by New Zealand in January 1930 and India in June 1932.

With the empire based on assumptions of white supremacy, it is significant that the first cricket side to visit England should be made up of Australian Aboriginal workers from Wimmera sheep stations. They made history in 1868 by undertaking an official tour, albeit with an Englishman, Charles Lawrence, as tour organiser and captain. Like many of the nineteenth-century tours, it was entertainment, falling somewhere between a circus show and a sporting competition. Prior to the opening fixture, *Sporting Life* resisted what was likely to be the common perspective, suggesting that 'it must not be inferred that they are savages; on the contrary …They are perfectly civilised, having been brought up in the bush to agricultural pursuits.'[7] There were 20,000 curious spectators at their first public game at The Oval, where the visitors were well beaten by Surrey but demonstrated they had some fine players, most notably Unaarrimin, a Wotjobaluk man known as 'Johnny Mullagh'. In the course of a gruelling 47-match tour, the team made a favourable impression in recording 14 wins, 14 losses and 19 draws. They provided further entertainment with a variety of activities that included boomerang and spear throwing. The tour's cricketing significance is widely acknowledged, but it proved to be a one-off venture. 'What it reveals,' said cricket historian Bernard Whimpress, 'is opportunity denied because there's nothing built on it.'[8]

Aborigine sportsmen, explained Ashley Mallett in *The Black Lords of Summer*, became victims of politics: 'While the White Australia policy held sway in Australia, the idea of a black man playing Test cricket for Australia was "unthinkable".'[9] But prior to this racist construction, the position was more fluid. Remarkably, a black cricketer represented Australia more than a decade before well-known Aboriginal cricketers Jack Marsh and Albert Henry came into consideration. He was Samuel Morris, born in Hobart, Tasmania, in 1855. His father, Isaac Morris, was from Barbados and had sailed to Australia during the gold-rush era. It was there that he met his wife, Elizabeth Ann McGuiness, who was Tasmanian of West Indian descent. Their son, Sam, played cricket in Daylesford, then moved to Melbourne where he became a professional with the Waverley club, carrying out the usual duties of groundsman and net bowler. He scored 280 for Richmond against St Kilda in February 1882. It was recorded as the first-ever double century by a cricketer of colour anywhere in the world. It also earned Sam Morris the chance to play first-class cricket for Victoria and he excelled in his second inter-colonial game against South Australia in Adelaide in 1884. It was a historic occasion as it was the first time six-ball overs were introduced. Morris claimed 4-82 from 40 overs in the first innings and scored an unbeaten 64 as Victoria chased down a fourth-innings total of 369.

Morris played just one Test, one of nine debutants in the second encounter of the 1884/85 series against England. A pay dispute involving players from the first Test meant an entirely new team was chosen under Tom Horan's captaincy. Morris became the first black Test cricketer, some ten years before Charles 'Buck' Llewellyn and

Kumar Shri Ranjitsinhji. England amassed 401 in their first innings at Melbourne, with Morris brilliant in the field. Horan noted that he 'was particularly swift in his movements and his correct and true returns from the farthest points of the outfield, combined with his dash in picking up, frequently brought down the house…As a fieldsman, especially at point, Sam has no superior among Australians.'[10] Morris also had Arthur Shrewsbury caught off his bowling for 72 and Billy Barnes bowled for 58. He was then asked to open the batting in the Australian first innings, scoring 4, and was undefeated on 10 in the second, batting at number ten as his side went down by ten wickets.

References were made to Morris as 'Darkie' in contemporary newspaper reports, and the omnipresent racism of the environment in which he operated required a strong character. During the Test, Johnny Briggs asked him on the field why he was wearing black kid gloves below his shirt buttoned to the wrist. Morris laughed it off, as he so often had to do. A popular member of the cricket community, he earned a living as a curator at various cricket grounds and continued to play first-class cricket until 1892/93. He played against the touring Englishmen again in 1886/87, when he scored an unbeaten 54 in his side's second innings, saving the match through an unbeaten 77-run last-wicket partnership with Jim Phillips. Then, against a strong South Australian side, he made two useful scores, while also capturing 4-59 and 5-21 to take a depleted Victoria side to victory. Morris, despite his colour, was accepted because, by virtue of his ancestry in the West Indies, white colonists saw him as a colonist himself – one of them and not an indigenous inhabitant of the continent around whom the noose of imperialism was being increasingly tightened. Prejudice became a common factor in the 1890s, and Australia, like South Africa, became increasingly reactionary, though each part of the empire went in this direction for its own specific reasons.

This 'tide of prejudice', as Mallett put it, would create problems at the turn of the century when two outstanding Aboriginal fast bowlers emerged. Jack Marsh from New South Wales and Albert Henry from Queensland were both considered good enough to play first-class cricket, but would suffer the indignity of being labelled as 'chuckers'. Umpires were beyond reproach, said Mallett, respected men whose decisions were never questioned, but he drew attention to the prejudice that existed and the fact that when 'an Aboriginal cricketer of Test potential turned up, officialdom stepped in'.[11]

Short in stature for a fast bowler – five feet seven inches – Jack Marsh was capable of dismissing the best batsmen in the game. In his early years, he clean bowled Victor Trumper and Monty Noble, two of the greatest names in Australian cricket. He was given the opportunity to play first-class cricket and captured 21 wickets for New South Wales at 17.38 in his first three Sheffield Shield matches. J.C. Davis, a leading cricket writer, observed: 'Marsh could make the ball do stranger things in the air than any other bowler I saw.'[12] He was a strong contender for a place in the national side, but, said Mallett, the Australia of the early 1900s was a racist and bigoted environment. Cricket historian Jack Pollard thought Marsh was the best Australian bowler of his time, but his name was scratched from the list of players by 'an official who was simply carrying out the racist customs of the day'.[13]

An outstanding athlete, Marsh was arguably the fastest sprinter in Australia in the early 1890s and reportedly ran the 100 yards in 9.8 seconds to equal the world record held by the American John Owen. It helped him generate pace as a bowler, but he couldn't escape the continual controversy surrounding the legitimacy of his action. At the time, there was a major campaign against throwing in Australia and England, and those who supported Marsh believed he was a soft target because of his race. Noble, the New South Wales selector, refused to include him in the state side, citing his controversial action. But then Noble also believed that the fast bowler 'didn't have class enough to play for Australia'.[14] Marsh, in his defence, was determined to prove his action fair and decided to challenge a leading umpire, William Curran, by famously arranging to encase his arm in a splint. Curran withdrew from the match believing he had been humiliated.

Archie MacLaren, captain of the touring English side in 1901/02, refused to play against Marsh at Bathurst. Two years later, Pelham Warner's team were bowled out for 176 against Bathurst – Marsh

5-55 – and were fortunate to escape with a draw. Warner called Marsh a 'shier' (thrower), but Albert Knight, who also played in the game, and like Warner had been dismissed by Marsh, provided a minority counterpoint to the racist consensus that dominated colonial consciousness and the cricket establishment. He thought Marsh was 'quite the best bowler in the Commonwealth' and that his delivery was 'not, one thinks, a throw or even essentially doubtful':

> Marsh may be said to literally possess those wrists of india-rubber which the cutting batsman is often credited with. His hand and wrist had the flabby flexibility of a heel-less slipper and could be elongated and manipulated by him after the eccentric fashion of some modern acrobatic comedian of the music hall. The pace and angle at which the ball came from the pitch owed nothing to a high delivery, for although of good height and build he dwarved himself to the height of the stumps with a delivery which followed his run up of swooping gliding strides. 'Foreign' cricket it truly is, as some black men play it, but we can learn a very great deal indeed from these exponents.[15]

Warren Bardsley, the Australian opening batsman, stated openly: 'The reason Marsh was kept out of big cricket was his colour.'[16] Les Poidevin, who played for New South Wales, Lancashire and London County, wrote:

> He is certainly a marvel with the ball. What a treasure, a gold-mine indeed he would be to an English county. But you will not see him because the absurd White Australia policy has touched or tainted the hearts of the rulers of cricket, as it has the political rulers ...[17]

When New South Wales met Queensland in March and November 1902, Marsh played against fellow Aborigine Albert Henry. The latter was tall and slim, and regarded as the fastest bowler the English side of 1903/04 had seen. He played seven first-class matches, but was also accused of throwing. He confronted umpire Albert Cossart with the claim, 'You bastard! You no-ball my good balls and the ones I throw you never!'[18] Henry was suspended, drifted out of the game and died from tuberculosis before he was 30. A little more than 20 years later, another exciting Aboriginal fast bowler emerged in Eddie Gilbert, but he too was no-balled for throwing. The stigma of being labelled a chucker brought an abrupt end to the cricket careers of all three players, all of whom had tragic lives. Marsh died violently, kicked to death by two white men who were subsequently acquitted. The jury did not bother to leave the box to discuss the verdict, and the judge ruled that 'Marsh might have deserved it, because he had been offensive'.[19] Gilbert was incarcerated in a mental institution where he stayed until his death almost 30 years later.

Sam Morris was the first cricketer of West Indian heritage to play in a Test match. It would be more than 40 years before the Caribbean islands achieved Test status in 1928. The problems and progress experienced in the West Indies were not entirely dissimilar to those that characterised the South African game during the latter part of the nineteenth century. Tours by three English teams in the 1890s not only tested standards and widened the interest base across the islands, but also raised questions about white attitudes towards black players. The key to the future success of West Indian cricket lay in the potential of black communities where, said Barbadian cricket historian Sir Hilary Beckles, the game became 'as instinctively cultural as religion and the performing arts'. The cricket of the 'plantation villages and urban ghettos was learnt at community level rather than formally through the school system'.[20]

In 1899, Lord Hawke invited the West Indians to tour England. Beckles believed that at that stage 'blacks were poised to force their way *en masse* into first-class colonial cricket and therefore to secure selection for West Indies teams'. He considered the tour in 1900 the grand 'international' debut of multi-racial West Indies cricket, with five black players among the 15 chosen in the touring party.[21] There were three black amateurs, Lebrun Constantine, Delmont 'Fitz' Hinds and Charles Ollivierre, and two black professionals,

'Float' Woods and Tommie Burton. The five players were treated exactly like the white members of the side and proved good tourists – Woods supposedly commenting at Crystal Palace: 'What a lot of white people they have got in this country.'[22]

W.L.A. Coleman, writing in *The Cricketer*, said of the 1900 tourists:

> Apparently the coloured members of the team were much impressed with England and they indicated that in the West Indies the question was being asked as to whether white and coloured cricketers should play together in the same team. It had been the form to allow only white cricketers to play in cup and inter-colonial matches in the West Indies.[23]

Coleman referred to comments made in the *Boy's Own Paper*, which had ventured to suggest that at a time when cricket was dominated by whites, the islands suddenly found themselves in an awkward position. If black players were good enough to represent the West Indies in an international context, said Coleman, 'it is difficult to see how they can be refused opportunities of playing at home'.[24]

The *Boy's Own Paper* reflected on English perceptions of the tour, stating that it had been anticipated the 'blacks would go on to the field without boots and in a very sparse attire'.[25] C.L.R. James took up the theme in his *Beyond a Boundary*, citing the tour match against Gloucestershire as a revealing moment in West Indian cricket history. The tourists' bowling was hammered – Gilbert Jessop struck 157 in an hour. According to James, fast bowler Float Woods eventually made 'the best response he knew to a truly desperate situation':

> He went to his captain and asked permission to take off his boots. West Indies captain Aucher Warner, a brother of Sir Pelham, asked him why; he replied that he could bowl properly only when barefooted … Warner promptly refused his request. Woods returned to the bowling crease. Jessop despatched his fast balls over the boundary, out of the ground, on to roof-tops.

> Woods made one last attempt. 'Mr Warner,' he pleaded, 'let me take off one – just one and I could get him – just one, sir.' 'Out of the question. You can't do that here, Woods.'[26]

To the West Indians, said James in 1963, it recalled 'the origin of many a fine bowler of 60 years ago. He came to the nets, often without shoes. He picked up a ball and bowled.'[27] In a contemporary report, Alfred Knight described the 'extraordinary suppleness in many of the coloured races which predisposes them for excellence in such a game as cricket... Even in the West Indian Olliverre... there is a certain allusive nuance, suggestive of a faraway glamour which no English player possesses'.[28]

The athletic West Indians would produce many of the finest fast bowlers the world has seen, but early defeats in their 1900 tour would result in little interest among the English press and public. It was also unfortunate that arguably the most interesting fixture of the original tour programme should be cancelled. The West Indies were scheduled to play South Africa at Lord's, but this became impossible when the latter's tour was delayed by the Anglo-Boer War.

Public interest in English cricket in 1900 was instead captivated by the brilliance of Kumar Shri Ranjitsinhji, who topped the national averages in scoring more than 3,000 runs for a second successive season. The noble Rajput, heir to the throne of Nawanagar, had earlier become England's first recognised player of colour. He began his studies at Cambridge in 1891 where, said Ramachandra Guha in *A Corner of a Foreign Field*, for his first two years, he 'was not given a trial at the University ground, Fenner's, on account only of the colour of his skin'.[29] He started his county career with Sussex in 1895, and was for some years the leading batsman in English cricket, noted for his timing and enchanting leg-glides. A place in the England team seemed certain, but the president of the MCC, Lord Harris, opposed his selection. Ranjitsinhji was not included in Lord Hawke's team that toured South Africa in 1895/96; Fry was sent in his place. Then, despite his outstanding batting form in 1896, he was not chosen by the MCC for the first Test against Australia at Lord's. The host committees selected teams in those years, so Lancashire seized the opportunity to name Ranjitsinhji in their side for the next Test at Old Trafford, where he scored 62 and 154 not out. It would have been difficult for England not to select him again. *The Field* observed: 'The MCC had ruled that a gentleman born in India, of a long line of distinguished ancestry, could not be an Englishman by any ingenuity of reasoning, however good a cricketer he might be. Lancashire and Surrey, however, ruled that he is an Englishman.'[30]

Lord Harris's previous role as governor of the Bombay Presidency has been noted in projecting the grand years of empire. It seemed a dream imperial appointment: after all, Harris was born in Trinidad, brought up in India, educated at Eton and Oxford, and went on to captain England at cricket. He was governor for almost five years, lending his support as patron to the Bombay Gymkhana – the European club run along the lines of the Western Province CC – which kept out all Indians and also whites of uncertain pedigree, such as petty tradesmen and soldiers without a commission. English writers later praised Harris for his great work in the development of cricket in India. Cecil Headlam wrote that no one did more than Harris to further the game in India,[31] and Rowland Bowen, rather bizarrely, claimed that Harris 'adopted on the cricket field the attitude that all cricketers are equal, regardless of colour, and this attitude became widely known and made him a much respected [governor of Bombay]'.[32] Such writing was misleading. English cricket historians – and notably Birley in his exaggerated account of Harris in *The Willow Wand* – generally seemed unaware of the governor's autocracy and racism and his failure to notice that 'native' cricket, despite a critical lack of space, was flourishing in Bombay when he arrived.[33] 'Indeed,' wrote Guha, 'had [Harris] played cricket more often with or against Indians, he might have been less disliked.'[34] The governor's racist administration made no exception for cricket. The captain of the local Parsi team was a Cambridge graduate, but in Harris's Bombay, this man and his team 'were not allowed to break bread with Englishmen or to enter any English club, merely because their skins were dark'. Guha mentioned that 'Harris was unwavering in his support for European polo over native cricket' and quoted the assessment of the local cricketers' leader, Sorabjee Shapoorjee:

> The whole 'spirit of generous concession' was expected by Lord Harris from one side only – the native cricketers – and none at all from the Gymkhana gentlemen, who sent their men to play polo on the native cricketers' ground to the entire destruction of its turf and surface and kept their own ground for their cricketers safe and untouched not only by their polo ponies but even by the native cricketers! A remarkably curious appreciation of justice and 'generosity' Lord Harris had![35]

When the time came for Harris to leave India, the introductory note to a publisher's book of press cuttings stated, 'Never during the last hundred years has a Governor of Bombay been so sternly criticised and never has he met with such widespread unpopularity.'[36]

Bowen's portrayal of Harris was one of many controversial views he put forward in his *Cricket: A History of Its Growth and Development Throughout the World* when it was published in 1970. Not all he said was totally accurate, and John Arlott noted that Bowen 'aired some unexpected theories'.[37] Bowen's arch-enemy among the English establishment, Irving Rosenwater, was critical, stating, 'One of the dangers of this book is that statements are made which are simply not true but made with such forthright authoritativeness as to make them seem facts.'[38]

Bowen was to make the stunning discovery that South Africa had fielded a coloured player – Charles Bennett 'Buck' Llewellyn – in Test cricket. He wrote that of all the cricketers who had represented South Africa, Llewellyn was 'the only man who has been openly avowed as a coloured man (there have been plenty who have not)'.[39] The *Cape Times* acknowledged shortly afterwards that this information was 'little-known' and it sparked a flurry of interest in a player who had made his Test debut for South Africa 75 years earlier.[40] Bowen was correct about Llewellyn, but his suggestion that 'plenty' of South African cricketers were in denial of their coloured origin was considerably more speculative, even if the flexible and subjective nature of who was or wasn't coloured makes his comment essentially unverifiable.

Further research by cricket historian Brian Crowley uncovered that Llewellyn's father was a Pietermaritzburg house painter and his mother a black woman from St Helena.[41] As a result of continued interest in the story and in the racially charged context of the struggle around apartheid, *The Cricketer* published articles on Llewellyn and the 'coloured question'. The content upset Llewellyn's daughter, Agatha Anderton, who asked, 'I wonder how it ever came about that he has been referred to as South Africa's only coloured Test cricketer. He was of white stock.'[42] It seemed that Anderton was either ignorant of or misled over her father's background, or herself unprepared to acknowledge the position. Death certificates record Thomas Buck Llewellyn (died 1914) as being 'European' and his wife, Ann Elizabeth Rich (died 1920), as having 'Mixed' origin. Christopher Merrett wrote a detailed piece for *The Cricket Statistician* in which he noted that Llewellyn had been born out of wedlock to Thomas Buck Llewellyn, who was born in Pembroke in 1844, and that the question of Llewellyn's race rested 'on the origins of his mother, born Ann Elizabeth Rich in 1845 at Jamestown, St Helena'. Merrett said that from 1838 onwards, 'hundreds of Saint Helenans emigrated to the Cape and some moved on to Natal' where, in the hierarchy of colonial society, they were 'regarded as being of mixed race'.[43]

The research undertaken on Llewellyn has direct relevance in understanding the position of Krom Hendricks. Their mothers came from St Helena, but both apparently believed that they were born of European parents. Anne Hendricks's death certificate noted that she was 'European', a view that was not contested. The critical difference between the two was that while Hendricks was born in the Cape, Llewellyn was born in Natal. The significance of race for whites in Natal reflected the huge African population of the territory and efforts to turn this into a compliant labour force. It also involved the evolution of a position towards the complex Indian community, which included indentured labourers and a small proportion of immigrant 'passenger' Indians who had paid their own way.

In the light of all this, the question of some degree of potential racial intermixture was far less of a problem. There was no 'Malay' community in Natal, so no basis for discrimination. And neither Milton nor Rhodes was in Natal. The issue of who was or wasn't coloured was also a subjective judgement. The real truth of racism and the categorisation of individuals by arbitrary and subjective criteria invariably made it difficult to form hard and fast judgements. Most did not try, allowing culture and class to settle the issue.

Not surprisingly then, according to Merrett, the *Natal Almanac*, in its categorisation of the population, would have considered Llewellyn 'grudgingly perhaps, a white man, but marked as different because of his mother's origins'.[44] Llewellyn, aware that the colour of his skin might cause comment, resented any allusions to his racial status. When the move towards union brought tighter racial restrictions during the 1900s, he must have realised that his position could change. In effect, it could become impossible for him to play in South Africa. He could be grateful that he was given a few years' grace to forge a cricket career in Natal. Hendricks, as Llewellyn would no doubt have been aware, was not as fortunate, but it is likely that the two men would have followed each other's progress with more than a passing interest.

Llewellyn was born in Pietermaritzburg, Natal, on 29 September 1876. He progressed through the Pietermaritzburg junior ranks where promising youngsters played matches and received coaching prior to being drafted into the town's well-organised club system. His progress was such that he was chosen for the Natal Currie Cup side that played against Transvaal at the City Oval, Pietermaritzburg, in April 1895. Transvaal defeated Natal, but the 18-year-old Llewellyn demonstrated his potential in a performance that was duly praised. Dropped catches prevented him from taking more than one wicket in the Transvaal first innings, but when they went in again to chase 203, he bowled superbly to capture 3-39 in 19 overs. The highlight was clean bowling Ernest 'Barberton' Halliwell, who had reached 30 and threatened to dominate proceedings. The wicket would have some bearing on Llewellyn earning his first Test cap.

In 1895/96, Lord Hawke's English team visited South Africa to play three Tests. The Transvaal selection committee, comprising Halliwell (chairman), Tommy Routledge, E.J.L. Platnauer, Bertie Rose-Innes and 19-year-old Jimmy Sinclair, chose the team for the second Test at Johannesburg. Among several changes from the side that had played the first Test in Port Elizabeth, they were keen to include Hendricks and Llewellyn. An outcry followed at the Cape with the Western Province Cricket Union duly preventing Hendricks from making the trip to the Rand. In contrast, publicity over Llewellyn's selection was low-key and there were no objections to his playing.

Hendricks's position was fundamentally different because he had played Malay cricket in Cape Town and for the representative Malay side against Read's English tourists in 1891/92. Moreover, he had specifically and publicly announced through the *Cape Times* that his mother hailed from St Helena. Llewellyn never played Indian or coloured cricket. He had developed his game through the establishment cricket structure, was not required to make public statements of any kind as to his background and was viewed by Natal's white cricket community as a highly promising prospect. To accept Hendricks in the side was to accept an acknowledged player of colour representing South Africa; to accept Llewellyn was to accept 'one of us'.

It was not what they were, but rather with whom they associated. This, of course, was one of the great truths of racism in South Africa. It was what people took you for that was important, and who accepted you defined your status. You were a coloured if enough people thought you were, hence Llewellyn's serious concern about any references to the issue. No wonder he was worried about whisperings in corridors and selection meetings – at any minute the weight of acceptance could change, totally transforming his life.

Llewellyn was dropped for the third Test at Cape Town and there might well have been an ulterior motive on the part of William Milton and his selection committee. A rumour that Llewellyn was not white could have been enough for Milton to simply block his selection, a decision he could have partly, if not convincingly, justified to some extent on cricket grounds. Llewellyn had made the second-highest score in the South African first innings in Johannesburg, but had little luck with his bowling, returning figures of 0-71 in 14 overs. The selection decision could also have been parochialism. The Cape selectors went, as they almost always did, for their man, and named Alf Richards – in his only Test – as captain instead of Halliwell. The Test was lost by an innings, as had been the case in Johannesburg.

The next few years would reinforce the view that Llewellyn was a tremendous prospect. At the Currie Cup in Johannesburg in March 1897, he captured 30 wickets at an average of 12.13. The following year in Cape Town, he was not quite as successful in collecting another 16 wickets, but impressed the Transvaalers again when he scored 63 and 12 and took six wickets. He twice clean bowled Sinclair before 'the hardest hitter anyone had ever seen' could get going.[45] Llewellyn was a certainty for the South African side when Lord Hawke brought out another English team in 1898/99. This time, he was older and better prepared. He took 2-35 and 3-89 in the first Test at the Old Wanderers – five catches were dropped off Llewellyn's bowling in the course of England's second innings in a match the South Africans should have won.

Llewellyn did not play in the second Test in Cape Town. Press reports indicated that he had declared himself unavailable. The *Cape Times* announced in a terse report: 'Mr B Llewellyn, the Natal bowler, has notified his inability to accept his place in the South African Test match on April 1 owing to business reasons.'[46] The Transvaal newspapers were not convinced, believing the sensitive Llewellyn had been upset by the machinations of the Cape. *The Star* commented:

> The one thing to be deplored is the absence of Llewellyn, undoubtedly the finest bowler in South Africa. Though he did not gain the best average in the Johannesburg Test match, the Englishmen were unanimous in awarding him the palm as the trickiest bowler of the lot; while as a batsman one might say he is as likely to make runs as anybody, and as a

> fielder there was not a man on either side that could compare with him. Llewellyn, youngster though he is, has proved himself the best all-round player in South Africa, and his absence from the representative team is a misfortune that some of the big wigs at the Cape, one may reasonably think, would have seen to.[47]

This unavailability may have been connected to Llewellyn's uncertainty as to how he might be treated by Western Province, that they would not select him for racist reasons and that he did not want the issue debated publicly. Yet his being unavailable did not have a detrimental effect on his career; on the contrary, within a few days much interest was being shown in his cricket. Major R.M. Poore had, while stationed in South Africa, been 'much struck with his play' and wrote to Hampshire 'advising them to offer the young cricketer an engagement'.[48] The county cabled their interest to Llewellyn, who was initially inclined to reject the offer. The great South African batsman, Herby Taylor, later recalled that the Natalians encouraged him to seize the opportunity: 'I do know that my father and some of his colleagues were so impressed with [Llewellyn's] potential that they raised the money to send him to England for a trial with Hampshire. In other words, he went to England on the same basis that Basil D'Oliveira did, and like Basil has done, he made a success of it. Mind you, I wouldn't say he was quite as educated or cultured as Basil is.'[49]

Upon arriving in England, Llewellyn proved himself an outstanding prospect. While qualifying for the county, he excelled against the 1899 Australians, scoring 72 and 21 in addition to taking 8-132. He impressed Kumar Shri Ranjitsinhji and was invited to join a strong MCC touring side to America, capturing 22 wickets at a cost of 11.13. His first season in the County Championship – 1901 – was also a great triumph for him: in all matches he achieved the 'double', scoring 1,025 runs (31.06) and taking 134 wickets (22.53). He played against Logan's South Africans for Hampshire in their opening match and, no doubt highly motivated by playing against his compatriots, pulverised their attack, racing to 216 in three hours. A small crowd was impressed and collected nine pounds and ten shillings for him. He was then asked to assist the touring side in later matches, scoring 4 and 88 and taking 13-241 against London County, and recording 51 and 10 and 12-130 against Liverpool and District.

Jimmy Sinclair, who toured with the South African side in 1901, spent additional time in England and was selected for 'Gentlemen'. The achievement contrasted with Llewellyn's inclusion in the 'Players' side the following season. It was a case of the two South Africans being quickly separated by English custom in a method not dissimilar to the way they might have been separated in South Africa. 'The same logic,' wrote Keith Sandiford, 'that dictated that amateur cricketers should have precedence over the professionals led the Victorians to conclude that Anglo-Saxons were ordained to have dominion over non-white peoples.'[50] At a time when relatively little heed was paid to residential qualification, Llewellyn came close to selection for the full English side in 1902. He was among the 14 players named in the English squad for the first Test against Australia at Edgbaston. He was omitted on the morning of the match, but the side that played could be described as one of England's finest teams: MacLaren, Fry, Ranjitsinhji, Jackson, Tyldesley, Lilley, Hirst, Jessop, Braund, Lockwood and Rhodes.

After losing just two of their 39 matches in England, the Australians set off for South Africa. Llewellyn, who had captured 170 wickets during the English season, also made his way to Johannesburg. Abe Bailey assumed control of Llewellyn's movements and his investment paid handsome dividends. Llewellyn compiled 90 in the first Test at the Old Wanderers and bagged a remarkable 25 wickets in the series at 17.92 runs apiece. His skilled variation of pace and spin, combined with immaculate length, troubled all the visiting batsmen. He took 6-92 in Australia's first innings of the first Test, captured 5-43 and 5-73 in the second Test, and ended with an innings return of 6-97 in the final Test. The first two Tests were both at the Old Wanderers, where *The Star* praised Llewellyn for his success on the field before adding, he 'is esteemed not only for his cricket ability but for his personal qualities'.[51]

There was no problem in Llewellyn playing in a Test at Newlands for the first time. The Cape administrators, who had worked assiduously to maintain an all-white policy in their cricket, were fortified by the English stamp of approval: Llewellyn had been in the English squad a few months earlier, while the local press frequently referred to him as the Hampshire professional. It was through similar reasoning – or so it seemed – that George Whitehead was able to play cricket for Cape Town CC two years later.

Bailey's influence continued to prevail. He financed the next South African tour to England in 1904, and Llewellyn was called upon to assist the side. His appearances were restricted to six matches because of county commitments, but he easily topped the batting averages (338 runs – average 56.33) and collected 16 wickets at 25.31. A more demanding challenge was the series played against Australia in 1910/11. Initial arrangements occurred at a time when Bailey was in the process of arranging for South Africa to gain equal partner status in the formation of the Imperial Cricket Conference. He knew that his country's credibility on the cricket field would be tested by the Australian tour as well as the triangular tournament with England and Australia that followed in 1912. An all-Transvaal selection committee regarded Llewellyn, who was in outstanding form in 1910 and named as one of *Wisden*'s 'Five Cricketers of the Year', as a key player.

The other cricket bodies had little say in developments. The Natal Cricket Association argued that after ten years in England, Llewellyn could no longer be looked upon as a South African player. They thought the invitation should be withdrawn. The *Cape Times* reflected on the extent of the decline in the Western Province Cricket Union's influence in cricket matters. Years of incompetent administration had taken their toll and they had just one player in the touring party. 'The Western Province,' said the newspaper report, 'has become so accustomed to the autocratic dictation of cricket policy from Johannesburg that we seem to take even the most outrageous decisions without even the proverbial grumble.' With some irony, the *Cape Times* added: 'Now a lot of piffle has been written regarding the eligibility of Llewellyn to play for South Africa, and the Natal Cricket Union has considered the matter so important that it has lodged a formal protest … Llewellyn is a South African. Why should the services of such a valuable player not be taken advantage of when he is willing and anxious and qualified under the rules for South Africa only?'[52]

Shortly before embarking on the tour, Llewellyn ended his high-profile role in county cricket to accept a more lucrative contract with Accrington Cricket Club in the Lancashire League. *Wisden* stated that 'a disagreement over terms resulted in his severing his connection with Hampshire',[53] but his daughter wrote that her father had 'left county cricket because with four daughters, he needed the money offered in league cricket'.[54] Jack Williams claimed that Llewellyn was 'a tenacious negotiator over terms but there is also a belief that his departure from Hampshire occurred in part because of his being refused accommodation in hotels and boarding houses when the team was playing away matches and racist comments from other players'.[55]

In Australia, Llewellyn initially experienced problems in adjusting to the harder wickets, but the left-armer's googly was soon working effectively. In the second Test, *The Star* recalled: 'The ball which took [Clem] Hill's wicket was a googly and completely mystified the batsman who did not attempt to play it.'[56] There were greater deeds to follow in the third Test, which *Sporting Life* described as 'the greatest day in the history of South African cricket'.[57] *The Star* headed their report for the Test 'Llewellyn's match'. He scored 43 and 80 (out of 200 in 218 minutes), took 4-107 in Australia's first innings and bowled Trumper relatively early in the second. The report stated that 'Trumper did not shape at all well. He was completely beaten by two balls from Llewellyn before he was dismissed by a googly.'[58]

There was never doubt that Llewellyn would continue to play in Tests overseas. He participated in the historic 1912 Triangular Tournament between Australia, England and South Africa that was severely affected by the weather and in which the South Africans performed poorly. Llewellyn played a fine knock in South Africa's second innings against England at Lord's in mid-June. He reached his 50 in an hour, and in an innings marked by fine driving and 'shots all around the wicket', he scored 75. Sir Home Gordon said in the *Daily Express*, 'Llewellyn batted superbly. Many a century has been made in first-class cricket of lesser merit.'[59] A defiant 59 followed against Australia at Lord's: 'The fine clean hitting of Llewellyn,' said the *Yorkshire Post*, 'pleasantly illumined the afternoon's cricket and it is probably not assuming too much to say that it was enjoyed by His Majesty.'[60] Unfortunately, Llewellyn was unable to make an impression in the remaining two matches, a period of disappointing cricket that coincided with off-the-field problems for him.

In late July 1912, the *Cape Argus* published a report from London to say that Llewellyn had asked to be released from his engagement with Accrington. 'His grievance is a remarkable one,' said the article, which referred to a keen rivalry existing between Accrington and neighbouring club, Church.[61] At the time, it was customary to record the results of games in whitewash on the boundary wall of the two towns, but an artist not content merely with whitewashing the scores of a recent game had added a caricature of Llewellyn.

A photograph was published locally of the artwork, which depicted Llewellyn standing over a cooking pot on a fire – a scene that might have had an African connotation – with an accompanying inscription stating, 'Llewellyn now warm'. He had earlier taken 6-49 and made the top score in a lost cause. The *Accrington Observer and Times* reported that 'the artist, a gentleman not unaccustomed to the tracery of fanciful design…has succeeded fairly well in his efforts. Some colour has been introduced – an innovation.'[62] The illustration and the wording of the article hinted at a racist slant, with Llewellyn's sensitivity about his colour leading to the belief that he was being 'held up to public ridicule and obloquy'.

The editor of the *Accrington Observer and Times* further noted that Llewellyn's initial objection to the picture resulted in 'the portion which had given offence being obliterated on Saturday night last – only to be followed ere Monday dawned by still another piece designed as a sequel to the one that had been blotted out'. The editorial expressed concern over the artwork and thought that the personal element would have been better left undone. Llewellyn argued that he would prefer to leave the club than be called upon to endure such publicity and the 'unjustifiable and ill-natured derision of any man who may choose to make him the butt for his pictorial jibes'. The editorial conceded that Llewellyn felt the matter acutely and that he and his family had taken it to heart, but thought it wrong to assume that the incident was a personal affront. It said of Llewellyn, 'He's a gentleman! – that is the popular estimate of the man, and one that no amount of gentle satire in whitewash will eradicate,' but claimed a problem had arisen because 'Llewellyn has spent the greater part of his life among a less robust and demonstrative people than the East Lancashire folk'.

Although Llewellyn subsequently backed down on his request to sever ties with Accrington, he did leave after his contract ended at the conclusion of the 1915 season. The editor of the *Accrington Observer and Times* had done his best to come to terms with the events as they occurred, but he did not understand the reality of Llewellyn's situation. There were occasions, such as the artist's caricature and his withdrawal from the Newlands Test in early April 1899, when Llewellyn may have overreacted in the belief that attention was being drawn to his colour. Such instances understandably hit a nerve. Llewellyn's apparent determination to resist any suspicion of being coloured made him vulnerable, given that his career may well have depended on statements made. Although the editor referred to the caricature incident impacting on the 'family', it also appeared that Llewellyn was conscious not to share issues that affected him so deeply. When, in more recent years, it was suggested that his daughter was hiding the truth over the colour question, her upbringing was probably such that the matter was never discussed.[63]

Similarly, Hendricks may have felt considerable anxiety as his children were growing up and perhaps discovering that their father had been considered coloured in the repressive Cape context. While Hendricks was open, honest and possibly naive in revealing details of his background to the press during the mid-1890s, the politically driven course of events that followed must have bewildered him. It is possible that he avoided recalling his cricket achievements in order to shield his children from the accompanying humiliation that he had experienced. He no doubt lived in fear that they too could be exposed to racial indignities. It is the ultimate indictment of the racist establishment that he should have been unable to do anything other than hold his head up high.

Epilogue

Hendricks, D'Oliveira and a cricketing tradition

> 'It was the English cricket establishment in Cape Town which turned on Hendricks ... 75 years later, in 1968, the South African Cricket Association would find itself caught up in strikingly similar controversy involving Basil D'Oliveira.'[1]
>
> – Peter Oborne

HENDRICKS IS A case study in social injustice, of one man caught in a colonial web and his extraordinary story. The racist colonial establishment saw Krom Hendricks's cricket career as the thin edge of the wedge that would open the exclusive preserves of their domain to the underclasses. The better he was, the more threatening to racially defined privilege he became. He was the first in a long list of sporting exclusions that denied his many successors, including Basil D'Oliveira, the right to represent South Africa.

In 1910, when South Africa became a union, Hendricks left his position at the Salt River railway workshops and became a clerk in the Harbour Cartage Department. This move was almost certainly facilitated by Frank Robb, his friend and mentor who had supported him on and off the cricket field for more than a decade. Robb had not only served briefly as president of the Western Province Cricket Union, but was also secretary to the Harbour Board for 20 years. He became docks manager during 1908, a position that included responsibility for transport. The job offered to Hendricks involved overseeing the stables, and it came with an on-site, galvanised-iron house at 4 Battery Street. This area was once part of District One in De Waterkant, strategically situated for transport workers amid the busy operations that served the docks. The houses, which were adjacent to the stables, were constructed for coloured employees of the South African Railways and Harbours – the white staff lived in double-storey homes near the City Tramways. Behind the Battery Street accommodation was a large square that accommodated carts, wagons and flatbed trailers that were used for transporting goods to and from the docks.[2] Hendricks, in his fifties, was happy to get a congenial new post that was at least a tacit reflection of his identification and engagement with the coloured community with whom he was playing cricket.

Not long after Hendricks's move to the Harbour Board position, his mother, who was referred to as Anne Hendrickse, died at the age of 77 after a long stay in the Old Somerset Hospital. She had been living on Barrack Street in central Cape Town when she was taken ill. Her death notice, signed by the surgeon-in-charge, reveals that she was born in the Cape Colony but that her parents were 'not known'. The section requiring details of her spouse was left blank. The death notice also mentions that she was a housewife and widow and mother of one child, 'William Hendrickse', who lived at 4 Battery Street. In addition, a 'Form of Information' was completed and signed by the clerk on duty. Unlike the death notice, it requested details of race, recording that she was European, but that her maiden surname was 'not known'.

Crucially, there was no reason to investigate 'race' systematically in the early 1900s, so the hospital administration placed no pressure on the Hendricks family to reveal ancestral details. The official record that Anne was European does, however, contradict her son's claim to separate newspapers in 1894 and 1896 that she was from St Helena. His mother had presumably told him so, and he had accepted the information. But by 1904, with the incentive of a new job, an English son-in-law and a growing but vulnerable family, he made his bold case to the Western Province Cricket Union that he was the son of European parents. This was probably not true, but there was no documentation to prove otherwise and no siblings or family members to contradict the new position. It is therefore odd that William Kingon, who supported Hendricks's case during the meeting, should have completely ignored the point.

The position of Anne Hendrickse is curious in other ways. The two certificates, which provide details of her death, state that she was born in the Cape Colony. The hospital would not have queried this information, but it does not fit with a key aspect of her background that passed into family legend. As a single mother with no indication of her child's father, it is perhaps not surprising that a myth arose of a poor pregnant Dutch girl trying to find her lover from Holland. It served to explain the less romantic reality of a single parent bringing up a child who would never know his father. The social significance of such details is important in that they may well explain the limited knowledge of Krom Hendricks, the 'coloured' cricketer, within the family. Such secrecy was to prove tragically necessary.

The stress of the potential impact of Hendricks's background may have created myths not limited to Anne's story. Hendricks became a committed family man who cared for his mother, but according to his descendants, he told the tale that he had jumped ship at Cape Town and adopted the name 'Hendricks'. This provided another variation on the theme of escaping his origins and shrouding his past in mystery. He may have fostered this ambiguity to shield his children from the discrimination he had suffered during his cricket career. His wife, Georgina, might not have read the accounts of the Western Province Cricket Union meetings in the newspapers, but she would have been aware of the trials that her husband was forced to endure. The family did move home on a regular basis, but there would have been some discussion in the communities in which they lived. The Hendricks children would have known of their father's enthusiasm for cricket, but may not have known of his treatment at the hands of the cricket authorities. Sophia, his eldest daughter who married John Rowland Trott, was 17 years old when he claimed 9-0 runs against Claremont in 1900, while William Henry (junior) joined his father in playing for Molteno CC and later at Sea Point CC. During the First World War, family members would have been proud of Hendricks's role in supporting the war effort, notably his selecting and leading invitational representative teams.

The Hendricks family, insofar as they took on a racial identity based on Krom's and Georgina's apparent origins, would have seen themselves as Christian and European, but living their lives as part of a broader non-racial, cross-cultural community. They would have been aware of the increasing pressure towards racial segregation. Two of Hendricks's children – Albert James, who moved to Australia, and Percival Findlay – changed their surname to Kendricks, possibly to avoid the connotations of the name Hendricks. His second eldest daughter, Winifred, was born in 1893 and classified 'coloured' according to her marriage certificate. This detail would resurface on her death. 'It was how South Africa worked in the 1970s,' recalled her granddaughter, 'that the classification caused problems with her being buried with my granddad.' Fortunately, 'one of my aunts got involved and money changed hands and she was re-classified as white'.[3]

The family remained closely connected to the Woodstock–Green Point–Mouille Point communities and supported one another at baptisms, weddings and funerals. Of the oldest children, Sophia Georgina and Winifred Maria married soldiers – John Rowland Trott and Melville Howard Priday respectively. William Henry (junior) married Sarah Jemima Keet from Moreland Terrace off Napier Street in De Waterkant, and George Edward met Alice Elizabeth (surname unknown) at Dock Cottages where the Hendricks family had resided for some years. Brothers and sisters of both the Hendricks and Myers families often stayed at 4 Battery Street.

Hendricks's children had large families: Sophia and William Henry (junior) each had 12 children; George Edward had five; Winifred Maria had three; Percival Findlay had seven with three different wives; and Irene May had five. There were numerous grandchildren and Hendricks would have enjoyed seeing them grow up. He probably saw the potential that Winifred's son, Robert Priday (born in 1925), had as a cricketer and footballer. It was in the latter game that Robert excelled, playing for Cape Town City before moving to Liverpool. He was chosen for the club's tour of North America in 1946 and made nine appearances for the side that won the First Division in 1946/47. He went on to make a further 25 appearances for Liverpool over the next two seasons before moving to Blackburn Rovers. On his return to Cape Town, he was a strong supporter of the coloured community.

In 1923, Krom Hendricks purchased a house at 13 George Street, Mowbray. His youngest daughter, Irene May, and her husband, Sidney Arthur Newton, lived there after they were married at St John's Evangelistic Church in 1924. He was a marine engineer with a trawling company, Irwin and Johnson, and they had four children.

Hendricks retired at the age of 75 in 1933, at the height of the depression, but he had prepared wisely. It was decided that the Newtons should take over his home while he spent his retirement years there.

Given Hendricks's previous involvement as a vice-president of the Western Province Coloured Cricket Union, it is likely that he followed matches at the nearby Mowbray Sports Club grounds, which were administered by the Cape District Cricket Union. He might have watched the outstanding coloured player of the twenties and thirties, Taliep Salie, a talent that Hendricks himself had identified for his invitation team as early as 1917. Salie led Western Province to five successive victories in the Barnato Trophy tournaments. Clarrie Grimmett, the famous Australian cricketer, came across him as a net bowler and thought he was good enough to play for any international side. Salie also received invitations to play professional cricket in England but turned them down. A fellow cricketer suggested he was reluctant to move overseas because 'he feared he would be unable to find a mosque close enough to the English grounds to enable him to properly observe the tenets of his Muslim faith'.[4]

In 1939, Hendricks became ill and for the last 15 months of his life he was under the care of a medical practitioner, Dr C. Shapiro. He died on 23 September 1940. His death certificate described him as 'European' and stated that he died of old age. Shapiro made a point of adding that Hendricks had been an employee of the Table Bay Harbour Board. In his will, Hendricks left Irene May £135.27 and his piano, with equal shares of £45.11 going to his remaining children at that time: Sophia Georgina, William Henry, Winifred Maria, Albert James, Percival Findlay and Edward Bairstow. The presence of the piano throws a rare ray of light on to Krom's domestic life. The piano was a mechanism for congeniality, at the cultural heart of his large family and a social centre for a wide circle of friends. Irene May established a gravestone at the family's Woltemade plot, while Hendricks's death notice in the *Cape Times* recorded:

> **Hendrickse** – 23 September 1940 – Passed away peacefully at his daughter's residence – 13 George Street, Mowbray, on the 23rd inst. William Henry in his 83rd year, late of Table Bay Harbour. Deeply mourned by his sorrowing daughters, sons, daughters-in-law, sons-in-law and grandchildren. Funeral leaves Goodall and Williams Chapel, Main Road, Observatory tomorrow (Wednesday 25th Inst) at 3.30pm for Woltemade No 1 (first gate). Relatives and friends are kindly invited to attend.[5]

There was no obituary for Hendricks. Most of his cricket achievements were already lost in the mists of time. He had played with marked success for establishment teams between 1894 and 1901, but administrators had subsequently seen fit to airbrush him out of their history. Records of his involvement in 'coloured' cricket are sketchy, both before and after the period when he played for 'white' clubs. By 1940, more than 20 years after he played his last match, the administration of coloured cricket had become fragmented as a result of deepening segregationist structures and increasing ethno-religious divisions. There was no structure in place to support and maintain records, while newspapers that catered for the coloured communities were invariably short-lived. One result of this lack of cricket coverage is that no details have been discovered for four out of the five Barnato cricket tournaments played in the decade between 1922/23 and 1931/32. Moreover, there are few facts and figures for players who represented Western Province in the first half of the twentieth century, including legends like Taliep Salie, Ivor J. 'Sakkie' Abrahams and A.J. 'Dol' Freeman.

The problems that cricket administrators experienced were not uncommon. They lived and worked in a time of unprecedented upheaval: the advent of economic imperialism after the Anglo-Boer War and the formation of the Union of South Africa; the struggle over labour; the involvement of the empire in two world wars; decolonisation; and finally, the expulsion of South Africa from the imperial fraternity. Syd Reddy and Benny 'Damoo' Bansda produced three 'Non-European' cricket almanacks during the 1950s and 1960s, but much research was still necessary to fill the gaps. When Basil D'Oliveira became one of the most famous cricketers in the world at the end of the 1960s, he had not heard of Krom Hendricks.

The parallels between Hendricks and D'Oliveira were remarkable, even though their treatment and experience were significantly different. D'Oliveira, who was of Indian-Portuguese descent, entered club cricket only 20-odd years after Hendricks's last season in the City Cricket League. The two men at different times lived in houses a few hundred metres apart in Bo-Kaap and trod the same cricket paths in early life. Like Hendricks, D'Oliveira was a member of a Christian minority within the majority Muslim community. Both applied to join prominent Muslim clubs in the area in which they lived. D'Oliveira was turned down; Hendricks was not. They were both modest, private men, whose cricket reflected formidable physical strength, outstanding athleticism and phlegmatic temperaments, plus enough fighting spirit to get to the top of the game open to them.

Like Hendricks, D'Oliveira caught the eye through his stellar performances for a South African 'Non-European' side. It is unknown whether Hendricks was ever offered the possibility of playing overseas. If he had, such an offer would probably have come too late given his family responsibilities. D'Oliveira famously grabbed at the chance of international fame. He was ultimately denied the opportunity to play Test cricket for England in South Africa, while Hendricks was denied the chance to play for South Africa in England.

Hendricks performed in front of his supporters at Newlands immediately following the conclusion of a Test match on the same pitch and against substantially the same opposition. D'Oliveira, by contrast, never had an opportunity to play on what should have been his home ground and watched white cricket longingly from the corrugated-iron railway stand reserved for coloureds. Hendricks and D'Oliveira were ultimately the standard bearers of a single tradition, shaping and reinforcing a cricket culture that continues to this day and is part of the lifeblood of South Africa.

The D'Oliveira family lived on Upper Bloem Street, the highest habitable point on the lower slopes of Signal Hill. It has a magnificent view of Cape Town. Further down the steep slope is Chiappini Street, where Hendricks had resided and probably learnt his cricket in his younger years. D'Oliveira wrote about playing street cricket – boys from one street playing against those from another. There was once a sloping field between the D'Oliveiras' home and the next row of houses on Upper Pepper Street. A neighbour recalled watching D'Oliveira and his friends playing cricket on a concrete slab. They also made use of a flight of steps on the tenements where they lived. Bouncing the ball from the top landing to one below was one of their improvised 'nets'. 'We were back-alley cricketers who broke windows and ran,' said D'Oliveira.[6] In later years, he recalled the value of the street games, not least in being able to cope with fast bowling. He also commented on the depth of talent, singling out the brilliance of wicketkeeper Lobo Abed. One of a great cricketing family, Abed would practise his skills behind an oil can hour after hour. D'Oliveira was convinced 'he would have been a Test player if he had ever had the chance'.[7]

In the immediate post-war period, a renewed effort was made by black cricket communities to counter the separatism of the 1930s. In the 1945/46 season, the South African Coloured Cricket Board was revived, and the Barnato Trophy tournament was staged for the first time since 1931/32. Salie, who was by then 51 years old, captained Western Province to victory over sides from Transvaal and Griqualand West at the Mowbray Sports Club. The tournament was a success and developments in non-white cricket were to move relatively quickly over the next few years. In 1947, three organisations that had broken away from the South African Coloured Cricket Board formed a new umbrella body for 'inter-race' cricket that became known as the South African Cricket Board of Control (SACBOC). It was made up of boards representing coloured Christians, Africans, Indians and Malays.

Despite the administrative progress, the outlook for black sportsmen was bleak as the new regime moved in precisely the opposite direction. In 1948, the National Party under Dr D.F. Malan took power at the (white) ballot box. The new government wasted no time in shaping South Africa using an ideology of apartheid, which sliced up society on the basis of racial differences. Apartheid entrenched white supremacy and privilege through the Prohibition of Mixed Marriages Act, the Immorality Amendment Act and the Population Registration Act, which formally separated people into white, coloured, Indian and African categories. Building on this racial categorisation, the 1950 Group Areas Act enforced residential and economic segregation with massive population relocations, and the Reservation of Separate Amenities Act enforced social segregation in all public areas.

With whom or against whom one could play, and where, were enshrined in law, not simply social practice. It was difficult for sportsmen to react effectively. 'I knew about the laws of the land,' wrote D'Oliveira, 'the "separate development" policy that became government policy in 1948, and we would have been foolish at that time if we had tried to buck the system.'[8]

D'Oliveira recalled that 'enthusiasm for cricket was massive in the non-white communities of South Africa'. Like Hendricks before him, he believed the game provided an opportunity to better himself. He wanted to prove that he was 'as good as anybody in the only place he felt at ease – the cricket field'.[9] When he was 16, he joined his father's club, St Augustine, for whom Hendricks had played some 30 years earlier. St Augustine still played at Green Point, where 20 or more matches were crammed together with overlapping boundaries and fielders.

Australian writer Ray Robinson went to see D'Oliveira play: 'On unfenced parkland players changed in the open if they could not squeeze into the over-crowded pavilion. The matting-over-gravel pitch was a rough old strip that no first-class player would normally have set foot on, even if his life insurance was doubled.'[10]

D'Oliveira would go to Newlands 'to watch the great white players'. Unaware that the South African coloured cricketers had played against Read's English tourists at Newlands in 1891/92, he expressed a desire 'to be the first coloured man to play on the major cricket fields of South Africa'.[11] How D'Oliveira and his friends would have delighted in the knowledge that Hendricks had unnerved some of South Africa's finest white batsmen at Newlands to the extent that they did not want to play against him. 'I always supported the visiting country,' admitted D'Oliveira, 'after all, they weren't denying me the chance to play in such a magnificent stadium.'[12]

SACBOC sought to play the game at the highest level. In 1955, an application was made to join the Imperial Cricket Conference as a full member, potentially forcing the ICC to choose between the white and non-white bodies or having two bodies from the same country. The ICC dead-batted the application. SACBOC was told 'to prove its ability to conduct tours and also obtain two sponsoring countries'.[13] SACBOC next applied to play matches against official South African Cricket Association tourists, but were again rejected. Their players would have strengthened South African cricket in the Test arena. One sportswriter, Sy Mogapi, chose an ideal 'all-South African' team to play England at Trent Bridge in 1955. His line-up included six players of colour – Chong Meyer, Basil D'Oliveira (vice-captain), Tiny Abed, George Langa, Essop Jeewa and 'Mac' Anthony – and five white players.[14]

Hendricks, like D'Oliveira, was only the tip of the iceberg. The 1894 first touring side to England for which he was seen as a certain selection, might profitably have included both Krom and Armien Hendricks, Ebrahim Ariefdien, Robert Grendon and Lamarah Samsodien. This team would have been more representative of South African cricket and provided a far more serious challenge to their English opponents than the depleted combination that eventually toured.

A mixed side was anathema in 1894. By the mid-1950s it was illegal. South Africa's policy was that whites and blacks should organise their sports separately (although inevitably unequally). Mixed sport was formally prohibited within South Africa, and no mixed teams could compete abroad. Any international sides competing in South Africa would have to be all white, though black sportsmen from overseas would be allowed to compete against South African blacks. Government consequently abrogated to itself the final say in the composition of foreign national teams, as D'Oliveira would discover a decade later.

Within this context, SACBOC arranged successful home and away series against Kenya. D'Oliveira described the matches as 'the … emancipation of the coloured African as international cricketers'.[15] Plans were put into motion to invite Frank Worrell's West Indies to visit South Africa in 1959 to demonstrate that South Africa possessed black cricketers good enough to play Test cricket. Worrell fully supported the tour and 'had readily accepted, feeling it would help to break down apartheid'.[16] It had the support of C.L.R. James, who thought the tour had the potential to expose the numerous disparities that prevailed in a racist system: 'A political bombshell … I want it to go on exploding and exploding. The only people who can be hurt are the South African jailers.'[17]

The Worrell visit did not meet with everyone's approval. The South African Sports Association headed by Dennis Brutus objected because the tour would take place within South Africa's racist structure, and playing only black cricketers would lend legitimacy to apartheid. SACBOC eventually gave up on the tour. Black South African cricketers suffered; as D'Oliveira put it, 'The heartbreak of the cancellation … so upset me that I decided to finish with cricket.' He did not give up, fortunately, though he was never reconciled to the South African Sports Association cause. 'Even if the coloured politicians were right ... their attitude still denied to the coloured Africans contact and communication with people from another country.'[18]

When D'Oliveira's morale was at its lowest, an opportunity arose for him to play for Middleton in the Central Lancashire League. Damoo Bansda began a fundraising campaign and wrote an article on D'Oliveira that was published in *World Sports* magazine. 'People of all races co-operated to give him the chance he deserved. Gerald Innes, who had toured Australia and New Zealand with the South African team in 1952/53, arranged a highly successful benefit match at Claremont. 'Never mind the laws, Bas,' he told D'Oliveira, 'we'll get you to England.'[19]

D'Oliveira landed in London on 1 April 1960 and moved quickly from club to county and then Test cricket, making his debut for England against the West Indies in 1966. In that series, he struck four 6s in a hectic 88 at Headingley, Leeds, one being a straight drive off fast bowler Wes Hall. His first Test century came on the same ground against India the following year, but his major ambition was to tour South Africa in 1968/69. 'Right from the day I'd been selected to play for England,' he said, 'this trip had been on my mind.'[20]

The summer of 1968 was one of intense speculation over whether D'Oliveira would be included in the tour party. Sir Alec Douglas-Home, the former British prime minister, and Lord Cobham, a former president of the MCC, met with the South African prime minister, John Vorster. Letters and messages flowed amid an attitude of evasiveness and secrecy among leading officials. Bribery, lies and political pressure prevailed. Throughout the summer, D'Oliveira maintained his dignity and demonstrated faith in the English establishment.

In the course of the season, D'Oliveira was chosen for the first Test against Australia at Old Trafford, scoring an unbeaten 87 and claiming 2-45 in 30 overs. He was promptly dropped and experienced a dramatic lack of form in the county championship. However, he was recalled for the fifth Test when Tom Cartwright and Barry

Knight were declared unfit and Roger Prideaux withdrew. Under enormous pressure, D'Oliveira scored a match-winning 158. He had made an incontestable claim for a place in the MCC's touring side – or so he thought. Colin Cowdrey told him, 'I want you in South Africa,' but the England captain failed to support D'Oliveira at the fateful Lord's selection meeting.[21] Discussion went on until nearly two o'clock in the morning, after which D'Oliveira was not named in the MCC tour party. In sympathy and perhaps in recognition of a wrong done, Mrs Cowdrey subsequently sent flowers to Mrs D'Oliveira.

The huge public outcry that followed in Britain was concerned with issues of far greater significance than quibbling over cricket technicalities. The MCC had apparently capitulated to South African political pressure. When Tom Cartwright subsequently pulled out of the tour, the selectors took less than ten minutes to name D'Oliveira as his replacement.

In South Africa, the National Party government could not risk one of the country's coloured cricketers returning home and proving himself against South Africa's best players. Their attitude was essentially the same as that which Hendricks had faced at the Cape in the 1890s, a time when the establishment would not tolerate the potential humiliation of a white Western Province or Cape Town CC batsman receiving a fearful working-over from a coloured bowler.

Cecil John Rhodes, then prime minister of the Cape Colony, had prevented Hendricks from accompanying the first South African side to tour England in 1894. Rhodes claimed to be protecting the cricketer from Englishmen who would treat him as a curiosity. In reality, cricket was a critical element in the Rhodes-imposed policy of segregation that concentrated economic and political power in establishment hands and restricted team representation at its various levels to whites, whatever the nature of their ties to the country itself. Established practice became enshrined in the law until, nearly 75 years later, it was exposed to a worldwide audience by another player of colour from Bo-Kaap.

In a mirror image of Rhodes's involvement in Hendricks's eligibility to represent his country, Prime Minister John Vorster was soon involved in the question of the inclusion of D'Oliveira in the English side. From early 1968, Vorster operated behind the scenes while the MCC colluded with his regime to keep cricket ties open. Only when D'Oliveira was belatedly drafted into the team did Vorster declare his position. He told a cheering crowd in Bloemfontein that the English were the guilty party, as the touring side had become 'the team of the Anti-Apartheid Movement, the team of the South African Non-Racial Olympic Committee and the team of Bishop Reeves'.[22]

In the same way Milton had worked closely with Rhodes, so Arthur Coy, the president of the South African Cricket Association, became Vorster's primary instrument. In both cases, government and cricket administrators worked together to implement and maintain segregated sport, whatever the consequences. Few questioned the mendacity of the establishments involved. The MCC's Billy Griffith stated that 'never at any time was pressure put on the selectors by anyone from South Africa'.[23] And on hearing the original news that D'Oliveira had not been chosen, Coy wrote to Vorster: 'I did so appreciate your telephone call to me on the evening of the 28th August when our respective problems were resolved ... Your courtesy, frankness and the trust with which you received me on behalf of the South African Cricket Association was also very much appreciated and we do indeed appreciate your help and guidance in a matter which was important to our country in so many respects.'[24]

The attitude of the Western Province Cricket Union at this time was important because of D'Oliveira's significance as a major figure in cricket history at the Cape. When the tour was cancelled, the president of the union, Ernest McKay, was questioned by the *Cape Times*. He responded with a statement that was published on the front page: 'I am disappointed, but I support Mr Vorster on this.'[25] They were words that not only echoed the views of the infamous clique that had governed Western Province cricket at the turn of the century, but also served as a horrifying reminder that the administration of cricket at the Cape – and indeed the country – had not progressed.

The decision to ban D'Oliveira from playing for England in South Africa created a major schism in international cricket. It forced the sporting world to focus on apartheid, and South African cricket was plunged into two decades of isolation. The 1968/69 tour was cancelled, as were South Africa's 1970 tour to England and their 1971/72 tour to Australia. As a desperate measure, the South African Cricket Association sought to include two of D'Oliveira's former team-mates, Owen Williams and Dik Abed, in their side for the Australian tour. The cricketers rejected the invitation. 'I refused to go as a glorified baggage master,' said Williams in 1971, uncannily echoing Hendricks's response when this possibility was extended to the latter in 1894. 'I wanted to be chosen on merit,' explained Williams, 'after having proved myself at club and provincial level against the best in the country. Unfortunately, the laws of the country didn't allow that.'[26] South Africa was excluded from Test cricket and, in time, the country was isolated from virtually all international sport.

Hendricks and D'Oliveira's stories inevitably had different outcomes. D'Oliveira fought tooth and nail for a chance to establish how good he could be and achieved this even if he was denied the chance to show his talent in his own country. Hendricks never had the opportunity to really test himself, apart from rare occasions when the establishment let its guard down. He was the unwitting victim of racism in cricket at the Cape; an archetypal example of social injustice. Despite this, the enduring popularity of the game has contributed to building a new society in South Africa where cricket heroes are judged on their ability and talents. At the time of writing, four cricketers called Hendricks are currently playing first-class cricket, and Beuran Hendricks and Reeza Hendricks have already represented South Africa. They would be proud of their spiritual forefather and namesake who, for more than 40 years, loved nothing more than to run in, gather himself and propel the ball at lightning pace into the base of the stumps.

Notes

FOREWORD

1. See, for example, A. Desai, V. Padayachee, K. Reddy and G. Vahed, *Blacks in Whites* (Pietermaritzburg: University of Natal Press, 2002); B. Murray and G. Vahed (eds), *Empire & Cricket: The South African Experience 1884–1914* (Pretoria: UNISA Press, 2009); A. Odendaal, K. Reddy, C. Merrett and J. Winch, *Cricket and Conquest: The History of South African Cricket Retold 1795–1914* (Cape Town: HSRC, 2016); A. Desai, *A Reverse Sweep* (Johannesburg: Jacana Media, 2016); A. Odendaal, K. Reddy and C. Merrett, *Divided Country: The History of South African Cricket Retold 1914–1950s* (Cape Town: HSRC, 2018) and B. Murray, R. Parry and J. Winch (eds), *Cricket and Society in South Africa 1910–1971: From Union to Isolation* (London: Palgrave Macmillan, 2018).

INTRODUCTION

1. A. Odendaal, 'Foreword' in B. Murray and G. Vahed (eds), *Empire & Cricket: The South African Experience 1884–1914* (Pretoria: UNISA Press, 2009), xvii.
2. W. Hammond, *Cricket My World* (London: Stanley Paul, 1949), 88.
3. R. Bowen, *Cricket: A History of Its Growth and Development Throughout the World* (London: Eyre and Spottiswoode, 1970), 149.
4. A. Odendaal and S. Reddy, 'SACBOC: Its Origins and Development' in A. Odendaal (ed.), *Cricket in Isolation* (Cape Town: Don Nelson, 1977), 325.
5. M. Biddiss, *Images of Race* (Leicester: Leicester University Press, 1979), 141–155. Charles Darwin successfully nominated Farrar for Fellowship of the Royal Society.

CHAPTER 1: ORIGINS OF A LEGEND

1. J. Bright-Holmes, *The Joy of Cricket* (London: Secker & Warburg, 1984), 241; A. Knight, *The Complete Cricketer* (London: Methuen, 1906), 271.
2. *Cape Times*, 29 December 1891.
3. *Ibid.*, 15 January 1890.
4. *Ibid.*, 27 January 1890.
5. *Ibid.*, 29 January 1890.
6. All matches described as Tests up to 1905/06 were retrospectively given Test status: M. Luckin, *The History of South African Cricket* (Johannesburg: W.E. Hortor and Sons, 1915), 715.
7. *Cape Times*, 23 March 1892.
8. *The Sportsman*, 5 January 1892.

9. *Cape Times*, 24 March 1892.
10. *Ibid.*
11. *The Cricket Field*, 25 November 1893, 490.
12. *Ibid.*
13. *Ibid.*, 10 June 1893, 164.
14. *Cape Times*, 13 October 1892.
15. *Ibid.*, 14 October 1892.
16. *Ibid.*, 24 March 1892.
17. *Cape Argus*, 25 March 1892.
18. *Ibid.*, 26 March 1892.
19. Knight, *The Complete Cricketer*, 271.

CHAPTER 2: A PLACE NOT INHABITED BY WHITE MEN

1. I. Trott, correspondence with Rootsweb, March 2005.
2. H. Clarke and W. Jones, *The Life and Times of Thomas Fothergill Lightfoot* (London: Simpkin, Marshall, Hamilton, Kent & Co., 1908), 1, 67, 69.
3. *Ibid.*, 105, 130, 135.
4. *Cape Argus*, 18 May 1865.
5. *South African Advertiser and Mail*, 19 May 1865; Clarke and Jones, *The Life and Times of Thomas Fothergill Lightfoot*, 133–138.
6. *Cape Argus*, 3 October 1871.
7. An Old Peripatetic, 'Cape Town and Cricket' in *Cape Monthly*, Volume VI, 1873, 16–63.
8. *Ibid.*
9. *Cape Argus*, 6 March 1873.
10. R. Ballantyne, *Six Months at the Cape or Letters to Periwinkle from South Africa* (London: Nick Hodson, 1876), Letter 13.
11. A. Trollope, *South Africa (Volume 1)* reprint (Stroud: Nonsuch Publishing, 2005), 13, 45.
12. B. Frere, 'Native races of South Africa' in *Transactions of the South African Philosophical Society* 1, No. 2 (1877–1888), xxii–xxiv.
13. S. Dubow, 'South Africa and South Africans: Nationality, Belonging, Citizenship' in R. Ross, A. Kelk Mager and W. Nasson (eds), *The Cambridge History of South Africa, Volume 2, 1885–1994* (Cambridge: Cambridge University Press, 2011), 20, 25.
14. A. Trollope: Letter to John Blackwood, 21 July 1877.
15. Trollope, *South Africa*, 51.
16. Clarke and Jones, *The Life and Times of Thomas Fothergill Lightfoot*, 189–191. Sophia Georgina's birth certificate gives her surname as 'Hendrickse', which is the Afrikaans spelling.
17. *The Lantern*, 23 September 1882.
18. V. Bickford-Smith, *Ethnic Pride and Racial Prejudice in Victorian Cape Town: Group Identity and Social Practice 1875–1902* (Cambridge: Cambridge University Press, 1995), 39.
19. *Cape Times*, 29 January 1884.
20. R. Guha, *A Corner of a Foreign Field: The Indian History of British Sport* (London: Picador, 2002), 12–14.
21. *Cape Argus*, 31 October 1890.
22. *Ibid.*, 1 November 1890.
23. S. Marks, 'Class, Culture and Consciousness in South Africa, 1880–1899' in R. Ross, A. Kelk Mager and W. Nasson (eds), *The Cambridge History of South Africa, Volume 2, 1885–1994* (Cambridge: Cambridge University Press, 2011), 102.

CHAPTER 3: OPPOSITION TO THE 'MCC OF THE CAPE COLONY'

1. Luckin, *The History of South African Cricket*, 46, 47.
2. Letter from 'Old Cricketer', *Daily Independent*, 25 April 1888.
3. *The Lantern*, 23 April 1888.
4. *Cape Argus*, 2 April 1888.
5. C. Muller (ed.), *Five Hundred Years: A History of South Africa* (Pretoria: Academica, 1981), 190.
6. The *Cape Argus* published the resolution after it was presented to the annual general meeting of the Cape Town CC on 18 August 1890.
7. *Cape Argus*, 1 August 1890.
8. P. Lewsen, *John X. Merriman: Paradoxical South African Statesman* (New Haven: Yale University Press, 1982), 83.
9. M. Tamarkin, *Cecil Rhodes and the Cape Afrikaners: The Imperial Colossus and the Colonial Parish Pump* (London: Routledge, 1996), 73.
10. *Daily Independent*, 28 January 1889.
11. Marks, 'Class, Culture and Consciousness', 141.
12. *Cricket: A Weekly Record of the Game*, 24 January 1889.
13. *Port Elizabeth Telegraph*, 3 January 1889.
14. *Diamond Fields Advertiser*, 21 January 1889.
15. *Imvo Zabantsundu*, 28 February 1889.
16. D. Slater – correspondence with authors.
17. *Cape Times Weekly*, 5 January 1890.
18. *Cape Argus*, 10 November 1890.
19. *Ibid.*, 14 November 1890.
20. *Cape Times*, 15 February 1891.
21. *Ibid.*, 25 February 1891.
22. *Ibid.*
23. *Ibid.*, 23 March 1891.

CHAPTER 4: THE TALK OF THE TOWN

1. *South African Review*, 3 November 1893.
2. *Diamond Fields Advertiser*, 15 December 1888.
3. *South African Review*, 6 October 1893.
4. *Cape Times*, 13 September 1880.
5. *Cape Argus*, 26 May 1881.
6. *Ibid.*, 4 July 1881.
7. *Ibid.*, 5 July 1881.
8. J. Winch, *England's Youngest Captain: The Life and Times of Monty Bowden and Two South African Journalists* (Windsor: Windsor Publishers, 2003), 53.
9. *Cape Argus*, 1 November 1886.
10. *Cape Times Weekly*, 23 February 1887.
11. *Cape Times*, 9 April 1891.
12. *The Star*, 9 April 1890.
13. A. Darter, *Pioneers of Mashonaland* (Bulawayo, Books of Rhodesia, 1977), 149.
14. *Rhodesia Herald*, 18 September 1914.
15. R. Blennerhassett and L. Sleeman, *Adventures in Mashonaland* (Bulawayo: Books of Rhodesia, 1969), 226–227.
16. *Cape Times*, 20 November 1892.
17. *Cape Argus*, 3 October 1893.
18. *Cape Times*, 17 October 1893.

19. *Ibid.*, 18 October 1893.
20. *Imvo Zabantsundu*, 4 October – 30 December 1888.
21. *Ibid.*
22. *Cricket: A Weekly Record of the Game*, March 1893.
23. *Cape Times*, 11 January 1894.
24. M. Tamarkin, *Cecil Rhodes and the Cape Afrikaners*, 183.
25. Dubow, 'South Africa and South Africans', 32.
26. R. Parry, 'Black Cricketers, White Politicians and the Origins of Segregation at the Cape to 1894' in Murray and Vahed (eds), *Empire and Cricket*, 40–41.
27. J. Hofmeyr with F. Reitz, *The Life of Jan Hendrik Hofmeyr (Onze Jan)* (Cape Town: Van de Sandt, 1913), 436–437.
28. *Cape Times*, 30 December – 7 January 1894.
29. T. Lewis, *Double Century: The Story of MCC and Cricket* (Sevenoaks: Hodder & Stoughton, 1987), 100.
30. *The Cricket Field*, 4 August 1894.
31. *Cape Times*, 17 October 1893.
32. *Ibid.*, 11 November 1893.
33. *Ibid.*, 27 October 1893.
34. N. Ferguson, *Empire: How Britain made the Modern World* (London: Penguin, 2003), 227.
35. *South African Review*, 3 November 1893, authors' emphasis.
36. *Ibid.*, 15 December 1893.
37. *Ibid.*

CHAPTER 5: 'WHY AM I TERMED A MALAY?'

1. *Standard and Diggers News*, 14 February 1894.
2. *South African Review*, 8 December 1893.
3. *Cape Times*, 1 and 11 November 1893; *The Press*, 9 January 1894.
4. *The Press.*, 11 January 1894.
5. *Ibid.*, 29 January 1894.
6. *Cape Times*, 11 January 1894
7. *Ibid.*, 12 January 1894.
8. *Standard and Diggers News*, 13 January 1894.
9. *Ibid.*, 14 February 1894.
10. *The Star*, 15 January 1894.
11. R. Rotberg, *The Founder: Cecil Rhodes and the Pursuit of Power* (Oxford: Oxford University Press, 1988), 459–460.
12. *Cape Argus*, 4 January 1894.
13. Rotberg, *The Founder*, 459–460.
14. *South African Review*, 1 December 1893.
15. *Cape Times*, 10 February 1894.
16. *South African Review*, 11 August 1893.
17. *Ibid.*, 12 January 1894.
18. P. Warner, *Lord's 1787–1945* (London: Sportsman's Book Club, 1951), 60.
19. P. Warner, *Long Innings* (London: George G. Harrap, 1951), 36–37.
20. Dubow, 'South Africa and South Africans', 32.
21. Rotberg, *The Founder*, 476–477.
22. *Cape Times*, 21 February 1894.
23. Reported in the *South African Review*, 9 February 1894.
24. *Standard and Diggers News*, 17 February 1894.
25. *South African Review*, 2 March 1894, author's emphasis.

26. *Standard and Diggers News*, 21 February 1894.
27. *The Press*, 5 and 17 February 1894.
28. *Natal Mercury*, 23 February 1894.
29. R. Blake, *A History of Rhodesia* (London: Eyre Methuen, 1977), 152.
30. Reported in the *South African Review*, 23 February 1894.
31. *Cape Times*, 9 February 1894.
32. Hofmeyr with Reitz, *The Life of Jan Hendrik Hofmeyr (Onze Jan)*, 473.

CHAPTER 6: 'COURTING' A DISASTER FOR THE SAKE OF PREJUDICE'

1. *Standard and Diggers News*, 29 March 1894.
2. *Cape Times*, 12 March 1894.
3. *Standard and Diggers News*, 1 March 1894.
4. *South African Review*, 16 March 1894. Following the *South African Review* report, drawings appeared in *The Cricket Field* depicting the touring side as African warriors brandishing assegais.
5. *The Cricket Field*, 31 March 1894.
6. *Cricket: A Weekly Record of the Game*, 3 May 1894.
7. *South African Review*, 2 March 1894.
8. *Natal Mercury*, 22 March 1894.
9. *Standard and Diggers News*, 27 February 1894.
10. *Bloemfontein Express*, 9 March 1894.
11. *Standard and Diggers News*, 27 February 1894.
12. *Cape Times*, 27 February 1894.
13. *Standard and Diggers News*, 27 February 1894.
14. *Cape Times*, 5 March 1894.
15. *The Press*, 27 February 1894; *Standard and Diggers News*, 27 February 1894.
16. *Standard and Diggers News*, 27 February 1894.
17. *Cape Times*, 17 March 1894.
18. *Cape Argus*, 30 March 1894.
19. *Table Talk*, 18 October 1894.
20. *Cape Argus*, 27 February 1894.
21. *South African Review*, 16 March 1894.
22. *Ibid.*, 6 March 1894.
23. *Natal Mercury*, 9 and 15 March 1894.
24. *Standard and Diggers News*, 22 February 1894.
25. *South African Review*, 16 March 1894.
26. *Cape Times*, 16 March 1894.
27. *Ibid.*
28. *Standard and Diggers News*, 29 March 1894.
29. *Ibid.*, 13 April 1894.
30. *Cape Argus*, 30 March 1894.
31. *Standard and Diggers News*, 29 March 1894.
32. Rotberg, *The Founder*, 461–462.
33. *Cape Times*, 16 March 1894.
34. *Cape Argus*, 30 March 1894.
35. *Cape Times*, 30 March – 3 April 1894.
36. *Cape Argus Weekly*, 11 April 1894.
37. *South African Review*, 13 April 1894.
38. *Cape Times*, 12 April 1894.
39. *South African Review*, 31 August 1894.

40. *Ibid.*, 16 November 1894.
41. *The Cricket Field*, 4 August 1894.
42. *Ibid.*
43. *Cricket: A Weekly Record of the Game*, 13 September 1894.
44. Knight, *The Complete Cricketer*, 271.
45. *The Standard and Diggers News*, 2 October 1894.
46. *Ibid.*
47. *Ibid.*, 31 August 1894.
48. *South African Review*, 31 August 1894.
49. *Standard and Diggers News*, 2 October 1894.
50. *South African Review*, 6 July 1894.
51. *Ibid.*, 14 September 1894.
52. *Ibid.*, 30 November 1894.
53. *Standard and Diggers News*, 15 September 1894.
54. *Cape Times*, 17 September 1894.
55. *Ibid.*
56. *The Cricket Field*, 8 December 1894.

CHAPTER 7: THE HENDRICKS CONTROVERSY COMES HOME

1. *Cape Times*, 30 October 1894.
2. *Ibid.*
3. *Ibid.*, 2 November 1894.
4. *Ibid.*, 3 November 1894.
5. *Standard and Diggers News*, 2 November 1894.
6. *Cape Times*, 6 November 1894.
7. *The Cricket Field*, December 1894.
8. I. Goldin, *Making Race: The Politics and Economics of Coloured Identity in South Africa* (London: Longman, 1987), 23.
9. V. Bickford-Smith, *Ethnic Pride and Racial Prejudice in Victorian Cape Town: Group Identity and Social Practice 1875–1902* (Cambridge: Cambridge University Press, 1995), 124–125.
10. *Cape Argus*, 14 June 1895.
11. *Natal Mercury*, 3 January 1895.
12. *South African Review*, 8 March 1895.
13. *Cape Times*, 23 December 1895.
14. *Ibid.*, 19 April 1895.
15. *Ibid.*, 18 September 1895.
16. B. Dobbs, *Edwardians at Play* (London: Pelham, 1973), 140.
17. B. Green (ed.), *The Wisden Book of Cricketers' Lives: Obituaries from Wisden Cricketers' Almanack* (London: Queen Anne Press, 1988), 316.
18. I. Wilton, *C.B. Fry: King of Sport* (London: Metro, 2002), 78, 415.
19. D. Birley, *A Social History of English Cricket* (London: Aurum Press, 1999), 165.
20. Wilton, *C.B. Fry*, 77–78, 84–85.
21. *Natal Mercury*, 25 January 1896.
22. *Cape Times*, 20 December 1895.
23. *Ibid.*, 21 December 1895.
24. *South African Review*, 26 December 1895.
25. E. Longford, *Jameson's Raid* (London: Weidenfeld & Nicolson, 1982), 61.
26. Rotberg, *The Founder*, 539, 542.
27. *Natal Mercury*, 25 January 1896.
28. *South African Review*, 24 January 1896.

29. *Standard and Diggers News*, 25 January 1896.
30. *Cape Times*, 20 February 1896.
31. *South African Review*, 31 January 1896.
32. *Ibid.*, 14 February 1896; S. Horwood's Scrapbook (Cape Town CC).
33. *Cape Times*, 18 February 1896.
34. *Ibid.*, 1 February 1896.
35. *The Standard and Diggers News*, 14 February 1896.
36. *Cape Times*, 18 February 1896.
37. *Ibid.*, 27 February 1896.
38. *Standard and Diggers News*, 7 March 1896.
39. *South African Review*, 7 February 1896.
40. *Cape Times*, 11 February 1896.
41. *South African Review*, 21 February 1896.
42. *Cricket: A Weekly Record of the Game*, 20 August 1896.
43. *South African Review*, 7 February 1896.
44. *Cape Times*, 21 February 1896.
45. *South African Review*, 28 February 1896; *Cape Times*, 25 February 1896.
46. *Cape Times*, 16 March 1896.
47. *South African Review*, 31 January 1896.
48. G.H. Tanser, *A Scantling of Time: The Story of Salisbury, Rhodesia 1890–1900* (Salisbury, Manning: 1965), 178.
49. *Cape Argus*, 3 August 1896.
50. *Ibid.*
51. Luckin, *The History of South African Cricket*, 365.
52. *Cape Times*, 8 March 1930.
53. Rotberg, *The Founder*, 685.

CHAPTER 8: 'LET THEM LOOK TO GOD FOR JUSTICE FOR MAN HAS REFUSED IT'

1. *Cape Times*, 6 November 1897.
2. *Ibid.*
3. A. Badham, 'Rediscovering Woodstock' in which she also refers to the A. Keen Collection (Cape Archives Depot, Cape Town, A1839) and L. Green, *Growing Lovely, Growing Old* (Cape Town: Howard Timmins, 1954), 21.
4. *Woodstock Parish Magazine*, December 1904.
5. J. Hodgson, *A History of Zonnebloem College, 1858–1870: A Study in Church and Society* (Cape Town: University of Cape Town), 453.
6. J. Hodgson and T. Edlmann, *Zonnebloem College* (Cape Town: African Lives, 2018), 196–198.
7. The wording of the resolution is outlined in the *Cape Times*, 6 November 1897.
8. *The Owl*, 31 October 1896.
9. *South African Review*, 27 November 1896.
10. *Cape Times*, 21 November 1896.
11. *Ibid.*, 23 November 1896.
12. *South African Review*, 27 November 1896.
13. *The Owl*, 19 December 1896.
14. *Cape Times*, 26 December 1896.
15. *The Owl*, 19 December 1896.
16. *Ibid.*, 7 November 1896.
17. *Ibid.*, 9 January 1897.
18. *South African Review*, 5 February 1897.

19. *The Owl*, 6 February 1897.
20. *Ibid.*
21. *Ibid.*, 13 February 1897.
22. E. Hayden in the *Licensed Victuallers' Gazette*, reported in the *Cape Times*, 27 May 1897.
23. *Daily Independent*, 16 May 1890.
24. Luckin, *The History of South African Cricket*, preface, 5.
25. *Cape Times*, 19 October 1897.
26. *The Owl*, 23 October 1897.
27. *Cape Times*, 28 October 1897.
28. *Ibid.*
29. *Cape Times*, 1 November 1897.
30. *Cape Argus*, 1 November 1897.
31. *South African Review*, 4 November 1897.
32. *The Owl*, 6 November 1897.
33. *Cape Argus*, 3 November 1897.
34. *Ibid.*
35. *Cape Times*, 5 November 1897.
36. *Cape Argus*, 10 November 1897.
37. *Cricket: A Weekly Record of the Game*, 22 July 1897.
38. *Cape Argus*, 10 November 1897.
39. All quotations from the meeting come from the *Cape Times*, 6 November 1897, although the authors also consulted the *Cape Argus*, 10 November 1897, which carried the same story.
40. A.C. Parker, *W.P. Cricket: 100-Not Out* (Cape Town: Western Province Cricket Union, 1990), 21.
41. *Cape Times*, 6 November 1897.
42. *Cape Argus*, 10 November 1897.
43. *Ibid.*, 5 November 1897.
44. *Ibid.*, 9 November 1897.
45. *South African Review*, 11 November 1897.
46. *Ibid.*
47. Letters published in the *Cape Times*, 7–11 November 1897.
48. *Ibid.*, 13 November 1897.
49. *Cape Times Weekly*, 2 September 1896.

CHAPTER 9: 'ANY CLUB COULD OBJECT TO ANY MAN'

1. Marks, 'Class, Culture and Consciousness in South Africa', 144.
2. *The Times*, 27 July 1925.
3. Jan Smuts's description in a letter to Emily Hobhouse: H. Giliomee and B. Mbenga, *New History of South Africa* (Cape Town: Tafelberg, 2007), 224.
4. *South African News*, 4 April 1901.
5. S. Trapido, 'The Origins and Development of the African Peoples' Organisation' in *Collected Seminar Papers on the Societies of Southern Africa in the 19th and 20th Centuries, Volume 1* (London: Institute of Commonwealth Studies, 1970), 92–93.
6. Rotberg, *The Founder*, 611.
7. A. Marx, *Making Race and Nation: A Comparison of South Africa, the United States, and Brazil* (Cape Town: Cambridge University Press, 2003), 88.
8. *Cape Argus*, 23 March 1900.
9. *Juta's Directory of Cape Town* (Cape Town: J.C. Juta & Co., 1881–1910); Rev. M. Weeder, 'The Palaces of Memory – a Reconstruction of District One, Cape Town

before and after the Group Areas Act' (MA thesis, University of the Western Cape, May 2006), 119.
10. *Cape Times*, 20 December 1897.
11. *Cape Argus*, 17 January 1898.
12. *Ibid.*, 14 January 1898.
13. *Ibid.*, 15 January 1898.
14. *Cape Times*, 17 January 1898.
15. *Ibid.*
16. Given the earlier treatment of Harry Cadwallader, it may be more than a coincidence that Frank Robb, Hendricks's major supporter in establishment cricket, was omitted from the list of presidents in the white historical record.
17. *The Owl*, 22 January 1898.
18. *Cape Times*, 28 January 1899.
19. *Ibid.*, 21 November 1898.
20. *The Owl*, 3 March 1899.
21. *Cape Times*, 27 February 1899.
22. *The Owl*, 3 March 1899.
23. *Cape Times*, 21 March 1899.
24. *South African Review*, 24 March 1899.
25. *Cape Argus*, 17 October 1899.
26. *Ibid.*
27. *Ibid.*, 21 October 1899.
28. *Ibid.*
29. *Ibid.*, 27 October 1899.
30. *South African Review*, 27 October 1899.
31. *Ibid.*, 2 February 1900.
32. *Cape Times*, 6 March 1900.
33. *Ibid.*, 7 March 1900.
34. *Cape Argus*, 16 March 1900.
35. *South African Review*, 23 March 1900.
36. *Cape Times*, 19 March 1900.
37. *South African Review*, 23 March 1900.
38. *Ibid.*, 26 October 1900.
39. *Ibid.*, 2 November 1900.
40. *Ibid.*, 14 December 1900.
41. P. Wynne-Thomas, *The Complete History of Cricket Tours at Home and Abroad* (London: Hamlyn, 1989), 231.
42. *Cape Times*, 15 April 1901.
43. *Ibid.*, 21 February 1901.
44. *Ibid.*, 22 March 1901.
45. *Cricket: A Weekly Record of the Game*, 1 August 1901.
46. J. Morris, *Farewell the Trumpets: An Imperial Retreat* (Harmondsworth: Penguin, 1982), 71–72.
47. N. Ferguson, *Empire: How Britain Made the Modern World* (London: Penguin, 2004), 280.
48. B. Spies, 'Reconstruction and Unification, 1902–1910' in T. Cameron and B. Spies (eds), *An Illustrated History of South Africa* (Johannesburg: Jonathan Ball, 1986), 219.
49. *Juta's Directory of Cape Town.*
50. *Cape Times*, 6 October 1904.
51. *Ibid.*, 12 January 1894.
52. All quotations from the meeting come from the *Cape Argus*, 17 November 1904,

although the authors also consulted the *Cape Times*, 17 November 1904, which carried the same story.

CHAPTER 10: 'CRICKET UNDER A CLOUD WITH NO SILVER LINING'

1. *Cape Times*, 20 December 1904.
2. *Ibid.*
3. *Ibid.*, 24 December 1904.
4. *Ibid.*, 28 December 1904.
5. *Ibid.*, 29 December 1904.
6. *Ibid.*, 11 January 1905.
7. *Ibid.*, 11 February 1905.
8. *Ibid.*
9. *Ibid.*, 15 February 1905.
10. *Ibid.*
11. *Ibid.*
12. *Ibid.*, 10 November 1904.
13. *Ibid.*, 7 and 8 March 1905.
14. *Ibid.*, 16 March 1905.
15. In 1874, South African College was separated into the South African College (which became the University of Cape Town) and South African College Schools (today's SACS). The history of cricket at the South African College, prior to the First World War, including its rivalry with Bishops, is described in an article by 'An Old Collegian' in Luckin, *The History of South African Cricket*, 797–799.
16. *Cape Times*, 1 April 1905.
17. *The Cape*, 10 January 1908.
18. *Cape Argus*, 24 March 1905.
19. *Cape Times*, 11 December 1905.

CHAPTER 11: 'THE GREAT AND MIGHTY HENDRICKS'

1. Letter dated 17 October 1900 reproduced in *South African News*, 6 April 1901.
2. *South African News*, 6 April 1901.
3. *Cape Times*, 22 February 1902; 30 December 1901.
4. *Ibid.*, 30 December 1901.
5. Goldin, *Making Race*, 26.
6. Rules of the South African Coloured Cricket Board, Clause 25, 1903, KZNCU Archives, Krish Reddy Collection, n.d.
7. *Cape Times*, 7 March 1907
8. *Ibid.*, 9 March 1907.
9. *APO*, 7 February 1914.
10. *Cape Times*, 13 December 1913.
11. *APO*, 14 November 1914.
12. *Ibid.*, 10 August 1912.
13. *Cape Argus*, 26 March 1915.
14. *Cape Times*, 27 March 1915. The player referred to by the *Cape Times* was probably George Wallace Stephen from Green Point who represented Western Province from 1904/05 to 1910/11.
15. *Cape Argus*, 29 March 1915.
16. *Ibid.*, 3 April 1915.
17. Luckin, *The History of South African Cricket*, 639.
18. *Cape Times*, 8 December 1915.

19. *APO*, 2 October 1915.
20. *Cape Times*, 8 December 1915.
21. *Ibid.*
22. Odendaal, Reddy and Merrett, *Divided Country*, 26, 32.
23. *Cape Argus*, 11 April 1917.
24. *Cape Times*, 16 April 1917
25. *Ibid.*
26. *Cape Argus*, 16 April 1917.
27. National Archives: G.P. Taylor: Baptism Certificate, Beaufort West, Ecclesiastical Division of Victoria West, 440/30 July 1888; Robina Henderson Taylor: Death Certificate Cape Town 1248/11 April 1934.
28. It seems likely that Roslin College and the famous Roslyns cricket and rugby clubs were connected and took their names from Roslin (Roslyn) Castle in Scotland. See also Odendaal, Reddy and Merrett, *Divided Country*, 54.
29. *Cape Times*, 4 April 1918.
30. Odendaal, Reddy and Merrett, *Divided Country*, 28.
31. *Ibid.*, 27, 28, 32, 48.
32. *Cape Times*, 25 November 1918.
33. *Ibid.*, 22 November 1918.

CHAPTER 12: HENDRICKS AND THE WORLD: AN INTERNATIONAL PERSPECTIVE

1. Guha, *A Corner of a Foreign Field*, 11.
2. Rotberg, *The Founder*, 150, 5.
3. Rectorial address delivered to Glasgow University, 16 November 1900.
4. J. Williams, *Cricket and Race* (Oxford: Berg, 2001), 1, 17.
5. Birley, *A Social History of English Cricket*, 107.
6. D. Frith, *The Golden Age of Cricket 1890–1914* (London: Omega Books, 1978), 12.
7. *Sporting Life*, 16 May 1868.
8. L. Romensky, 'First XI: Is this the single most important cricket team in Australian history?', www.abc.net.au/news, updated 15 March 2018.
9. A. Mallett, *The Black Lords of Summer: The Story of the 1868 Aboriginal Tour of England and Beyond* (St Lucia: University of Queensland Press, 2002), 170.
10. A. Sengupta, *Cricket Country*, 25 October 2015.
11. Mallett, *The Black Lords of Summer*, 170.
12. *Ibid.*, 174.
13. D. Fraser, *Cricket and the Law: The Man in White is Always Right* (New York: Routledge, 2005), 389.
14. *Ibid.*
15. Knight, *The Complete Cricketer*, 272.
16. B. Whimpress, *Australian Dictionary of Biography, Supplementary Volume* (Melbourne: Melbourne University Press, 2005).
17. C. Tatz, *Obstacle Race: Aborigines in Sport* (Sydney: University of New South Wales), 74.
18. *Ibid.*, 70.
19. D. Heardon (ed.), *The Best Ever Australian Sports Writing: A 200 Year Collection* (Melbourne: Schwartz Publishing, 2001), 554.
20. H. Beckles, 'The Making of the first "West Indian" teams 1886–1896' in Beckles and B. Stoddart (ed.), *Liberation Cricket: West Indies Cricket Culture* (Manchester: Manchester University Press, 1995), 198.
21. *Ibid.*, 193–200.

22. H. Beckles, *The Development of West Indies Cricket, Volume 2: The Age of Nationalism* (Kingston: Pluto Press, 1998), 28.
23. W. Coleman, 'The First West Indians' in *The Cricketer*, June 1988.
24. *Ibid.*
25. *Ibid.*
26. C. James, *Beyond a Boundary*, (London: Serpent's Tail, 1994), 72–73.
27. *Ibid.*
28. Knight, *The Complete Cricketer*, 270.
29. Guha, *A Corner of a Foreign Field*, 94.
30. *The Field*, 15 August 1896.
31. C. Headlam, 'Cricket in India' in P. Warner (ed.), *Imperial Cricket* (London: London and Counties Press, 1912), 353–354.
32. Bowen, *Cricket*, 149.
33. D. Birley, *Willow Wand: Some Cricket Myths Explored* (London: Aurum Press, 1989), 115–117.
34. This and the following opinions of the Indian press on 'Lord Harris's Administration and the Hollowness of the Permanent Memorial in his Honour by his Friends and Admirers' in Guha, *A Corner of a Foreign Field*, 56–77.
35. *Ibid.*
36. *Ibid.*
37. E. Swanton (ed.), *Barclays World of Cricket* (London: Collins, 1980), 576.
38. P. Wynne-Thomas quoted Rosenwater in his article, 'The man who made history', in *Cricket Lore*, Vol. 2, Issue 5, 18.
39. Bowen, *Cricket*, 150.
40. *Cape Times*, 15 January 1972.
41. A. Odendaal (ed.), *Cricket in Isolation: The Politics of Race and Cricket in South Africa* (Stellenbosch: The Author, 1977), 325.
42. *The Cricketer*, February 1976, 21.
43. C. Merrett, 'Sport and Race in Colonial Natal: C.B. Llewellyn, South Africa's First Black Test Cricketer' in *The Cricket Statistician* No. 128 (Nottingham: Winter 2004), 17.
44. B. Murray and C. Merrett, *Caught Behind: Race and Politics in Springbok Cricket* (Johannesburg/Scottsville: Wits University and University of KwaZulu-Natal Press, 2004), 22–23.
45. T. Gutsche, *Old Gold: The History of the Wanderers Club* (Johannesburg: Citadel Press, 1966), 88.
46. *Cape Times*, 23 March 1899.
47. *The Star*, 23 March 1899.
48. *Cricket: A Weekly Record of the Game*, 30 July 1908, 305.
49. *Ibid.*, 15 January 1972.
50. K. Sandiford, *Cricket and the Victorians* (Aldershot: Scolar, 1994), 153.
51. *The Star*, 13 November 1902.
52. *Cape Times*, 19 October 1910.
53. B. Green, *The Wisden Book of Cricketers' Lives: Obituaries from Wisden Cricketers' Almanack* (London: Queen Anne Press, 1986), 556.
54. *The Cricketer*, March 1976, 29.
55. Williams, *Cricket and Race*, 22.
56. *The Star*, 2 January 1911.
57. *Sporting Life*, 14 January 1911.
58. *The Star*, 13 January 1911.
59. *Daily Express*, 12 June 1912.

60. *Yorkshire Post*, 18 July 1912.
61. *Cape Argus*, 27 July 1912.
62. This and the following quotes are taken from the *Accrington Observer and Times*, various issues 16–27 July 1912.
63. *Ibid.* Llewellyn returned to Accrington CC from 1921 to 1925.

EPILOGUE: HENDRICKS, D'OLIVEIRA AND A CRICKET TRADITION

1. P. Oborne, *Basil D'Oliveira: Cricket and Conspiracy: The Untold Story* (London: Time Warner Books, 2006), 20.
2. Rev. M. Weeder included the detail in his MA thesis (University of the Western Cape), 'The Palaces of Memory – a Reconstruction of District One, Cape Town before and after the Group Areas Act' (May 2006), 102–103. In his thesis he referred to interviews with S. Krynauw and a resident of the area, R. Dudley.
3. V. Priday and H. MacAlister, personal correspondence with the authors, 17 January 2019.
4. B. Crowley, *Cricket's Exiles: The Saga of South African Cricket* (Cape Town: Don Nelson, 1983), 113.
5. *Cape Times*, 24 September 1940.
6. B. D'Oliveira, *An Autobiography* (London: Sportsman's Book Club, 1969), 40.
7. D'Oliveira, *An Autobiography*, 41–42; B. D'Oliveira, *The D'Oliveira Affair* (London: Collins, 1969), 28.
8. B. D'Oliveira with P. Murphy, *Time to Declare: An Autobiography* (London: J.M. Dent & Sons, 1980), 4.
9. *Ibid.*, 5.
10. D'Oliveira, *The D'Oliveira Affair*, 33–34.
11. *Ibid.*, 17.
12. D'Oliveira, *Time to Declare*, 4.
13. K. Sandiford and B. Stoddart, *The Imperial Game: Cricket, Culture and Society* (Manchester: Manchester University Press, 1998), 100.
14. D'Oliveira, *The D'Oliveira Affair*, 29.
15. *Ibid.*, 36.
16. I. Tennant, *Frank Worrell: A Biography* (Cambridge: Lutterworth Press, 1987), 47.
17. *The Nation*, 15 May 1959; C. James, *Cricket* (London: Allison & Busby, 1986), 90.
18. D'Oliveira, *The D'Oliveira Affair*, 38.
19. *Ibid.*, 7.
20. *Ibid.*, 61.
21. *Ibid.*, 138.
22. J. Vorster, Address to the Orange Free State National Party Congress at Bloemfontein, 17 September 1968.
23. Oborne, *Basil D'Oliveira*, 213.
24. *Ibid.*, 206.
25. *Cape Times*, 18 September 1968.
26. M. Allie, *More Than a Game: History of the Western Province Cricket Board 1959–1991* (Cape Town: *Cape Argus*, 2000), 93.

Bibliography

NEWSPAPERS, PERIODICALS AND ANNUALS

Accrington Observer and Times
APO (Cape Town)
Bloemfontein Express
Cape Argus
Cape Argus Weekly
Cape Monthly
Cape Times
Cape Times Weekly
Cricket: A Weekly Record of the Game.
Cricket Country
Cricket Lore
Daily Express
Daily Independent (Kimberley)
Diamond Fields Advertiser
Imvo Zabantsundu
Natal Mercury
Port Elizabeth Telegraph
Rhodesia Herald
South African Cricket Annual
South African News
South African Non-European Cricket Almanack
South African Review
Sporting Life
Standard and Diggers News (Johannesburg)
Table Talk (Melbourne)
The Cape
The Cricket Field
The Cricket Statistician
The Cricketer
The Lantern (Cape Town)
The Nation (Trinidad)
The Owl (Cape Town)

The Press (Pretoria)
The Sportsman
The Star (Johannesburg)
The Times
Wisden Cricketers' Almanack
Woodstock Parish Magazine
Yorkshire Post

BOOKS, ARTICLES AND THESES

Allen, D., *Empire, War and Cricket in South Africa* (Cape Town: Zebra Press, 2015).
Allie, M., *More Than a Game: History of the Western Province Cricket Board 1959–1991* (Cape Town: *Cape Argus*, 2000).
An Old Peripatetic, 'Cape Town and Cricket' in *Cape Monthly*, Volume VI, 1873.
Archer, R. and A. Bouillon, *The South African Game* (London: Zed Press, 1982).
Badham, A., 'Rediscovering Woodstock' in *Contree*, 21, 1987.
Ballantyne, R., *Six Months at the Cape or Letters to Periwinkle from South Africa* (London: Nick Hodson, 1876).
Beckles, H., *The Development of West Indies Cricket, Volume 2: The Age of Nationalism* (Kingston: Pluto Press, 1998).
——— and B. Stoddart (ed.), *Liberation Cricket: West Indies Cricket Culture* (Manchester: Manchester University Press, 1995).
Bickford-Smith, V., *Ethnic Pride and Racial Prejudice in Victorian Cape Town: Group Identity and Social Practice 1875–1902* (Cambridge: Cambridge University Press, 1995).
Biddiss, M., *Images of Race* (Leicester: Leicester University Press, 1979).
Birley, D., *A Social History of English Cricket* (London: Aurum Press, 1999).
———, *Willow Wand: Some Cricket Myths Explored* (London: Aurum Press, 1989).
Blake, R., *A History of Rhodesia* (London: Eyre Methuen, 1977).
Blennerhassett, R. and L. Sleeman, *Adventures in Mashonaland* (Bulawayo: Books of Rhodesia, 1969).
Bowen, R., *Cricket: A History of Its Growth and Development Throughout the World* (London: Eyre and Spottiswoode, 1970).
Bright-Holmes, J., *The Joy of Cricket* (London: Secker & Warburg, 1984).
Cameron T. and B. Spies (eds), *An Illustrated History of South Africa* (Johannesburg: Jonathan Ball, 1986).
Clarke H. and W. Jones, *The Life and Times of Thomas Fothergill Lightfoot* (London: Simpkin, Marshall, Hamilton, Kent & Co., 1908).
Crowley, B., *Cricket's Exiles: The Saga of South African Cricket* (Cape Town: Don Nelson, 1983).
Darter, A., *Pioneers of Mashonaland* (Bulawayo, Books of Rhodesia, 1977).
Davids, A., *The Mosques of Bo-Kaap* (Athlone: SAIAIR, 1980).
Dobbs, B., *Edwardians at Play* (London: Pelham, 1973).

D'Oliveira, B., *An Autobiography* (London: Sportsman's Book Club, 1969).
———, *The D'Oliveira Affair* (London: Collins, 1969).
——— with P. Murphy, *Time to Declare: An Autobiography* (London: J.M. Dent & Sons, 1980).
Farrar, R., *The Life of Frederic William Farrar, D.D., F.R.S., Etc., Sometime Dean of Canterbury* (London: James Nisbet & Co., 1904).
Ferguson, N., *Empire: How Britain Made the Modern World* (London: Penguin, 2003).
Forrest, D., *The Pacemen: 100 Years of South African Fast Bowlers* (Johannesburg: Macmillan, 2013).
Fraser, D., *Cricket and the Law: The Man in White is Always Right* (New York: Routledge, 2005).
Frere, B., 'Native races of South Africa' in *Transactions of the South African Philosophical Society* 1, No. 2 (1877–1888).
Frith, D., *The Golden Age of Cricket 1890–1914* (London: Omega Books, 1978).
Fry, C., *Life Worth Living* (London: Michael Joseph, 1939).
Giliomee, H. and B. Mbenga, *New History of South Africa* (Cape Town: Tafelberg, 2007).
Goldin, I., *Making Race: The Politics and Economics of Coloured Identity in South Africa* (London: Longman, 1987).
Green, B. (ed.), *The Wisden Book of Cricketers' Lives: Obituaries from Wisden Cricketers' Almanack* (London: Queen Anne Press, 1988).
Green, L., *Growing Lovely, Growing Old* (Cape Town: Howard Timmins, 1954).
Guha, R., *A Corner of a Foreign Field: The Indian History of British Sport* (London: Picador, 2002).
Gutsche, T., *Old Gold: The History of the Wanderers Club* (Johannesburg: Citadel Press, 1966).
Heardon, D. (ed.), *The Best Ever Australian Sports Writing: A 200 Year Collection* (Melbourne: Schwartz Publishing, 2001).
Hodgson, J., *A History of Zonnebloem College, 1858–1870: A Study in Church and Society* (Cape Town: University of Cape Town, 1975).
Hofmeyr, J. with F. Reitz, *The Life of Jan Hendrik Hofmeyr (Onze Jan)* (Cape Town: Van de Sandt, 1913).
Honey, J., *Tom Brown's Universe: The Development of the Public School in the 19th Century* (London: Millington, 1977).
James, C., *Beyond a Boundary* (London: Serpent's Tail, 1994).
———, *Cricket* (London: Allison & Busby, 1986).
Juta's Directory of Cape Town (Cape Town: J.C. Juta & Co., 1881–1910).
Kilburn, J., *Overthrows: A Book of Cricket* (London: Stanley Paul, 1975).
Knight, A., *The Complete Cricketer* (London: Methuen, 1906).
Lewis, G., *Between the Wire and the Wall: A History of South African 'Coloured' Politics* (Cape Town: David Philip, 1987).
Lewis, T., *Double Century: The Story of MCC and Cricket* (Sevenoaks: Hodder & Stoughton, 1987).
Lewsen, P., *John X. Merriman: Paradoxical South African Statesman* (New Haven: Yale University Press, 1982).

Longford, E., *Jameson's Raid* (London: Weidenfeld & Nicolson, 1982).
Luckin, M., *The History of South African Cricket: Including the Full Scores of All Matches since 1876* (Johannesburg: W.E. Horton and Sons, 1915).
Mallett, A., *The Black Lords of Summer: The Story of the 1868 Aboriginal Tour of England and Beyond* (St Lucia: University of Queensland Press, 2002).
Mangan, J., *The Games Ethic and Imperialism* (Harmondsworth: Viking, 1985).
Marks, S. and A. Atmore, *Economy and Society in Pre-Industrial South Africa* (London: Longman, 1980).
Marx, A., Making Race and Nation: A Comparison of South Africa, the United States, and Brazil (Cape Town: Cambridge University Press, 2003).
Merrett, C., 'Sport and Race in Colonial Natal: C.B. Llewellyn, South Africa's First Black Test Cricketer' in *The Cricket Statistician* No. 128 (Nottingham: Winter 2004).
Morris, J., *Farewell the Trumpets: An Imperial Retreat* (Harmondsworth: Penguin, 1982).
Muller, C. (ed.), Five *Hundred Years: A History of South Africa* (Pretoria: Academica, 1981).
Mulvaney, D., *Cricket Walkabout: The Australian Aboriginal Cricketers on Tour 1867/68* (Carlton: Melbourne University Press, 1967).
Murray, B. and C. Merrett, *Caught Behind: Race and Politics in Springbok Cricket* (Johannesburg/Scottsville: Wits University and University of KwaZulu Natal Press, 2004).
——— and G. Vahed (eds), *Empire & Cricket: The South African Experience 1884–1914* (Pretoria: Unisa Press, 2009).
———, R. Parry and J. Winch (eds), *Cricket and Society in South Africa 1910–1971: From Union to Isolation* (London: Palgrave Macmillan, 2018).
Oborne, P., *Basil D'Oliveira: Cricket and Conspiracy: The Untold Story* (London: Time Warner Books, 2006).
Odendaal, A. (ed.), *Cricket in Isolation: The Politics of Race and Cricket in South Africa* (Stellenbosch: The Author, 1977).
———, K. Reddy, C. Merrett and J. Winch, *Cricket & Conquest: The History of South African Cricket Retold 1795–1914 Volume 1* (Cape Town: HSRC, 2016).
———, K. Reddy and C. Merrett, *Divided Country: The History of South African Cricket Retold 1914–1950s Volume 2* (Cape Town: HSRC, 2018).
Parker, A., *W.P. Cricket 100 Not Out* (Cape Town: Western Province Cricket Union, 1990).
Parry, R., '"In a Sense Citizens, But Not Altogether Citizens ...": Rhodes, Race and the Ideology of Segregation at the Cape in the Late Nineteenth Century' in *Canadian Journal of African Studies*, 17(3), 1983, 377–392.
Romensky, L., 'First XI: Is this the single most important cricket team in Australian history?', www.abc.net.au/news, updated 15 March 2018.
Ross, R., A. Kelk Mager and B. Nasson (eds), *The Cambridge History of South Africa, Volume 2, 1885–1994* (Cambridge: Cambridge University Press, 2011).
Rotberg, R., *The Founder: Cecil Rhodes and the Pursuit of Power* (Oxford: Oxford University Press, 1988).

Sandiford, K., *Cricket and the Victorians* (Aldershot: Scolar, 1994).
——— and B. Stoddart, *The Imperial Game: Cricket, Culture and Society* (Manchester: Manchester University Press, 1998).
Schulze, H., *South Africa's Cricketing Lawyers: Biographical Notes on the 32 Lawyers who Represented South Africa in Cricket* (Halfway House: Interdoc Consultants, 1999).
Swanton, E. (ed.), *Barclays World of Cricket* (London: Collins, 1980).
Tamarkin, M., *Cecil Rhodes and the Cape Afrikaners: The Imperial Colossus and the Colonial Parish Pump* (London: Routledge, 1996).
Tatz, C., *Obstacle Race: Aborigines in Sport* (Sydney: University of New South Wales, 1995).
Tennant, I., *Frank Worrell: A Biography* (Cambridge: Lutterworth Press, 1987).
Thornton, A.P., *Doctrines of Imperialism* (New York: John Wiley & Sons, 1965).
Trapido, S., 'The Origins and Development of the African Peoples' Organisation' in *Collected Seminar Papers on the Societies of Southern Africa in the 19th and 20th Centuries, Volume 1* (London: Institute of Commonwealth Studies, 1970).
Trollope, A., *South Africa (Volume 1)* reprint (Stroud: Nonsuch Publishing, 2005).
Van der Ross, R., *Myths and Attitudes: An Inside Look at the Coloured People* (Cape Town: Tafelberg, 1979).
Walsh, F., *A History of South Africa* (London: Harper Collins, 2000).
Warner, P. (ed.), *Imperial Cricket* (London: London and Counties Press, 1912).
———, *Long Innings* (London: George G. Harrap, 1951).
———, *Lord's 1787–1945* (London: Sportsman's Book Club, 1951).
Weeder, Rev. M., 'The Palaces of Memory – a Reconstruction of District One, Cape Town before and after the Group Areas Act' (MA thesis, University of the Western Cape, May 2006).
West, S. and W. Luker, *Century at Newlands: A History of the Western Province* Cricket Club (Cape Town: WPCC, 1965).
Wilburn, K., *The Life of Statesman and Industrialist Sir James Sivewright of South Africa, 1848–1916* (Lewiston: Edwin Mellen Press, 2010).
Wilde, S., *Ranji* (London: Methuen, 1990).
Williams, J., *Cricket and Race* (Oxford: Berg, 2001).
Wilton, I., *C.B. Fry: King of Sport* (London: Metro, 2002).
Winch, J., *England's Youngest Captain: The Life and Times of Monty Bowden and Two South African Journalists* (Windsor: Windsor Publishers, 2003).
Worden, N., E. van Heyningen and V. Bickford-Smith, *Cape Town: The Making of a City* (Cape Town: David Philip, 1998).
Wynne-Thomas, P., *The Complete History of Cricket Tours at Home and Abroad* (London: Hamlyn, 1989).

Index

'Had it not been for the forensic feat of Jonty Winch and Richard Parry, the compelling story of Hendricks and the nefarious shenanigans of Rhodes would not have been unearthed in their fascinating book *Too Black to Wear Whites*.'

Mushtak Parker, *Cape Times*

STORIES OF
CRICKET'S FINEST PAINTING
KENT v LANCASHIRE 1906
SPORTS BOOK AWARDS 2020
SHORTLISTED
A CORNER OF EVERY FOREIGN FIELD
CRICKET'S JOURNEY
FROM ENGLISH GAME TO GLOBAL SPORT
TONY GREIG
A reappraisal of English cricket's most controversial
DAVID T
ENGLAND ON THIS DAY
HISTORY, FACTS AND FIGURES FROM EVERY DAY OF THE YEAR
RICHARD MURPHY
THE TRANSFER MARKET
THE INSIDE STORIES
ALAN GERNON
FOREWORD BY JIM WHITE
Nick Weatherhogg
The Diary of Sport
History, Facts & Figures from Every Day of the Year
MARK PEE
PLAYING THE GAME
CRICKET'S TARNISHED IDE
From Bodyline to presen
NEIL FITZSIMON
Rhapsody in Blue
WHY ARE WE ALWAYS ON LAST?
Running Match of the Day and Other Adventures in TV and Football
PAUL ARMSTRONG
MATT PIPER
OUT OF THE DARKNESS
MY STORY IN FOOTBALL
DAVIE WILSON
AND ALISTAIR AIRD
Wilson ON THE WING
The Davie Wilson Story
FOREWORD BY WALTER SMITH OBE
An A to Z of Sporting Collectibles
Priceless Cigarette Cards and Sought-after Sports Stickers
CARL WILKES
AN ENGLISHMAN, A SCOTSMAN AND AN IRISHMAN WALKED ONTO A FOOTBALL PITCH
GROWING UP WITH THE TRINITY
BRENDON McGUIRE
JOHN SMITH AND DAN TRELFER
BOOKED! THE GOSPEL
ACCORDING TO OUR FOOTBALL HEROES
MARK HODKINSON
THE OVERCOAT MEN
How Two Unsung Heroes Staved off the Bulldozers and Saved their Football Club from Oblivion
'Comprehensively researched and honest to a fault. Recommended.'
When Saturday Comes
LANCASHIRE
TURF WARS
A FOOTBALL HISTORY
RETIRED